A Contribution to the
Theory of the
TRADE CYCLE

A Contribution to the Theory of the
TRADE CYCLE

BY

J. R. HICKS

CLARENDON PRESS · OXFORD

Oxford University Press, Walton Street, Oxford OX2 6DP

OXFORD LONDON GLASGOW
NEW YORK TORONTO MELBOURNE WELLINGTON
KUALA LUMPUR SINGAPORE JAKARTA HONG KONG TOKYO
DELHI BOMBAY CALCUTTA MADRAS KARACHI
IBADAN NAIROBI DAR ES SALAAM CAPE TOWN

ISBN 0 19 828416 0

First Edition 1950
Reprinted 1951, 1956, 1959, 1961, 1965, 1967, 1972, 1978

Printed and bound in Great Britain by
REDWOOD BURN LIMITED
Trowbridge & Esher

PREFACE TO THE THIRD IMPRESSION

DURING the two or three years after this book was first published (in 1950) it called forth quite a remarkable collection of review-articles, in something like a dozen different journals, in England, in America, and in several other parts of the world. The ideas which I put forward have thus received a very searching examination. Though several of my critics would prefer approaches which are different from mine, I think it may be said that the various approaches point broadly in the same direction; thus I think I may claim that my analysis has stood up to the test to which it has been submitted quite reasonably well. It has indeed achieved about as much as I expected of it; for though there are pages in the book in which I have allowed myself to be carried away by the excitement of a voyage of discovery, I did not hope to be explaining everything, and on the whole I tried to avoid setting my sights unduly high.

In spite of all that has been written, I have not felt that the book calls for revision on reprinting. It is an exercise in a particular method, and if I were to adopt a different method (as some of my critics would desire) I should have to write a different book. Nor, I think, would it be useful on this occasion if I were to attempt the arduous task of replying to my critics in detail. I shall acknowledge my indebtedness to them in another way. I shall take the opportunity of this second preface to make some comments on the (unamended) text which follows, mainly in order to clear up points which have proved troublesome, but in some cases in order to insert qualifications, the necessity for which I have come to accept.

(1) The first of these comments relates to the change in the character of my argument at the end of Chapter IV. Nearly everything which is said up to that point belongs, in my view, to the most general sort of economic dynamics—or, at the least, to any sort of dynamics which should retain any connexion whatever with the work of Keynes. The theory of the lagged multiplier (Chapters II and III) and the general theory of induced investment (Chapter IV) must have a place, in some form or other, in

any modern analysis—whether that analysis is ultimately concerned with the elucidation of historical patterns, or with the provision of tools for policy. (I should like to emphasize that the inducement of investment, as I conceive it, and as it is described in Chapter IV, is not a mere matter of technical necessity; it works through the state of mind of entrepreneurs, having a close connexion with what I have called in another place the 'elasticity of expectations'.) But in the last section of Chapter IV there is a change. From that point onwards, I am concentrating upon the explanation of historical patterns; I accordingly make the hypothesis that we shall get a representative pattern if we take a standard form of entrepreneurial reaction, the form which looks like being typical, though it is certainly not necessary. This form of reaction is then embodied, for purposes of manipulation, in the highly artificial device of the 'period', as there defined. This device has the advantage that it facilitates the analysis of the chapters which follow (especially Chapters V–X); on the whole I think that that advantage, in this particular context, was worth getting. But its disadvantage is that it makes the analysis *look* more mechanical than it is intended to be. Though I did make attempts, as I returned towards realism (in Chapters VIII–X), to move as freely as I could within the strait-jacket into which I had put myself, it was impossible to attain a perfectly free movement, so that it may well be that there are possibilities which ought to have been considered but which remained out of reach.

(2) Of all the concepts which are used in this book, that which has caused the most trouble is *Autonomous Investment*; and here I must admit to having brought the trouble upon myself, for I do not think that I was entirely consistent in the use which I made of the term. The basic thing which I wanted to emphasize is that the inducement of investment (as described in Chapter IV) does not wholly explain why the amount of investment is what it is. While the amount of investment, at any given time, is partly to be explained by the current level of business activity, and by the course which activity has followed in the recent past, it cannot be wholly explained by such factors. There are other things which affect the volume of investment (quite apart from monetary factors): technical progress, changes in wants (such as those which result from population changes), and public policy

itself being the chief. From the point of view of analysis such things are exogenous, but they are not therefore to be neglected. So far I do not expect that there will be any disagreement. I was, however, too often tempted to express the two sets of factors affecting investment as two parts of investment (just as Keynes himself expressed the various sets of factors affecting the demand for money as parts of the demand for money). As an expository device, a separation of this sort is at times hardly avoidable. But one should remember that it is an expository device and no more. I am afraid that I do occasionally talk as if one could tell whether a particular piece of investment was autonomous just by looking at it; this is quite wrong. 'Autonomy' is a matter of the causes which have brought the investment about, never a matter of its technical character; there is no reason why any sort of investment, fixed, circulating, constructional or what not, should not on occasion be autonomous.

Then there is another, more serious, trouble. Autonomous investment, in this sense, is not adequately distinguished from something which is nearly the same thing for my purpose here, but is by no means the same thing for other purposes. This is the investment which is geared, not to current activity, nor to the activity of the economy in the recent past, but to the trend growth of the economy, the average rate of growth over long periods. Here we do have something which can be identified with a particular sort of investment—long-range investment, which is expected to pay for itself over a long period, but not necessarily within a short time. I would now agree that from a long-period point of view such investment is *not* autonomous; it is necessary that it should proceed at a rate which is appropriate to the growth of the economy, if a steady growth is to go on. Thus if we are confining our attention to the conditions for long-term stability, and if we neglect the other sort of autonomous investment (or look after it in other ways), then we may properly take as our model one in which all investment is induced; so that Mr. Harrod's model (the 'regularly progressive economy without autonomous investment') becomes the right model to use. I would now grant this, and would consequently modify some of the statements in my Chapter V; but I still feel that the framework which I use is the right framework for my purposes.

For there is a real convenience, in cycle analysis, if we agree
to treat the exogenous factors as producing one sort of autonomous investment; and for cyclical purposes long-term investment itself can be regarded as having a fairly autonomous
character. It will be relatively unaffected by a short depression
(so far as the incentive to undertake it is concerned); it does
accordingly provide a 'floor' below which investment is re-
strained from falling, as autonomous investment is shown to do
in my diagrams. But the same may not be true, for this long-
range investment, if the depression goes on for a long time, since
prolonged depression may alter people's views about the trend.
In a long depression, long-range investment may disclose itself
as induced, not autonomous. Thus it is important, and not sufficiently emphasized, that in a short depression recovery may be
expected to start from a fairly high 'floor' (based upon long-
range investment as well as on that which is more truly autonomous); but the longer the depression continues, the less is the
help which can be expected from long-range investment, so
that it is only the purely autonomous investment, based for the
most part on relatively non-economic changes, which remains
to provide a 'floor' and in the end a way out.

(3) Finally, I think I would now agree with some of my critics
that the analysis of induced investment in terms of the delayed
effects of *output* changes does not, in all cases, tell quite enough
of the story. I was to some extent aware of this when writing
(see the footnote on p. 99 and several passages in Chapter X);
but though what I have said in these places goes some way to
meet the difficulty, I doubt if it goes far enough. The following
reflections may take the matter a little farther on.

I would certainly not admit that there was anything wrong, *in
general*, with my interpretation of induced investment in terms
of output changes—that I ought to have worked throughout in
terms of demand, not output. Apart from stock changes (which
are looked after by my device of the 'period') demand as a whole
and output as a whole can ordinarily be taken to be one and the
same thing. This remains true, even when prices are varying, so
long as we insist on working in real terms—and so long as price-
movements keep the supplies and demands of commodities in
balance with one another. Ordinary disequilibria between supply

and demand (involving accumulation or decumulation of stocks) are looked after by the 'period' device; but one sort of disequilibrium remains which is not looked after in that way. This is the case in which demands are persistently ahead of supplies at the ruling prices, the disequilibrium being met by postponement of delivery. It is true that in such a case the inducement to invest may be stronger than would be expected from the actual course of sales; a long order-book provides an incentive to invest, in addition to that which arises from the fact that actual sales are running at a high level. It is, however, still more important that in such circumstances buyers are likely to be saving some portion at least of the funds which they are at present unable to spend as they would desire; thus the saving coefficient is likely to be boosted, for the time being, above its normal level. It follows from this that the completion of a particular piece of investment may not exercise its usual depressive effect so quickly as it would otherwise do, the slack being taken up by a back-log of orders to be worked off; or in other words, the system may be kept from bouncing off the ceiling by a temporary fall in the saving coefficient, due to expenditure on deliveries that had previously been postponed. If this mechanism is at work, the period of the Full Boom may be stretched out for a longer duration than appears probable from the analysis of Chapter X below; though it should be observed that this stretching-out carries with it the persistence of inflationary pressure, as a necessary consequence.

At the time when I was writing this book (in 1948–9) the postwar boom had not lasted long enough for its peculiar characteristics to be clearly discernible. All that was clear was that the boom would not be prematurely cut off by monetary restriction —as I believed the corresponding boom to have been cut off in 1920–1. Otherwise, I was inclined to think of it as being explicable in terms of a hump in autonomous investment, which had (for the time being) pushed the equilibrium line right above the ceiling. I still feel that this interpretation holds good for the late forties—and this hump was then prolonged by a further hump, due to the Korean war and its aftermath. The earlier part of the Long Boom is quite adequately accounted for in this way. It does, however, seem to me quite evident that in its later stages

(say since 1952) the boom is coming nearer to the traditional
pattern. A larger part of investment is now induced, a smaller
part is autonomous. Investment which is reasonably autonomous
is still running at a higher level than in the old days, but it is not
carrying so much of the boom on its back as it did in the first
years after the war. In this later phase, the extent to which the
boom can be supported by back-logs, such as that just discussed,
is particularly important. Nevertheless it should be emphasized
that these back-logs are themselves a form of inefficiency—inefficiency which the system is always tending, in one way or
another, to overcome. When it does overcome them (and the
time when it does so may not be far away) the increased control,
which we ought to have won by our improved understanding of
these phenomena, will be put to a test.

J. R. H.

December 1955

PREFACE

THE title of this book is at once a claim and a disclaimer. I do believe that the argument which I am going to set out is quite likely to be the main part of the answer to the great question with which I am concerned—why it is that these rather regular fluctuations in trade and industry have gone on occurring, from the beginnings of industrialism up to the present. That is claim enough; but I want to make it clear at the outset that I am not claiming any more. I am not by any means positive that the answer which I have found is the right answer; one cannot begin to be sure of that until one has tested one's theory against the facts, and I am well aware that any testing which I have been able to do has been extremely superficial. If the theory which is here offered stands up to theoretical criticism, the next stage will be the concern of statisticians, econometrists, and (most of all) economic historians, who will have to see whether it does prove possible to make sense of the facts in the light of these hypotheses. All I hope to have shown is that the theory is reasonable in itself, and that it would serve to explain the kind of phenomenon which has been experienced.

Even on the purely theoretical side, I am very conscious that much remains to be done. If a provisional answer is given to the main question, that answer raises further questions, and many of these are left unexplored. The main argument itself has got some weak links, which need strengthening. But there are plenty of people whose hands will itch to get on with these jobs. At the point where I leave it, the inquiry looks like branching out in many directions. That is a good point at which to write a progress report, which is all that this 'contribution' claims to be.

What I have not felt inclined to do, on the basis of a theory which is little more than an untested hypothesis, is to make much in the way of policy prescriptions; while the diagnosis is still unconfirmed, it is early to think of cures. Of course cures will be tried, are being tried, and must be tried; but on the track I am following, the time for confident prescription still lies ahead. The most I hope to have done is to have brought it a little nearer.

The central idea, round which my argument is built, was first set out by me in a review article, 'Mr. Harrod's Dynamic Theory' (*Economica*, May 1949).[1] But hardly had that article been published (at about the same time as this book was finished) when I began to find indications that others had been thinking along the same lines. In the Proceedings volume of the *American Economic Review* (May 1949) there is a paper by Professor W. Leontief (of Harvard) entitled 'Recent Developments in the Study of Inter-industrial relationships'. On pp. 219–20 of that paper there is a passage which will be of distinct interest to the readers of this book. Even more explicit is the abstract of a paper by R. Goodwin (also of Harvard), which is printed on pp. 184–5 of the April 1949 number of *Econometrica*. Evidently we are all of us very close on each other's heels.

Another recent publication, to which I should like to draw attention (as I should have done in the text of this book if it had been available to me earlier), is the paper by F. Modigliani 'Fluctuations in the Saving-Income Ratio', which appears in volume XI of *Studies in Income and Wealth* (National Bureau of Economic Research). Although Modigliani's hypothesis about the Consumption Function is not the same as mine, it is practically very similar, and is no doubt more convenient for statistical testing than the more generalized hypothesis with which I work. (There is a page or two of discussion with Professor Leontief at the end of the Modigliani paper, dealing with this precise point.) The fact that he gets good results from the use of his hypothesis is a thing from which I also can derive encouragement.

My obligations to particular writings of fellow economists have been set out in their places as the argument proceeds. But there is one obligation which could not adequately be acknowledged in this manner, because it is of so general a character; it extends right through the whole development of my thinking on these matters, from start to finish. In a review article 'The Monetary Theory of D. H. Robertson' (*Economica*, 1942), I indicated

[1] I have also incorporated the substance of two of my earlier articles, 'Mr. Keynes and the Classics' (*Econometrica*, 1937) and 'La Théorie de Keynes après neuf ans' (*Revue d'économie politique*, 1945).

something of the debt which I owed to Professor Robertson's work, as the account then stood; but that was before I had begun to think on the particular lines here developed. The seed-bed had been prepared, but the plant had not yet begun to grow. The debt which I now owe to him is much greater. It is now a good many years since I have enjoyed the privilege of submitting everything I have written on these subjects—whether it proved in the end to be publishable or not—for his kind but searching criticism. The knowledge that he would be the first reader of these pages has been a salutary discipline and a continual encouragement. If I have succeeded in getting any way beyond the formal model-building, which has inevitably constituted the skeleton of my argument, it is to his influence that I mainly owe it.

I have to thank Miss K. Sarginson, of Somerville College, Oxford, for giving me a professional verdict on the mathematical adequacy of the methods used in my Appendix. And I must add an acknowledgement to my secretary at Nuffield College, Miss P. Rathbone, whose work on this book was much more than secretarial, especially in connexion with the awkward job of preparing the diagrams.

J. R. H.

NUFFIELD COLLEGE
OXFORD
October 1949

CONTENTS

LIST OF FIGURES

I

ANTECEDENTS

1. KEYNESIAN economics, in spite of all that it has done for our understanding of business fluctuations, has beyond all doubt left at least one major thing quite unexplained; and that thing is nothing less than the business cycle itself. We do now understand, more or less, what it is that determines the level of economic activity at any particular time; and having acquired that knowledge, we are naturally tempted to rush on to devise means of making that level what we would like it to be. The invitation to such a rush was broadcast by the *General Theory*, and economists in general have not been reluctant to accept the invitation. Yet it may well be that the invitation was premature, and the rush was premature. For Keynes did not show us, and did not attempt to show us, save by a few hints, why it is that in the past the level of activity has fluctuated according to so very definite a pattern. And until we understand that, we run serious risks in the application of his theory. It is only if we have complete confidence in our ability to control economic pressures, whatever their strength (and to control them at the precise time when they need to be controlled), that the sort of understanding given by Keynes is enough. Otherwise we must know something about the longer-run consequences of policies; we must have an assurance that the policies adopted, to deal with a momentary emergency, will not set up, in the longer run, pressures which are greater than we can hope to withstand. We must therefore know, not only how it is that an economy becomes more or less 'active', but why it is that its activity tends to fluctuate over time in such a very particular way.

2. That the economic systems of modern times are liable to fluctuations of a particular sort, which can properly be called cyclical, is a very obvious inductive generalization from the main facts of economic history. Statistical theorists may warn us that purely random sequences of events (when those events are marked by quantitative characteristics) have a definite tendency to build up into cyclical patterns;[1] and practical statisticians may demonstrate that the facts of economic history can be analysed to show a bewildering variety of cycles, few of which would leap to the eye unaided by calculation.[2] The plain economist must, I think, conclude that these investigations cancel one another out. The economic history of the last 150 years organizes itself so easily into a series of 7- to 10-year cycles, with certain interruptions traceable to major wars, that the reality of the cycle seems to him unmistakable. The cycles are not uniform; they differ among themselves quite considerably; but there can surely be no doubt of their family likeness. The definition of their common characteristics is certainly no easy matter. It is, I think, a mistake to begin one's investigation with a definition of the kind of fluctuation which one is going to regard as basic—deciding whether one is going to regard the cycle as being fundamentally a fluctuation in employment, or output, or prices, or interest rates, or money supplies. It is better to allow the definition to emerge as the theory develops.

3. The theory of the cycle, which I shall develop in this book, is not new in the sense that it introduces some completely new explanation, previously never thought of, or previously neglected. Its constituent parts are all of them fairly familiar. But they have, to my knowledge, never been put together in the precise way which I am going to propose. Several writers have got very near to it, but none seems to have taken the final step. When that step is taken, we get something which may have a better claim to be regarded as *the* theory of the cycle than any which have preceded it. For the 'assumptions' which we have to make in order to get our cycle are nearly all of them things which can hardly fail to be true; the most doubtful is something which in itself is distinctly more likely to be true than not. With a comparatively short list of such 'assumptions' I can show that a cyclical sequence, which is (to say the least) remarkably similar to that which is experienced in practice, is *inevitable*. The exact

[1] Cf. E. Slutsky, 'The Summation of Random Causes as the Source of Cyclic Processes' (*Econometrica*, 1937). M. G. Kendall, *Advanced Theory of Statistics*, vol. ii, p. 381.
[2] Cf. A. R. Burns and W. C. Mitchell, *Measuring Business Cycles*.

form of the cycle is not uniformly determined. There is plenty of room for those divergences from a standard model which are needed in order to cover the historical facts, but the underlying repetitiveness of the phenomenon seems to be adequately explained. It would therefore seem that we can point to a short list of fundamental facts which are sufficient to account for the cycle; and that surely is the first thing which a theory of the cycle ought to be able to do. It is, however, perfectly possible that there may be other forces at work, which are of a more or less cyclical character, so that they are (as it were) superimposed upon those first identified. *Secondary* cycle-makers of this sort are by no means ruled out. They would not, I think, be sufficient of themselves to induce a regular cycle, but they have some tendency in that direction. Granted the existence of the main cycle, it will attract these secondary forces to it, and the secondary forces may then intensify the fluctuations very seriously. I shall not explore this possibility very far; most of what I have to say will refer to the *main* cycle; but in two concluding chapters, which deal with the 'Monetary Factor', I shall examine the working of one secondary force which must almost infallibly play a significant part in the story.

4. Although the ancestry of what I am going to say (as is inevitable in such a well-worked field) goes far back, its immediate progenitors are three and three only. First of all, there is Keynes, from whom I take the saving-investment mechanism and the multiplier theory. I shall not at first be concerned with his interest theory (Liquidity Preference and the interest-investment schedule called the Marginal Efficiency of Capital); not that I want to deny anything of importance which Keynes has said on these matters, but that they belong to the forces which I treat as *secondary*. It is now very commonly accepted, even among the most faithful Keynesians, that the particular way in which the doctrine of the *General Theory* was arranged tends to exaggerate the importance of interest; thus it is fully in accordance with the dominant trend of economic thinking to push this side of Keynes's work a little into the background. Apart from this change of emphasis, I am broadly prepared to accept the *General Theory* as a short-period theory, and I shall use it in that capacity. But I shall have to emphasize some consequences of Keynes's teaching which he himself did not bring out sufficiently, and I shall have to do some significant reshaping of the foundations so as to fit them for a place in a structure which is different from that for which they were originally designed.

5. This first of my lines of descent has to be associated, quite inevitably and unmistakably, with the name of Keynes; though one must never forget that the *General Theory* is in essentials a formalization (and sometimes an over-formalization) of the great Cambridge tradition in monetary economics, which descends from Marshall to Keynes, not without significant contributions from Pigou and Lavington, Robertson and Kahn. To associate it solely with Keynes is something of a personification. My second line is not capable of being personified even to this extent. The dependence of trade fluctuations on the 'Acceleration Principle' (the effect on Investment of *changes* in the level of real income or output) was perceived by the economic intuition of John Maurice Clark,[1] and was defended by him for a considerable period before the mathematical possibilities of the principle were noticed. When this happened (the crucial step was taken in 1934 by Ragnar Frisch),[2] a new phase of development opened. What Frisch had done was to show that the acceleration principle established an analogy between economic fluctuations and the 'waves' which are so elaborately studied in physics; thus a vast amount of knowledge and technique acquired for other purposes by applied mathematicians and physicists suddenly became relevant to the economic problem. This was a most exciting thing to happen, but it had its inconveniences. The new technique was such that only a minority of economists could have the leisure, or perhaps the ability, to acquire it; while those who did possess it had often acquired it in another setting than that of economics, so that their grasp of the technique was not always matched by their sense of the

[1] *Economics of Overhead Costs*, ch. 19. The modern discussion of the point undoubtedly goes back to Clark, and he seems to have been the first who fully appreciated its importance. But the point itself had been observed before; cf. D. H. Robertson, *A Study of Industrial Fluctuations*, p. 123, and the paper by Aftalion there mentioned (*Journal d'Economie Politique*, 1909).
[2] 'Propagation and Impulse Problems', in *Essays in honour of G. Cassel*.

peculiarities of the economic material on which they sought to exercise it. The non-mathematical economist has indeed been given plenty of excuse for his neglect of these developments; but to allow that is not necessarily to allow that the neglect has been justified. For my own part, I cannot pretend to have delved very deeply into the now extensive literature of Frischian 'macrodynamics'; but I have learned enough to be convinced that economists can only neglect it at their peril. I believe that Frisch and his followers (among whom Kalecki[1] and—in this connexion—Samuelson[2] need special mention) have isolated and investigated at least one vital element in the causation of the cycle. The attempt which I shall make in this book to state their reasoning on this point in the simplest possible terms, so as to make it as widely understandable as possible, is one of the more important parts of the task which I have before me.

It will be noticed that the Frisch paper was written and published before the publication of Keynes's *General Theory*; it is therefore not surprising that in some respects its argument should be pre-Keynesian. But in fact it turns out that these relics are of little importance. It is a relatively simple matter to re-state the 'macrodynamic' analysis in Keynesian terms; what then emerges is a notable extension of the Keynes theory, but nothing which is essentially inconsistent with it, at least in formal structure. Some of the econometrists (as, for instance, Kalecki) have not hesitated to draw essentially Keynesian morals from the system which they get in this way; whether they are justified in so doing is one of the things on which our work may throw some light. But first of all we must consider the 'macro-dynamic' system itself; and in view of the self-denying ordinance which I propose to maintain against any but a very limited use of mathematics in the text of this book, even to describe the main lines of that system is a considerable undertaking.

The 'macrodynamic' theory, compounded out of Keynes and

---

[1] *Essays in the Theory of Economic Fluctuations*, and *Studies in Economic Dynamics*.

[2] 'Foundations of Economic Analysis', Part II, and numerous earlier articles. The best general description of the modern 'acceleration' theory, based on Samuelson's work, is to be found in A. H. Hansen, *Fiscal Policy and Business Cycles*, ch. 12. An account in terms of fairly elementary mathematics, which I have found very useful, is in A. Smithies, 'Equilibrium Analysis and Process Analysis', *Econometrica*, 1942.

Frisch, has a claim to be regarded as a complete theory of the cycle; but I do not myself believe that that claim is justified. The econometrists have revealed to us an engine which is capable of inducing general fluctuations, and one must admit that there are strong grounds for supposing that that engine is in fact at work. Nevertheless, the fluctuations which it generates do not look quite like the actual fluctuations which we know, in history and in contemporary experience.[1] There still seem to be some missing pieces. These are unlikely to be anything very subtle; the fluctuations which we experience are so general and pervasive that it is much more natural to interpret them in terms of the major than of the minor characteristics of the modern economy. What one wants to do is so to enlarge the econometrists' model that it takes into account, or can take into account, all the major aspects of the economic process which look like being relevant. So far that does not seem to have been done.[2]

6. And so I come to the third of my 'progenitors', who is Mr. Harrod. I have certain very definite obligations to Mr. Harrod, which I should like to make quite explicit. They relate to some essential features of the following argument, though I must frankly admit that the work which has gone into this book had been carried a long way before I realized their importance.

[1] A good deal of evidence in this direction is presented in J. Tinbergen, 'Statistical Evidence on the Acceleration Principle', *Economics*, 1938.

[2] Although I have drawn so heavily upon the econometrists' work, and may often appear to be constructing a 'model' like theirs, I should like to make it clear at the outset that my purpose is different from theirs. If econometrics is defined (to borrow a definition which I once gave myself in another connexion) as 'the use of statistical methods to establish functional connexions between economic magnitudes'—it seems to me that this definition does describe the characteristic work of the econometric school—then I have very little faith in econometrics when it is applied to phenomena of the magnitude and complexity of those which here concern us. The weakness due to the shortness of economic time-series is notorious; but another weakness, due to the lack of reason for supposing that the relevant parameters are at all likely to remain constant for considerable periods, seems to me to be at least as damaging. I am therefore not seeking to find a formula which can subsequently be fitted by regression analysis to the recorded statistics; I am not seeking to fit curves, I am trying (in a more old-fashioned sense) to explain. In spite, therefore, of the use which I make of the 'models' in the earlier stages of my argument, it becomes (at least in spirit) more 'literary' as it goes on.

In the course of my work, I was coming to feel an increasing dissatisfaction with the 'macrodynamic' model; but it was not until I read Mr. Harrod's book[1] that I realized what it was that I had overlooked. Then everything began to fall into place. The theory which I am going to present is the result of the consequential transformation.

I could kick myself for not having seen it before. After all, the essential ideas which I am taking from Mr. Harrod are not new ideas, put forward by him for the first time in 1948; if one had had eyes to see, one could have seen them nearly a decade ago.[2] It is, however, quite clear why it is that neither I myself, nor (as far as I know) anyone else, seems to have seen them. To anyone who comes to the Harrod theory from the theory of the econometrists, it looks at first sight to be nothing more than a weaker, and less usable, version of the 'macrodynamic' model. What Mr. Harrod seems to be doing, if one comes to his theory from that side, is simply to be elaborating one of the cases which, on the other line, had been passed by and rejected in favour of a more interesting alternative. And this impression is not without foundation. The Harrod theory lacks some of the virtues of the econometrists' model, and it suffers severely from its lack of them. The first thing about it which strikes one is this deficiency, and having seen that, it is easy to be blinded to its countervailing merits. Yet these merits are very real. Once we decide to treat the Harrod theory as a supplement to the econometrists' theory, instead of a rival, it begins to look much more attractive. It does then appear that Mr. Harrod has emphasized a few simple and central points, which the econometrists could have taken into account, but which, in fact, they have generally tended to overlook. And if he has not been altogether successful in working those points into a coherent theory, he has at least given us some help in that direction.

7. The first of these points, which we have to attribute to Mr. Harrod, is of course his insistence on the propriety, indeed

[1] *Towards a Dynamic Economics* (1948), especially Chapter III.

[2] The ideas in question first appeared in his 'Essay in Dynamic Theory' (*Econ. Jour.*, 1939). They cropped up again in the apparently quite independent article by Evsey Domar, 'Capital Expansion, Rate of Growth, and Employment', *Econometrica*, 1946.

the necessity, of approaching the business cycle as a problem
of an expanding economy. What we have to study, he empha-
sizes, is not fluctuation as such, but fluctuation about a rising
trend. When we look at the problem in its historical context,
considering what it is that we have to explain, this precept is
obvious and compelling. Historically, the cycle began to appear
with the 'Industrial Revolution'—just at the stage, that is, when
expansion in the social output became a leading characteristic of
the economic system. The cycles which have been experienced
have all of them taken place against a background of secular
expansion. Thus we know, from inductive evidence, that cycles
can take place against the background of a rising trend; we do
not know, we can only guess, whether a stationary economy
could experience similar fluctuations. It is therefore wise to
begin by attempting to explain what has been experienced; anything else must be a matter of prophecy, or at any rate, extrapolation. The wisdom of such a course as this is evident; but
because the foundations of economic theory are static, economists are bound to have difficulty in extricating themselves from
a static framework. Nevertheless, it is possible to do so, and it is
essential that at the very threshold of a theory of the cycle, we
should make the effort.

8. The second of the points which I take from Mr. Harrod is
his contention that the study of an expanding economy proceeds
much more conveniently in the form of a theory of output than
of a theory of employment. This is a shaft which is, of course,
mainly directed against Keynes. Not all of the econometrists
have been very clear on the matter; but the proponents of a
theory which depends on the Acceleration Principle should here
be on Mr Harrod's side. For what that principle is concerned
with is the effect of changes in *output* on investment; it is not
evident that a rise in output will have any different effect in this
direction when it is due to increasing employment from what it
will have when it is due to many of the various causes which
can be grouped together as increasing productivity. It was
Keynes's neglect of the acceleration principle which enabled
him to push employment so much to the fore. A theory of the
other type can be, and should be, incidentally a theory of

employment; but it cannot be built around the unemployment percentage in the way Keynes's was. Having decided that, other things follow. The concept of the 'wage-unit', which Keynes introduced to buttress his employment approach, has to be abandoned. The concept of 'Full Employment' has to be looked at in a new way. We have throughout to go back to the pre-Keynesian (or rather, pre-*General Theory*) practice of thinking in real terms, in terms (that is) of money values corrected by the price-level of final output.[1] The Keynesian emphasis on employment, and all that went with it, turns out after all to have been a red herring.

9. The third of my debts to Mr. Harrod is more difficult to explain before we get down to detail. Stated rather roughly, it is something as follows. One cannot help feeling, as one works with the *macrodynamic* models in their simpler forms, that the most plausible value which one can give to the 'investment coefficient' (or coefficients) on which the whole theory turns, is *larger* than that which is needed to give the results which would conform most nearly to the cyclical phenomena which we experience. That is to say, the system looks as if it ought to be more unstable—even much more unstable—than it is. This difficulty has, of course, been noticed by the econometrists; some of them have been trying to find a way out by introducing new mathematical complications in the form of non-linear relations between the associated variables.[2] Formally, I suppose, the difficulty can be overcome in this way, but such a solution must always remain distinctly esoteric; it is hard to believe that it could possibly be made at all generally usable. Fortunately we can find another way out with the aid of Mr. Harrod. It is a

[1] My own conversion to this point of view has been largely the work of Professor Robertson, who had made much progress in reducing my fortifications before I finally succumbed to a flank attack from Mr. Harrod.

[2] See, especially, Samuelson, op. cit. A rather similar device, on a different level, has been proposed by Mr. Kaldor ('A Model of the Trade Cycle', *Econ. Jour.*, 1940). But Mr. Kaldor's model is not based on the acceleration principle (investment depending on changes in output); it is based on an assumed connexion between investment and the absolute level of output, a relation which seems to me to be much less defensible. Nevertheless, it must be said that the Kaldor theory is better than the assumptions on which it is formally based; for a certain amount of what is really 'acceleration' is allowed to go on, as it were, behind the scenes.

way which the mathematicians will not care for; but it is wholly in accordance with the general methods of *economic* analysis, so that economists will find that they can use it, at least for the most important of their purposes, without special difficulty.

10. I have now made my acknowledgements, and can get to work. There is, however, one thing which it has become conventional to do at the beginning of a work of this character, and which I may as well do in this place. This is to say something about the meaning of the term 'Economic Dynamics'. I have previously made a pronouncement on this subject myself, in quite a different context: I then said that dynamics was 'that part of economic theory in which all Quantities must be dated'.[1] Frisch has defined 'the essential characteristic of a dynamic theory' as follows: it is one in which 'we consider the magnitudes of certain variables in different points of time, and we introduce certain equations which embrace at the same time several of these magnitudes belonging to different instants'.[2] Mr. Harrod defines dynamics as the study of an 'economy in which rates of output are changing'.[3] All of these definitions (including my own) were introduced for special purposes; I think we can now begin to see what those purposes have been, and how they are related. I shall not in this place propose any new definition; I shall merely point out that the theory advanced in this book is dynamic in *all* of the senses which have thus been proposed. But whether it is therefore to be regarded as establishing a record in 'dynamism' is a matter which I shall leave to the judgement of the reader.

[1] *Value and Capital*, p. 115.
[2] Op. cit., p. 171.
[3] Op. cit., p. 4.

II

SAVING, INVESTMENT, AND THE MULTIPLIER

1. WE may now begin to drop our ingredients into the pot, beginning with the most familiar, namely, the Multiplier theory.

I shall assume that the reader is familiar with the multiplier theory, in the form Keynes gave it; nevertheless, we have to give it some discussion here, for two reasons. In the first place, we are committed to a certain change in approach, due to our decision to work in real terms (in terms, that is, of money values deflated by the price-level of output), not, as Keynes did, in terms of wage-units (money values deflated by the wage-level). This has important consequences, which require to be noticed. In the second place, we cannot avoid taking a hand in the prodigious controversy about the process of adjustment implied in the multiplier theory. For our 'dynamic' programme makes it quite impossible for us to allow any looseness of thought on this crucial matter.

2. There can be no multiplier theory unless the supply of output is to some extent responsive to the demand (or Effective Demand) for it.[1] This statement is true of Keynes's theory, as it is of the theory in the form we are going to give it; but in our version it needs, if anything, even greater emphasis. It is required in our version that the output of consumption goods, and the output of investment goods, should each be responsive to demand; and it is even desirable, if the theory is to be capable of its simplest statement, that they should each of them be so responsive that the ratio between the price-level of consumption goods and the price-level of investment goods should be approximately constant. This is a very drastic assumption, which can evidently not be valid at all generally; it would be unwise to accept it on anything but a very provisional basis. But it is convenient to make it in the opening stages of our argument, though we must not omit to take due account at a later stage of the

[1] Even if the supply of output was fixed, a process, analogous to the Multiplier process, could still occur; but it would not be convergent.

corrections which have to be introduced in those cases when it clearly becomes inapplicable.

The reason why it is so convenient to make this assumption is that it enables us to identify Real Investment (in the sense of investment deflated by the price-index of output in general) with real investment in the more natural sense (when it is deflated by its own price-index, the price-index of investment goods). So long as we are deflating both Investment and Saving by the same price-index, we can correctly express the Investment-Saving Equation in the form Real Investment = Real Saving. Of course we can always arrange things so that we do deflate them by the same price-index; but whenever it happens that the ratio between the sectional price-indices (the terms of trade, we may call it if we like, between the consumption goods and the investment goods industries) is not constant, we have continually to be reminding ourselves that either investment, or saving, or both, are not being deflated in the natural manner. It is obviously convenient to postpone such complications, and to begin by considering the case in which these 'terms of trade' can be treated as constant.

3. We can then argue substantially in Keynes's manner. In place of Keynes's Consumption Function, which expresses consumption in wage-units in terms of income in wage-units, we require a consumption function which shall express Real Consumption as a function of Real Income. This new consumption function is not the same as Keynes's, but the advantage of the change seems on the whole to be on our side. When the consumption function is expressed in wage-units, as Keynes expressed it, what is in fact being done is to say that we shall expect to find the same proportion between saving and income whenever income reaches a particular level in terms of wage-units; if the proportion changes, we shall have to say that there has been a change in the underlying conditions, a change in the 'ceteris paribus'. Approximately this means that we are to expect to get the same percentage of income saved whenever employment is at a given level. But in practice we should not expect to get the same percentage of saving in two cases where the level of employment was similar, if in the one case real income was high, and in the other it was very low. There is something to be said for a formulation which takes this into account.[1]

We can then proceed, or so it appears, exactly as Keynes did. We can note that Real Saving (S) is the difference between Real Income (Y) and Real Consumption (C). C is a given function of Y, and therefore S is a given function of Y. Social accounting considerations tell us that Real Investment (I) is equal to real saving. As soon, therefore, as I, the volume of real investment, is determined, Y, the volume of real income (or Output) will be determined. If investment must be equal to saving, and saving is a function of income, then the level of income corresponding to a given volume of investment must be that which engenders a volume of saving equal to the given volume of investment. If the level of income had been higher, saving would have been larger; thus if investment had been larger, income would have to have been so much larger as to engender a volume of saving equal to the larger volume of investment. If we suppose the consumption function to be such that a proportion c out of any increment of income is consumed, while the corresponding proportion $1-c$ is saved, income would have to increase so as to make $(1-c)$ of the increase in income equal to the given increment of investment. Thus the increment of income would have to equal the increment of investment multiplied by $1/(1-c)$. Thus it is this last expression which measures the 'multiplier'.

Before going farther, let us put this basic argument into diagrammatic form. We are going to have to develop the argument in a good many ways, and the diagram, which is not particularly necessary at this stage, will serve as a convenient instrument for the further developments. It is therefore worth our while to set it out rather carefully.

In Fig. 1, income (Y) is measured on the vertical axis, saving (or investment) on the horizontal. The curve S is the savings curve (or consumption function in reverse); it shows the

---

[1] We should clearly not expect the same effect on saving if total real income expanded as the result of a change in population, as would occur if the rise was due to a change in real income per head. On this account, as on others, population changes deserve special attention. See below, p. 36.

amount of saving corresponding to any given level of income. All magnitudes are taken to refer to the whole economy, and are measured in real terms (that is to say, at constant prices). It is, however, convenient to use a different unit of measurement on the two axes. For saving is unlikely to be more than a small

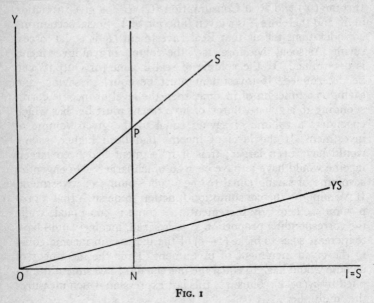

FIG. 1

proportion of income; thus if we used the same unit on the two axes, the savings curve would lie very close to the vertical axis, and the whole operative part of the diagram would be squashed up against the left-hand side, in a way which is very inconvenient for drawing. It is, therefore, convenient to measure saving in units which are (say) only one-tenth of the units in which we measure income; this gives us more room. We can mark this difference of scale by drawing a line *YS* through the origin at an angle which corresponds to the scale-ratio; this *scale-line* would be at an angle of 45° if the units on the two axes were the same, but is tilted over to the right in view of the scale adjustment. The economic meaning of the scale-line is that it shows the position which would be taken by the savings curve if the whole of income were saved.

A given volume of investment is marked on the diagram by a vertical line (I). The level of income which will engender a volume of saving equal to this given investment is shown by the vertical coordinate of the point P where the I-line intersects the S-curve. Thus it is Keynes's theory that in the given conditions the economy will take up a position which is represented by the point P. If investment had been larger, the I-line would have been farther to the right and the point of intersection correspondingly higher. Therefore the increase in income which corresponds to a given increase in investment depends upon the slope of the S-curve. It is this slope which measures the 'multiplier'.

4. When the multiplier theory is put in this form, one of the first things which strikes one is the parallelism between this diagram and that with which we are familiar in ordinary demand-and-supply analysis. Marshall taught us to regard the price and quantity of a single commodity as being simultaneously determined by the intersection of a pair of curves; Keynes is showing that the size of the whole social output may be regarded as being determined in the same way. And the resemblance is more than superficial, for when one thinks it out it becomes apparent that it is the same kind of 'curve' which is at issue. The savings curve (the only one which is so far operative) is itself a particular kind of demand curve—it shows the way in which the demand for consumption goods in general varies with income. This being so, it looks as if it would be correct to regard it in the same light as that in which we regard demand curves in general. We are familiar with the doctrine that the shortest of short-period demand or supply curves for a commodity does not necessarily indicate the price which will be paid on a particular date for the particular quantity of the commodity which is bought or sold. We have known (effectively since Adam Smith) that the market price will only coincide with the price which is determined by the curves if the market is in *equilibrium*. The equality between demand and supply must hold whether the market is in equilibrium or not. For every buyer there must be a seller, and therefore on every day the amount bought must equal the amount sold. But the amount which is bought and sold is not necessarily the equilibrium amount. In terms of the demand-and-supply diagram, all that the 'accounting' equality between demand and supply indicates is that any state of the market can be represented by a point on the diagram; but if the market is not in equilibrium, the corresponding point will not be at the intersection of the curves. But if the actual market situation lies off the demand curve, forces will be set to work which will pull it back to the demand curve; if it is off the supply curve, it will be pulled back to the supply curve; the combined operation of these forces will pull it towards the point of intersection.

There does not seem to be any reason why an analysis of this sort should not apply to the savings curve. It is not really sensible to regard the savings curve as a relation between saving and income which must hold in any period, however short; it is much more reasonable to regard it as a normal relation which will *tend* to be resumed if a departure is made from it. If, therefore, investment increases from ON to ON', income will not necessarily rise at once from PN to $P'N'$. If investment has been steady for a considerable time at ON, then we should expect that income would have come to approximate to the level PN; and after investment has remained for some time at ON', we should expect that income would approximate to $P'N'$. That is all that can reasonably be said.

This *static* interpretation of Keynes would, I think, have been generally accepted as the correct interpretation if it were not for one thing. It does not really answer the question we want to have answered. For what we are usually interested in is not the effect of a single simple shift in investment from one steady level to another steady level; what we want to understand (especially as we approach the theory of the Cycle) is the effect of continuous changes. And for that purpose the static interpretation does not give us enough help. The static interpretation is itself an improvement upon the erroneous interpretation which was too much countenanced by Keynes—the interpretation according to which the system is in equilibrium all the time. It shows us that the accounting identity can still hold, so that actual saving can remain equal to actual investment, and yet that the saving which is a function of income may not be equal to investment. This is an important and useful result, but it does not go as far as we need to go. It does not throw any light upon the *path* by which the system moves from one *equilibrium* to another; and this means, as we shall see, that it is not really well adapted for the study of a process of change—whether that process is one of continuous advance, or of fluctuation.

5. At any point on such a path saving will be equal to investment, in the accounting sense; but this actual saving will not necessarily be the saving which is functionally related to the ruling level of income, the saving which is proper to this level of income, or 'proper saving' as we may call it for the moment.[1] The fact that actual saving is equal to actual investment means that the actual position of the system can be represented by a point on the diagram; but if actual saving is not equal to proper saving the position taken up will not be an equilibrium position. The path to equilibrium can therefore be represented on the diagram; if it proceeds from one equilibrium point P to another equilibrium P', it will be shown by a line proceeding from P to P'. But it will not necessarily be the *straight* line PP'. It is easy to construct very reasonable assumptions under which the line will take different forms.

The simplest of these is the assumption which lies behind Mr. Kahn's famous 'convergent series'.[2] There will only be a direct movement from P to P' if consumption varies in its normal manner with the income which is being earned contemporaneously. It is, I suppose, conceivable that this might happen, but it is clear that in practice it does not happen, at least if the period to which the income and consumption refer is a short one. People earn their incomes and *then* spend them. Now it is quite consistent with the existence of a savings curve, interpreted as an equilibrium relation, if we assume that on a

---

[1] My 'proper saving' corresponds to what in another setting is called '*ex ante* saving'. But the latter term has connotations which I prefer to avoid, and it fails to bring out the analogy with value theory which to me is important.

[2] R. F. Kahn, 'Home Investment and Unemployment', *Econ. Jour.*, 1931. In D. H. Robertson's, *Banking Policy and the Price Level* (1928), the same assumption was more explicitly made, but for rather different purposes.

closer view consumption does not depend upon the income of
the current period, but on that of the period before. This is the
basis of Mr. Kahn's construction.

On this assumption, the 'saving' which is a function of income
is not the difference between current consumption and current
income but the difference between current consumption and
the income of the preceding period. It is 'saving' in this sense

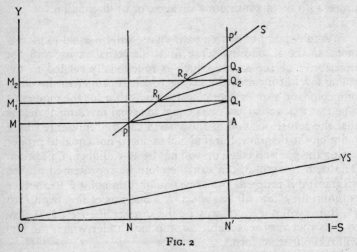

FIG. 2

(considered as a function of the income of the preceding period)
which will be shown by the S-curve. But 'saving' in this sense
is not the saving which is equal to investment by the accounting
identity. In each definition, saving is the difference between
income and consumption, and it is the same *consumption* which
enters into each definition. But in the one case it is current
income from which consumption has to be deducted, in the
other case it is the income of the preceding period. Thus the
difference between the two definitions is equal to the change in
income between the two periods. Since it is actual saving which
is equal to investment, we may put this principle thus: that the
increase in income between two successive periods is equal to
the difference between investment and 'saving'.

Let us look at this in terms of our diagram. In Mr. Kahn's

model, the economy begins from a point of equilibrium at P (Fig. 2); investment is then suddenly increased from ON to ON', being subsequently held constant at its new level. In the first period after the change investment is equal to ON', but 'saving', being dependent on the income of the *preceding* period, remains at ON. Investment minus 'saving' is thus equal to NN', and income will increase in the first period by an amount equal to this. Remembering our convention about the scale-line, we can show this increase in income by drawing a line through P parallel to the scale-line, intersecting the vertical through N' at Q_1. $Q_1 N'$ is therefore the income earned in the first period after the change; since investment in this first period is already equal to ON' (which also measures actual or accounting saving), we may say that the situation of the economy in the first period after the change is represented by the point Q_1.

For the second period after the change, 'saving' can be read off from the S-curve by finding the point at which the horizontal through Q_1 intersects the S-curve (R_1). $R_1 M_1$ is then the 'saving' corresponding to an income of the preceding period $Q_1 N'$. The gap between investment and 'saving' in the second period is $Q_1 R_1$, and this will be the amount by which income earned in the second period increases above the income earned in the first. Income earned in the second period is therefore shown on the diagram by drawing a line through R_1 parallel to the scale-line, to intersect the vertical at Q_2. $Q_2 N'$ is therefore the income of the second period, and the position of the economy in the second period is represented by the point Q_2.

The same construction can now be repeated for subsequent periods. In the third period, 'saving' will be $R_2 M_2$; the gap between investment and 'saving' will be $Q_2 R_2$; and the position of the economy will be represented by Q_3, where $R_3 Q_3$ is parallel to the scale-line. And so on, more or less indefinitely.

It will, however, be obvious, in view of the upward slope of the S-curve, that the successive intercepts $Q_n R_n$ will get smaller and smaller, so that the change in income between successive periods ultimately becomes negligible. When this happens (assuming, of course, that investment remains constant for long enough to enable it to happen) the position of the economy will be represented by the point of equilibrium P'.

Thus, under Mr. Kahn's assumption, the system does not proceed at once from the old equilibrium P to the new equilibrium P'; it goes there by the *path* $PQ_1Q_2Q_3...P'$. It is because we have assumed (a questionable assumption, which we are only making provisionally) that investment does go at once from its old volume ON to its new volume ON' that the intermediate positions all lie on the vertical line $P'N'$. They creep up that vertical towards the new equilibrium position.

6. We have now seen what will happen when consumption is lagged one period behind income—for that is what the Kahn assumption amounts to. However, when the argument is put in this way, it is easily capable of a good deal of generalization. We have seen that if there is no lag in consumption, there will be a direct movement from P to P'; if there is a uniform lag of the Kahn type, the system will move towards the new equilibrium by a path of the kind which has been described. It is easy to see that if the system reacts in a way which is intermediate between these two cases, some consumption reacting without lag, and some reacting with a certain uniform lag, we are bound to get a result which is intermediate in character. In the first period, the system will go to a point which is intermediate between P' and Q_1. In the second period, it will move to a second point which is intermediate between P' and the first point—and which is actually nearer to P' than the point which would have ensued upon the first point, if the first point had happened to have been reached in a Kahn process. And so on through later periods. This amounts to saying that we get a more rapid convergence than we got in the Kahn case, with the whole of consumption lagged; but we shall not get the immediate passage to the new equilibrium which would take place if there was no lag at all.

Again, since the 'period' for which consumption is lagged in the Kahn model is arbitrary in length, the Kahn process can evidently be slowed up by lengthening the time for which consumption is lagged. If consumption is lagged for three *months*, and we consider the situation at the end of each month, then at the end of the first month the system will already have reached Q_1, but it does not go on to Q_2 until three months have elapsed.

We get a simple Kahn process with a pause of three months between one step and the next.

Now suppose that instead of all consumption being lagged for three months, some is only lagged for one month. It is obvious that this will hurry up the movement to equilibrium. Arguing in this way, we see that however we vary our assumptions about lags—however complex we make them—we shall always get a process of the Kahn type, converging faster or slower according as less or more of consumption is lagged, and according as the average length of lag is smaller or greater. It will be noticed that the final position of equilibrium depends upon the marginal propensity to save outright (for it is this saving—the only net saving which would occur if income were stationary—which is the proper saving expressed in our S-curve), while the rate at which equilibrium is approached depends upon the characteristics of the transitory saving which is only deferred consumption.

This generalization of the multiplier is only a very slight generalization, but it does already do something to put the theory into the form which we need for our further inquiries. There can be no doubt at all that in practice the response of consumption to changes in income is lagged; indeed, the multiplier theory cannot be stated in a compelling form unless the lags are recognized. Of the two classical formulations, it is the 'lagged' version of Mr. Kahn which is the more easily intelligible; the 'lagless' version of Keynes, in spite of its technical simplicity, is not acceptable except to a mind which has already undergone some preliminary sophistication. But the lag between the payment of wages and the spending of them—which it is useful to emphasize for purposes of exposition—is, of course, not the lag which is practically important. If we had nothing but this wage-lag to take into account, we could deal with it quite adequately by taking a unit period long enough to straddle across it (a period of one month might already be long enough) and we could then treat the system as having an instantaneous adjustment in the Keynesian manner. It is with the consumption out of non-wage incomes (salaries and—most of all—profits) that much more important lags occur. Here we have to distinguish (1) the length of time which elapses between the effective economic earning of an income and its passage into the control of the consumer, (2) the length of time between the consumer's acquisition of spending power and his utilization of it. Both of these lags may be very considerable. The former is largely a matter of accounting necessity, which causes delay between the earning of profits and their ascertainment, and between ascertainment and distribution. The latter is mainly a matter of deliberate equalization by the consumer himself, who will ordinarily make some effort to ensure that his expenditure does not fluctuate to the same degree as his income fluctuates. It is, however, clear that equalization of this sort is nowadays an important factor in the former lag also. Undistributed profits are in principle temporary, rather than permanent, saving; and although we may suspect that the temporary saving has some tendency to become permanent, it is one thing to say this and quite another to say that undistributed profits have altogether lost their *temporary* character. A large part of undistributed profits must surely still be regarded as temporary saving.

An interesting econometric study by Professor Tinbergen,[1] based on British data of the pre-1914 period, suggests that at that time non-wage consumption was normally lagged behind income by a period of something like one year. I do not myself put great confidence in such results, but in this case the conclusion agrees very well with what might have been expected on general grounds. We may therefore feel fortified by it. My guess would be that the disturbances of the last thirty years have provided an additional stimulus for equalization policies, which would presumably mean that the lag would have tended to increase. We seem, therefore, to be amply justified on this ground alone in concluding that consumption lags are a matter of real importance; and we need little more than that for most of the work which follows.[2]

To sum up. We have so far done no more than examine the

[1] 'Does Consumption Lag behind Incomes?', *Review of Economic Statistics*, 1942.
[2] When we come, in a later chapter (p. 53 below), to consider the effects of changes in stocks, we shall find that there is a case for re-interpreting the multiplier analysis so as to allow for these; but when we do so, we get another reason for consumption lags, of perhaps even greater importance.

effects of a once-for-all increase in investment; we have concluded that even when the lag-structure is complex, we shall
nevertheless expect to find a convergence to equilibrium by
something which is broadly similar to the Kahn process. We
can always satisfy ourselves that this must be so in the following
way. We know that if all consumption reacted instantaneously,
we should get an immediate movement to the new equilibrium.
We know, on the other hand, that if all consumption was lagged
as much as that part of consumption for which the lag is greatest,
we should get a regular Kahn progress with a very long period,
which would mean a very *slow* convergence to equilibrium. Any
other distribution of lags must lie between these limits, and
must therefore produce something intermediate between these
two results. As long as some consumption is lagged, the convergence will not be immediate; as long as some consumption
reacts more rapidly than it does in the *slow* case, we shall get a
more rapid convergence than in that case. There is no more to
be said. But there is much more to be said as soon as we begin
asking about the effects of more complicated changes in the rate
of investment. To those problems we must now turn.

III

THE MULTIPLIER IN A CHANGING ECONOMY

1. WE have now to ask how the Multiplier mechanism will work, not in the relatively 'static' case of a single change in the rate of investment, but in the cases which, for the theory of the cycle, are much more interesting—when investment is continuously expanding, continuously contracting, or changing over from one motion to the other.[1] It will be convenient to begin with the simplest case, that of a uniform expansion, and to start by exploring it on the Kahn assumption of a single uniform lag. We have already seen enough to be able to guess that once this case has been mastered, further generalizations will not be too difficult.

Let us therefore assume, as in our previous diagram, that consumption is always determined by the income of the preceding period, and let us investigate what happens if investment increases from period to period *by equal amounts*.[2] The course which the system will then follow is shown on Fig. 3, which is simply an elaboration of Fig. 2. We suppose, as before, that the process begins from a static equilibrium at P (investment being ON_0 and income PN_0). In period 1, investment increases to ON_1, exactly as before. But now we do not assume that in period 2, investment remains constant at ON_1; instead it increases to ON_2, and so on through later periods. What happens?

In the first period things proceed as before. The movement will therefore be from P to Q_1 (as in Fig. 2), PQ_1 being parallel to the scale-line. In order to find the point reached in the second period, we calculate 'saving' by drawing a horizontal through Q_1 to the S-curve at R_1 and we then draw a line through R_1

---

[1] It will be noticed that the theorem with which we concluded the preceding chapter was already *dynamic*, in the sense of Frisch; but in the sense of Harrod it was quite definitely static. It is at the present point that our theory begins to be dynamic in Harrod's sense.

[2] It is easier to begin with the assumption of expansion by equal amounts (in an arithmetical series); the assumption of expansion by equal proportions (geometrical series) is more interesting, but is a shade harder to handle. See Mathematical Appendix, p. 176.

parallel to the scale-line to meet (now) the vertical through N_2 at a new Q_2. (For Q_2 must lie above Q_1 by an amount which measures the difference between investment *in the second period* and the lagged 'saving'.) The course of the economy in the second period is therefore from Q_1 to Q_2. Now since it is $R_1 Q_2$

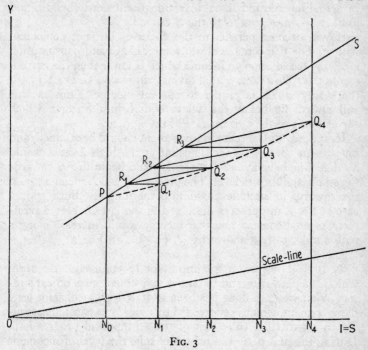

FIG. 3

which is parallel to the scale-line, $Q_1 Q_2$ must be steeper than the scale-line. In fact, income increases in the second period not merely by the amount of the increase in investment during that period; it also increases because of the 'first round' of the multiplier effect coming from the increase in investment in the first period. Similarly, when we pass to the third period, $Q_2 Q_3$ must be steeper than $Q_1 Q_2$. For now there is the 'second round' of the first period's multiplier effect to be taken into account. But (as is readily apparent from the diagram and is verifiable from these general considerations) the slopes of the successive segments do not increase beyond a certain point; they converge (just as the original Kahn series converged, and for the same reason). If investment goes on increasing regularly for a large number of periods, the course $PQ_1 Q_2...$ which is traced out by actual income and actual investment will slowly bend round until it becomes *parallel* to the S-curve.

It will become parallel to the S-curve, but not coincident with it. For if income is steadily increasing, and consumption is always based upon an income which is lower than the current income, it follows that actual saving will always be greater than the saving which is proper to current income. Thus income will always lie below the 'static equilibrium' income which corresponds to the current rate of investment.

If, indeed, the increase in investment should be stopped, and investment then remained constant at the high level it would by that time have attained, income would begin to rise towards the static equilibrium level. The process by which income would rise towards its static level would be nothing else but a special case of the Kahn process discussed in the last chapter. Investment is now constant, so that income would increase along a path similar to that shown by $Q_1 Q_2 Q_3...$ in Fig. 2.

2. It is, however, more important to emphasize the form which the path will tend to take if investment goes on expanding. What we have done has been to start with a constant level of investment, which is succeeded by a steady expansion according to a particular rule (that of the arithmetical progression). During the first periods after the change the level of income is much affected by the previous static condition. But, after a while, that influence drops into the background, and the system adjusts itself to the state of steady expansion. This, it will be noticed, is exactly analogous to what happened in the more *static* problem which we analysed in the last chapter. There we began with a system which was adjusted to a particular level of investment, and we inquired what happened when the level of investment was changed. We found that in the first periods after the change, income still clung to a certain extent to its old equilibrium level; it only adapted itself to the new equilibrium level by degrees. Given sufficient time, the adjustment to the new level would become practically perfect. We now see that a similar adaptation can take place to a process of expansion. But in this case the system does not settle down to a new static equilibrium; that would obviously be impossible. What it does is to settle down to a 'dynamic' or 'moving' equilibrium, in which it is adjusted to the expansion. By the time it settles down to its *moving equilibrium* it has, as it were, *forgotten* the static equilibrium from which it emerged; the static equilibrium has receded into the immemorial and ineffective past.

In the first periods after the change, income at Q_1 and Q_2 is *higher* than it would have been if the system had already reached its new moving equilibrium during those periods. (This can be seen at once if we extend the equilibrium path, already approximately reached by the fourth or fifth periods, in a backwards direction.) And this is as it should be. For if, during the periods before the change took place, investment had been increasing according to its new plan instead of being stationary as it was in fact, it must, during those periods, have been *lower* than it was in fact. If it had only reached ON_0 at the end of a previous expansion, its level in earlier periods must have been lower than ON_0. Thus, in our diagram, the path begins at a point which is *above* the moving equilibrium level, and only comes down to it by degrees. The process of adjustment to the moving equilibrium is exactly similar to the adjustment to a static equilibrium—the process with which we are familiar in the Kahn model. The system *converges* in exactly the same way.

3. Here again we have a principle which enables us to generalize very readily.[1] In the first place, we can do as we did at the end of the preceding chapter; we can drop the assumption of the single uniform lag. If there is no lag in consumption, then it is obvious that the moving equilibrium path must simply lie along the S-curve; and since equilibrium is on the S-curve in the static case also, there is no process of adjustment when a passage has to be made from one to the other. If there are

---

[1] To prove the *existence* of a moving equilibrium in the more complex cases to which we now come is not at all a simple matter; but it can be proved. (See Math. App., pp. 174 ff.) I am assuming that non-mathematical readers will accept it intuitively.

complex lags, some consumption being lagged (let us say) only a few weeks, some a few months, and some as much as a couple of years, then there will still be a moving equilibrium path, to which the system will converge if it is displaced from it. The convergence takes place for essentially the same reasons as in the static case; but it is the properties of the moving equilibrium which more deserve attention. When once the moving equilibrium has been reached, income must increase steadily; for investment is increasing steadily, and income has become adjusted to investment; thus income also must be increasing steadily. But since consumption is based, at least in part, upon the income of preceding periods, and in those periods income was running at levels which were lower than current income, the current level of consumption must be lower than that which is proper to current income. Actual saving is therefore greater than proper saving, and the actual position must be lower than the static equilibrium position. As a result of the lags, whatever form the lags take, income is kept at a lower level than that of the static equilibrium which would correspond to the current rate of investment.

The same argument would evidently hold if investment was increasing according to some other rule than the arithmetical progression which we have so far assumed. It would hold, for example, if investment of each period exceeded that of the previous period by a constant percentage. (This is the case which Mr. Harrod[1] describes by the expression 'a constant rate of growth'.) In the moving equilibrium, income must be adjusted to investment, with the same relation between them persisting from period to period; and in this case the adjustment must inevitably fail if their rates of growth were not the same. Any divergence between rates of growth must ultimately cause an unlimited divergence between the two magnitudes. But the ratio between current income and current investment will be made smaller by the existence of lags—the reduction being larger the longer the lags, and the larger the proportion of consumption which lags behind income.

Again, we could use a similar argument for the case of a decline in investment. Here the effect of the lags will be to slow

[1] *Towards a Dynamic Economics*, p. 77.

up the *decline* in income. In the moving equilibrium consumption, depending in part on the income of preceding periods, will be higher than it would have been if it depended on current income alone. Thus the moving equilibrium path will lie above the *S*-curve.

4. We can best approach the remaining case, that of fluctuating investment, in the following way. Let us examine what would happen in an economy in which phases of expansion and contraction followed one another according to the following pattern. Suppose that investment expanded uniformly for *m* periods, then remained constant for *n* periods, then contracted uniformly for another *m* periods, then remained stationary for another *n* periods. And suppose that a 'rectangular' cycle of this kind has gone on long enough for the economy to have become adjusted to it, so that after the four phases were completed, income and investment would be back at their starting-point. (This means, it will be noticed, that the system has already attained a moving equilibrium, in a rather wider sense than we have had to give that term in previous applications; the system is now to be adjusted, not to a steady expansion or steady contraction, but to a fluctuation of a peculiar kind.)

Applying our principles, we can see that the system will have to follow a track of the kind which is drawn out (with distinction of two subspecies) in Fig. 4. Looking first of all at the left-hand variety, we find the system starting at a point of static equilibrium (*A*). The upswing will then proceed as in Fig. 3. The path will begin by running parallel to the scale-line, and will gradually bend round until it approaches the moving equilibrium appropriate to a continued expansion. When the expansion in investment ceases, the path will run vertically upwards towards an upper static equilibrium at *C*. But here we come to the distinction between our two varieties. If the upper static equilibrium is actually to be reached, the stationariness of investment will have to go on for a considerable number of periods; in the left-hand diagram we suppose that it does so. In that case, when the downswing begins, the path will again begin by proceeding parallel to the scale-line, and will approach the moving equilibrium appropriate to continued contraction, as it gets to D. This point D, it will be noticed, is well above the S-curve; the contraction in income, which leads the path back to the S-curve, only takes place after the contraction in investment has stopped. This is the character of the course which will be pursued when the stationary phases are rather long.

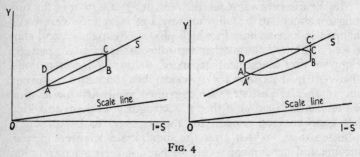

FIG. 4

The alternative case is distinctly more interesting. If the stationary phases are short, the path will not have got back to the S-curve before the new movement sets in; we shall then get a process of the type shown in the right-hand diagram. The curved parts of the path will still be approaching their 'moving equilibria' at B and D; there is no difference here. But at the other ends of these stretches there is an important difference to be noted. If, as in our first case, static equilibrium had already been reached at A, the upward path would begin, as it began in Fig. 3, by moving parallel to the scale-line. But if static equilibrium has not yet been reached at the time when the rise in investment begins, there will still be some fall in income, due to the delayed effects of the preceding fall in investment, to be taken into account. The path AB will then begin by moving upwards more slowly than the scale-line, or may even (if the lags are long relatively to the stationary phase) move downward a little before it turns upwards. A similar movement (in the opposite direction) will take place at C.

A bulge of this sort is perhaps not very likely under the conditions of our 'rectangular' cycle, in which investment changes, when it does change, at a uniform rate. But if we smooth off the corners of our 'rectangle', as we obviously must do in order to fit it to any practical case, the point which we have just made increases in significance. If the stationary phase is short (in a completely smoothed fluctuation it would presumably be on the point of vanishing), and if investment, when it started to contract, contracted at first very slowly—then it is clearly probable that the expansion in income, due to the lagged effects of past expansion in investment, will at first more than offset the effect on income of the current contraction in investment. What this means is that the maximum of income will be reached later than the maximum of investment. And similarly the minimum of income will be reached later than the minimum of investment.

The other general characteristic of a fluctuating system, which can be distinguished as a result of the present discussion, emerges with sufficient clarity from the case of the 'rectangular' cycle. The general effect of lags in consumption is to diminish fluctuations in income. If there were no lags in consumption, income would fluctuate between its upper and lower static equilibria (that is to say, between the points A' and C' in Fig. 4). If there are lags, these points can only be reached if there are long pauses at the lower and upper investment levels. Otherwise it is certain that income will turn upwards before it reaches its lower static limit, and it is certain that it will turn downwards before it reaches its upper limit. The postponement of the turning-points in income until after the turning-points in investment can obviously make no difference to this rule.

5. We have now completed our generalization of the multiplier theory, and the time has come when we may draw a few consequences from it. In the first place, it has become clear that the multiplier theory does in itself offer no shadow of an explanation why fluctuations occur; indeed, its tendency is rather in the other direction. It is true that in the absence of lags, fluctuations in income would be a magnification of the fluctuations in investment; to that extent the suggestion made by the term multiplier is appropriate. But lags in consumption tend to damp down the fluctuations in income which result from given fluctuations in investment; if the lags are complex, and if their length is considerable, relatively to the period of the fluctuations,

the damping may be very effective. Thus if investment fluctuated in a very random manner, up one period and down the next, consumption (if it depended upon the incomes of several past periods) would be relatively stable. This can be convincingly proved by assuming the opposite. If, during several past periods, income had fluctuated in the same random manner as investment is being supposed to fluctuate, nevertheless in the current period consumption would be based upon an average of these past levels of income, and current income must therefore tend to differ from its trend to a relatively smaller extent than current investment does. Current income would thus be pulled back towards its trend. After some periods in which this had happened, the past incomes on which current consumption is based would themselves have become stabilized in the same manner, so that the relative stabilization of present consumption would follow *a fortiori*.

It can, I think, hardly be doubted that a principle of this sort is at work in the real world. One of the most noticeable features common to nearly all actual cycles is the relative stability of the consumption goods trades; consumption seems to fluctuate less than investment. Now this observed fact can only be made consistent with an 'instantaneous' multiplier theory (according to which the system is always, at least approximately, in a position of equilibrium situated on the S-curve) by assuming that the S-curve has a very low inclination to the horizontal, which implies that the marginal propensity to save is very high. It has, indeed, been widely accepted among the more orthodox Keynesians that this is the case; but it is a hypothesis which raises serious difficulties. For with an S-curve of this type, any big drop in income would make saving negative; and even a moderate drop would reduce aggregate saving to so low a figure that it could hardly be reached without dissaving from a substantial portion of the population. Now it is certainly the case that actual saving does behave in this kind of way in the depths of a violent slump; but it must be questioned whether it is correct to regard a situation of this sort as one of static equilibrium. Large-scale negative saving must surely be of necessity a transitory phenomenon. It is therefore important to notice that we can overcome this difficulty, and still explain the facts, if we regard present consumption as being determined, to some considerable extent, by past incomes rather than by current income.

6. These considerations have an important bearing on the famous story of the econometric consumption function. That the consumption function should offer an attractive opportunity for analysis of the Statistical Demand Curve type was inevitable; there is, as we have seen, a close analogy between the consumption function and a demand curve, so that the methods which had been evolved for the statistical analysis of demand were bound to be turned on to the new problem, so much more important in practice than the demand study of any single commodity could be. But what was not to be foreseen was that the new problem, when the econometric technique was applied to it, would appear so deceptively easy. The only country for which reasonably reliable figures of aggregate saving were available, for any period of years before the beginning of the Second World War, was the United States, for which the Department of Commerce has issued a series of figures beginning in 1929. Now when these American figures are put against corresponding figures of disposable incomes for the same years (that is, private incomes[1] after tax), the points so plotted approximate with remarkable regularity to a straight line. It even makes very little difference whether or not we work in terms of constant prices, and whether or not a time-trend is eliminated. The temptation to conclude that *the* consumption function was found proved irresistible. The statistical tests were so good that some people were even unable to avoid the further temptation of concluding that the same consumption function would hold valid after the war as had held before. It was on the basis of such extrapolation that the famous prediction was made, of 8 million unemployed within a few months of VJ day, which had so misleading an effect on policy in the early days of reconstruction; while it was by the prestige of the American calculation (in the days of its glory) that projectors in other countries were tempted to lay down, in precise quantitative terms, the necessary

---

[1] Private incomes being defined as personal incomes plus undistributed profits. Savings also include undistributed profits.

requirements for a full-employment policy, in spite of the fact that the past statistical data on which their projections were based were in nearly all cases vastly more inadequate than these which were at the disposal of the Americans.

Let us look at this matter in terms of our own analysis. It is quite sufficient, for this purpose, if we consider it in terms of the 'rectangular' cycle (Fig. 4). If we had an economy which actually followed a path like that shown in Fig. 4 (either version), and we tried to deduce its S-curve from observation of this path, correlating income and saving in the usual manner, is it not highly probable that the path which we should fit would be appreciably flatter than the true (or static) S-curve? A least-squares regression line, fitted to these observations, must be deflected from the true S-curve in a clockwise direction. Its actual position and slope would depend not only on the character of the lags but also on the character of the fluctuation. If the periods of stationary investment were long, relatively to the up-swing and downswing (so that the left-hand version of the diagram was appropriate), then the bulk of the observations would be on the vertical stretches of the track, and it might happen that they were heaped up near the 'ends' of these vertical stretches, that is, near A and C respectively. In this case the regression line would not be materially divergent from the S-curve. Again, if the lag of consumption behind income were a very short one, and if the upswing and downswing were long (so that, in terms of our construction, investment continued to expand, and to contract, for a large number of periods), then we should find that most of the observed points on the oblique stretches would lie on those parts of the oblique stretches which tend to parallelism with the S-curve; this again would pull the regression line into conformity with the S-curve. But in a regularly fluctuating economy with fairly long lags, neither of these things would happen. The observed points would tend to be spaced out at fairly regular intervals round the circuit $ABCD$ (right-hand diagram). The parts of the path which would show a smaller apparent multiplier than the 'proper' multiplier would then be important, and the deflexion of the regression line would be a serious matter. It seems to me that this is the sort of thing which one would expect to find in a violently fluctuating eco-

nomy, such as that of the United States in the 1930's. If the
S-curve were fixed in position, the circuit would of course be
visible from the observed points; but it might not be visible if
the curve were moving.

It may perhaps be objected by some of my readers that
even if there is this deflexion, it does not much matter. If
we are concerned with a fluctuating economy, then what
we want to know about is the marginal propensity to save in
that fluctuating economy; what would happen if the economy
ceased to fluctuate is a hypothetical question, about which we
need not concern ourselves. Now for certain limited purposes
this may be true. If we are to take it for granted that the economy
is to continue to fluctuate, and desire only to predict the future
course of the fluctuations, then the propensity which assumes
fluctuations may be all that we need. But obviously in practice
we want more than that. The object of economic policy, as
generally admitted nowadays, is not merely to attain a high level
of employment, but to secure stability at that level. For the purpose of such a policy, it is the static S-curve which is relevant.
If we base our assumption on the statistical regression line,
treating it as if it were the static S-curve, we shall exaggerate
the amount of investment which is needed in order to *maintain*
a high level of employment. It seems very likely indeed that a
systematic exaggeration of this sort has been characteristic of
most of the projections which have been made by the econometrists as a contribution to 'Full Employment Policy'.

7. If the statistical consumption function has this systematic
bias, what can be said on other grounds about the probable
form of the true, or static, S-curve? It has been a characteristic
doctrine of Keynesian economics that the marginal propensity
to save is greater than the average propensity, so that the proportion of income saved rises as income rises. This hypothesis
was introduced in order to explain the relative stability of the
consumption-goods trades, for which purpose, as we have seen,
it is not necessary; it has been buttressed by statistical evidence,
which we have seen reason to regard with suspicion. How much,
then, is left of it? In the diagrams which I have drawn up to
the present, I have implicitly accepted Keynes's hypothesis,

because I knew that my readers would have it in their minds, and I was not yet ready to disturb them. At the point we have now reached, it is certainly impossible to say that the doctrine is wrong—but we do seem to lack firm grounds for saying that it is right. I do not know any convincing theoretical reason why the proportion in which income is divided between consumption and saving should change in one way or the other with a change in income; it would be perfectly consistent with fundamental demand theory if the proportion changed in the opposite direction to Keynes's. I think that my own private guess would be that the proportion probably does change in Keynes's direction, though certainly to a much smaller extent than has usually been supposed. But I have no confidence in this guess; until better evidence is produced, it is probably wise to remain in a state of conscious ignorance.

If it were the case that the proportion of income saved was independent of the level of income, the S-curve would become a straight line through the origin. There is something to be said for envisaging it in this form, in default of better information. One advantage of doing so is that it enables us to avoid a complication which would otherwise become awkward. If there were solid reasons for expecting some particular systematic variation in the proportion of income saved, we should have to pay a good deal of attention, in what follows, to the distinction between changes in total real income which are due to changes in income per head, and those which are due to changes in population. For there could hardly be the same systematic variation in these two cases. But since our attitude to the whole matter must be one of nescience, this qualification need receive no particular attention. It is fortunate that what is left of this issue seems to be of little importance for the main problems with which we shall be concerned.[1]

---

[1] Doubtless, I do not need to draw the reader's attention to what he may regard as a flagrant omission in the above discussion—its lack of any attention to changes in distribution. The omission is, of course, deliberate. Most of the distribution changes between large classes, which take place during the cycle, are in my view themselves a part of the 'lag' process, and have therefore been implicitly taken into account. Most of the changes for which this is not true do not seem to me to be essential parts of the cyclical mechanism. They do not affect the general character of the cycle.

IV

INDUCED INVESTMENT

1. Our discussion of the multiplier, useful as it will be in what follows, has itself thrown no light at all upon the causes of fluctuations. The fluctuations in consumption, which result from the multiplier mechanism, can at the most only reflect initiating fluctuations in investment; in fact, as has appeared from our analysis of lags, the fluctuations in consumption are likely to be damped down. Thus the multiplier mechanism, when it is analysed completely, proves after all to be a stabilizing influence; its general tendency is to diminish the propensity to fluctuate. The causes of fluctuations must be sought elsewhere.

It will, however, prove as we go on that we made no mistake in beginning with the multiplier theory. For the forces making for fluctuations, which we are now going to study, are exceedingly strong forces; if they did not operate in a medium by which their action is heavily damped, they might not result in fluctuation at all, but in complete breakdown. As it is, they do rock the boat but they do not altogether upset it. Since we did not want to waste our time in the contemplation of 'explosions' which in fact do not occur, it was as well to begin by familiarizing ourselves with some of the stabilizing forces. There was no point in letting the 'accelerator' loose until we had examined some of the chains by which it is in fact bound.

It will be my contention, in the following chapters, that the main cause of fluctuations is to be found in the effect of changes in output (or income) on investment. There is nothing new in this contention; it is, as we have seen, nothing else but the familiar 'Acceleration Principle' which already has a long history. But it does not seem to me that the consequences of this principle have hitherto been developed in a completely convincing manner. In order to do that (or to have any chance of doing it), we need to examine the nature of the induced investment very carefully. It is this examination which will be the subject of the present chapter.[1]

[1] It is *not* assumed that all Investment is Induced Investment. See below, p. 58.

2. Before we begin our systematic discussion there are two general points which need to be made. In the first place, it should be understood that what we are now going to do is simply to discuss the effects of output on investment, just as (in the preceding chapters) we discussed the effect of investment on output. The theory of the multiplier and the theory of the accelerator are the two sides of the theory of fluctuations, just as the theory of demand and the theory of supply are the two sides of the theory of value. In the theory of the multiplier we took investment for granted (either assuming it to be given in amount or to be changing in given ways) in order to study the consequential level of output or movement of output. Similarly, in this place, we are going to take output (or income) for granted, in order to study the consequential effects on investment. The theory which results can only be a half-theory, for the same reason as that which makes the multiplier (when properly understood) only a half-theory. The full theory must be that which shows both sides in operation; but we shall not begin to consider that full theory until we reach Chapter V.

Secondly, it will be noticed that I have posed the problem in terms of the effect on investment of changes in *output* as a whole (which of course includes investment); not, as has perhaps been more usual,[1] in terms of the effect of changes in consumption only. In spite of the apparent circularity in my formulation, it seems to me to be the right one. The building of houses, for instance, reckons as investment activity; but an increase in the demand for new houses induces investment in brickworks, saw-mills, and glassworks, just in the same way as an increase in the demand for cigarettes induces investment in cigarette-making machinery. And so on all along the line. It is true that in the case of investment we can, if we choose, lump together the induced investment with that which induces it, for both belong on the investment side. But it seems to me to be distinctly inconvenient to do so. In practice it is only too easy to allow ourselves to forget that a programme (say) of public investment can only be carried through efficiently if it is allowed to induce other investment to support it; a theoretical frame-

[1] Cf. for example, Hansen, *Fiscal Policy and Business Cycles*, ch. 12.

work which continually reminds us of this has much to be said for it.[1]

3. So long as we were concerned with the multiplier theory, in which investment is given, it was possible to be rather free and easy about the nature of the investment; even the essential reminder that the only investment which *can* equal saving is net investment did not need to be particularly stressed. Here we have to be much more careful. When we are considering induced investment in fixed capital we have to pay a great deal of attention to the depreciation factor, so that the distinction between gross and net investment becomes of vital importance. For this reason, among others, it is desirable to treat investment in fixed capital and investment in working capital separately. I shall begin with the case of fixed capital.

We shall proceed in the usual way, building up the theory by stages, beginning from simple cases and going on to the more complex. It is thus convenient to start from the situation with which theoretical analysis has made us most familiar—that of the stationary state. In the stationary state output is constant, and the capital stock is fully adjusted to the production of that constant output. There is no incentive to do anything else but to maintain that constant volume of capital. Net investment is therefore nil. Part of the capital stock falls due for replacement in every period, and is replaced. Gross investment is therefore not nil, but is constant, being equal to the constant allowance made for depreciation.

Now, suppose that there is an increase in output (we need not inquire for what reason), and that the increase is expected to be permanent—the new level is to be maintained indefinitely. For the production of the new output the existing capital stock will no longer be appropriate. In the *short period*, the enlarged output can be produced, but only by using the capital equipment at more than its optimum intensity, and therefore (in all probability) increasing its effective rate of depreciation;[2] this provides

---

[1] It must, however, be admitted that our formulation causes considerable difficulties with regard to induced investment (and disinvestment) in stocks. But we are postponing this question for the present. See below, pp. 52–4.

[2] That is to say, the user cost. It will, however, often happen that the output which can be produced in this way in the short period will be less

a motive for increasing the stock of equipment. Thus the increase in output induces investment; investment occurs as part of the process of moving from one equilibrium to the other.

In the new stationary equilibrium, when it is reached, net investment will again be zero; but capital has increased, so that in the process of moving to the new equilibrium net investment must have occurred. It seems reasonable to suppose that the net investment will not take place all at once—it will be spread over a certain length of time, partly because business men will not react at once to the need for new capital goods, partly because the process of making the new capital goods itself takes time. But even if the new capital goods could be produced at once (if, that is to say, they could be produced within a single 'period'), even so the new stationary equilibrium would not be attained at once. A further process of adjustment would still be required.

During the first period gross investment would rise above its previous stationary level by the value of the new capital goods; since depreciation would be unchanged (being based upon the pre-existing capital stock), net investment must be considered to rise from zero to the same amount. In the next period (assuming that the making of the new capital goods is already completed) gross investment must fall back to its pre-existing level; but now there is the extra depreciation on the new capital goods to be considered. Depreciation will rise from its old level by the amount of this extra depreciation; net investment will therefore become negative by this same amount. The negative net investment will continue until the time comes for the new capital

---

than the output which will be producible when the new equipment has come into operation. The natural course of events, as Professor Robertson reminds me, is that there should be 'some increase in output of final goods, then investment decisions, then the investment process (increase in output of capital goods), and then a large further increase in output of final goods'. It must, I think, be agreed that this increase in capacity is very important; but an increase in output does not follow as a necessary consequence of an increase in capacity. It is necessary that the goods which have now become capable of being produced without strain, should also be capable of being sold. In this chapter, where we are concentrating on the effects of changes in the demand for output, changes in capacity are not directly relevant. Where they do become relevant is at a later stage of our argument, where we introduce the 'Ceiling' (chs. 8–10). I am not sure that this particular effect has been adequately allowed for in that place, but that is where it belongs.

goods to be replaced. If they all have to be replaced at the same time, there will then be another period in which gross investment rises to a high figure, and net investment to a rather high figure (but not so high as in the first period, as the extra depreciation charge goes on being deducted). And so on, so far as one can see, indefinitely. The course followed by net investment will be such as is illustrated in the curve A in Fig. 5.

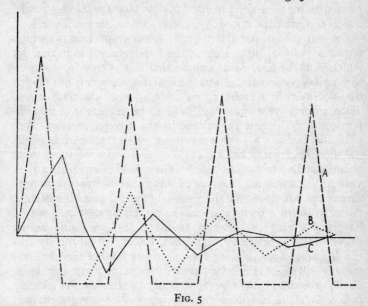

FIG. 5

This picture is not substantially altered if we take into account the fact that the various sorts of capital goods which comprise the additional investment will probably have different 'lives'. If there is one part which has a life of two years, another of three years, and so on, all that will happen is that we shall have a curve of the type A corresponding to each part of the initial investment, and that these curves will have to be superimposed. Doubtless that will do something to even out the fluctuations; but we shall still have to expect the repeated occurrence of periods which are common multiples of the separate 'lives', so that in them an exceptionally large proportion of the whole stock will fall due for renewal. (Thus if there is one part which has a life of three periods, and another which has a life of five periods, the whole amount would fall due for renewal in every fifteenth period.) While this can happen there can be no tendency for the system to settle down to a definitive equilibrium.

What does make a difference is uncertainty of the life of a particular piece of equipment. Suppose that the capital goods, which comprise the initial investment, have a *normal* life of four years, but that in practice there is some proportion (a) which requires renewal after three years, and some proportion (c) which lasts for five. And suppose that this is true, not only of the capital goods which form the initial investment, but also of the successors by which they are replaced when the time comes. Then in each year there will have to be replaced: (1) a proportion a of the new capital goods which were installed three years before, (2) a proportion $1-a-c$ of the capital goods installed four years before, (3) a proportion c of the capital goods installed five years before. The gross investment in each year is thus a weighted average of the gross investments in these three previous years; the successive figures for gross investment are derived from their predecessors by this process of repeated weighted averaging. Now it stands to reason (and can be proved[1]) that repeated averaging of this sort will ultimately iron out any sort of fluctuation; applied to any kind of initial movement it will begin at once to have a recognizably damping effect. Gross investment will, therefore, tend to settle down to a steady figure, equal to the depreciation charge. Net investment will follow a curve of the type shown by B in Fig. 5, with positive and negative swings, gradually settling down to zero.

The damping is only intensified when we take into account the further qualification, that the initial investment is itself unlikely to take place all at once, but will tend to be spread over an appreciable period of time. We then get a curve of the type C, with the initial hump already spread out, and the subsequent damping still more effective. This is the realistic case; and here it looks as if we should be safe in assuming that after (say) a couple of swings, the remaining oscillations would be quite negligible.

[1] See Appendix, p. 182.

4. It has been easiest to discuss this problem in terms of a single change in the level of output in a stationary state; but it would not have been worth while to discuss it in detail if the argument did not have a much wider application. There are good reasons for supposing that any rise in the level of output which business men regard as 'normal' will tend to induce an investment in new capital to support that increased output;[1] and if it does so, it will induce a stream of additional net investment with a time-shape something like our C-curve. But since in practice the change will not supervene upon a situation which is already stationary, there is no reason why the total of net investment throughout the economy should follow a course of this sort. All that our curve can be taken to show is the course of the net investment which is directly due to the particular increase in output. We have to think of our curve as being superimposed upon the curve showing the net investment or disinvestment which would have taken place otherwise. The stream which is shown by our curve is a 'marginal' stream.

We should get a very simple case of this compounding if we supposed that the increase in output in period o, which induced a stream of net investment with the time-shape C, was followed by a further increase in output in a later period. (It should be repeated that we are at present paying no attention to the changes in output which will naturally arise as a consequence of the induced investment—through its multiplier effects; these effects, which will be a main subject of our following work, will not be brought into the discussion until the next chapter.) A second increase in output, occurring, let us say, in period 2, will induce a second stream of net investment with the same time-shape; but since it only begins in period 2, it must be thought of as being bodily displaced to the right. Thus when the two curves are compounded together there may be some tendency for the peaks in one to offset the troughs in the other. But obviously we cannot count upon this happening. However much offsetting there is, the general tendency for a phase of increasing output to induce a hump of net investment, followed

---

[1] Evidently, this will not be true for a chance fluctuation, expected to be short-lived, such as the case of a good harvest; and maybe there are other exceptions.

by minor fluctuations which die away to zero, cannot be over-borne.

5. It thus appears that the effect of an increase in output is always likely to be of this standard type. We have now to ask whether the argument is reversible, whether the effects of a fall in output can be analysed in a corresponding way. It seems likely that this is not so, for well-known considerations suggest an important difference.

Let us, for the same reasons as before, begin by going back to the stationary state. Thus we start off with output remaining constant at a particular level, and the capital stock adjusted to the production of that output; gross investment is equal to depreciation and net investment is zero. Now suppose that there is a decline in demand, so that the level of output falls. The capital stock is now too large for the output which is to be produced, and a downward adjustment is necessary. But the downward adjustment can only take place by a cessation of re-investment, so that gross investment, while remaining positive (or at the worst zero) becomes less than depreciation.[1] If the initial fall in output was small, a partial cessation of re-investment, spread (perhaps) over two or three periods, may be sufficient to complete the first stage of the adjustment. After this the rest of the process would (in principle) proceed just like our C-curve, turned upside down. For after the initial adjustment in the capital stock had been made, by the partial cessation of reinvestment for a limited period, a time would come in which gross investment would return to its old level (or thereabouts), while depreciation would be reduced by the fall in the capital stock which had already occurred. Thus the first phase, with its negative net investment, would be followed by a second phase in which net investment would be positive (though, of course, small). Further oscillations similar to those of curve C would follow in later stages—for essentially similar reasons.

It is, however, much more important to notice that this symmetry between the effects of contraction and the effects of

---

[1] It should be remembered that we are still considering the case of investment in fixed capital.

expansion in output only holds good when the contraction in output is small. For the only way in which the capital stock can be reduced is by a cessation of reinvestment. Thus, if the contraction in output passes a certain figure, the necessary adjustment in the capital stock cannot be completed within a short period, even by shutting gross investment down to nothing. The initial disinvestment must accordingly be spread out over a longer time; and this flattening of the initial trough (just like the flattening of the hump which transformed curve B into curve C in Fig. 5) must reduce the amplitude of the fluctuations in the 'tail'. In such a case we may be sure that the 'tail' will be of little importance, and the curve of net disinvestment will follow a course such as that shown by curve D in Fig. 6.

A flattening of this sort will occur in practice even if gross investment does not fall to zero throughout the whole system. For it is of course unrealistic to suppose that a change in the level of output will induce a proportionate change in the stocks of all the different sorts of capital goods—not even when its effects are fully worked out. In practice, some kinds are bound to be affected more than others. It is therefore possible, and indeed highly likely, that gross investment in some sorts of capital goods will be reduced to zero, while at the same time some reinvestment in other sorts is continuing. A considerable amount of flattening can occur in this way, even while the total gross investment in the whole economy remains at a positive figure.

Now suppose (in imitation of the order of development which we followed when considering the consequences of an expansion) that our previously stationary economy has experienced one fall in output, which has induced a disinvestment of time-shape D; and that after that, perhaps a couple of periods later, there is a further fall in output. How is the further 'stream' of induced disinvestment to be compounded with the first? Evidently we cannot merely superimpose them, as in the expanding case; the limit to the amount of disinvestment which is possible at any one time prevents that. What must happen is that the initial trough is prolonged in length. Instead of the second 'stream' of disinvestment being added contemporaneously to the first, it is displaced in time and is added on *after* the first. Thus a

continued fall in output may not cause the rate of disinvestment
to be increased; what it is likely to do is to cause the process
of disinvestment to last longer. This is a profoundly important
difference between the cases of expansion and of contraction;
it has, as we shall see, profoundly important consequences. It

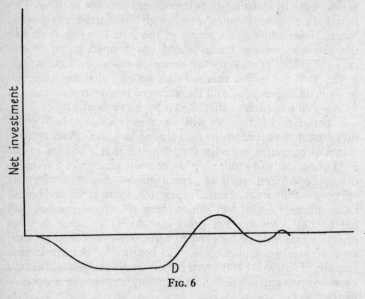

Fig. 6

is easy to recognize some of these consequences at once, in the
form of the 'surplus capacity' which is so familiar a feature of
trade depressions.

Finally, to complete our procedure, we must relax our
assumption that the contraction has supervened upon a stationary economy, in which the capital stock is fully adjusted to the
stationary output. In general, it will not be true (even if output
is stationary) that the amount of capital falling due for replacement is constant over time; we must ordinarily expect that it
will be varying in accordance with the complex history of investment in the past. Thus it may happen that the decline in output
takes place at a moment when the capital falling due for replacement is abnormally large; a larger amount of disinvestment can

then be induced in the short run by the fall in output than would otherwise be the case. Alternatively (and it is this alternative which is practically the more interesting) it may happen that the contraction supervenes upon a recent period of expansion, so that there is an abnormally large proportion of the existing capital goods which are rather new, and the proportion of those which are due, or nearly due, for replacement is abnormally small. In this event the flattening of the disinvestment curve D will be even more pronounced than it was in our standard case.

6. We have now before us a fairly complete theory of Induced Investment in fixed capital; but we have still to make a similar analysis for the other parts of the capital stock. We shall find that there is a theory of induced investment in these other kinds of capital, which is basically similar to that for fixed capital; but it raises some awkward problems of its own, which will need special attention.

I shall distinguish (more or less as Keynes did in the *Treatise*) between *Working Capital*, which is to include goods in process as well as such minimum stocks of materials and half-finished goods as are technically necessary in the productive process, and *Liquid Capital*, in the sense of reserve stocks not technically necessary. Liquid capital will include finished goods as well as unfinished; some minimum amount of liquid capital must be considered to be economically necessary if production is to be carried on at all 'comfortably'.

Let us begin, as before, with a situation in which output is constant, while both working capital and liquid capital are adjusted to that constant output. The demand for the product[1] then increases, and remains constant at a higher figure. The first thing to notice is that it will be technically impossible to increase output without some investment in working capital (as defined). For suppose that the period of production is three months. Then the stream of outputs can only be expanded if the stream of inputs is expanded three months earlier; the additional inputs during those three months, which will not be balanced by any contemporaneous increase in output, form the investment in

[1] When we leave the case of fixed capital it becomes important to begin with changes in *demand*. For the consequences of this see below, p. 53.

question. If production is continuous, so that inputs have to be made at all stages in the productive process, the rate of investment will rise from the beginning to the end of the three months. At the end of the three months the investment will fall sharply away to nothing.[1]

It seems to be inevitable that induced investment in working capital should proceed according to a pattern which is more or less of this character. And a decline in demand will have an exactly corresponding effect. For there will then be a period in which output is coming out of the 'sausage-machine' at a greater rate than input is going in; this signifies disinvestment. For the same reasons as before, the rate of disinvestment will go on increasing until the period of production is complete, and will then fall to nothing—as before.

7. Induced investment (or disinvestment) in working capital must be governed by this simple rule; but its behaviour is in practice largely masked (or at least modified) by the very different behaviour of the liquid capital component. If, as in our example, an article takes three months to produce, and the production of additional units is only begun at the moment when demand increases, there will be an interval of three months in which the additional demand cannot be met out of current output. If the demand is to be met at all, it must be met out of stocks. Thus it is very likely that during the same period in which there is the investment in working capital, there will be a disinvestment in liquid capital. And the disinvestment of liquid capital will normally be the larger; on the assumption of inputs going in at a uniform rate during the productive

---

[1] If labour is the only input, while 10 units of labour are needed during the first month, 10 during the second, and 10 during the third, in order to produce a unit of output, the investment in working capital due to an increase in output by one unit will proceed as follows. There will be an investment of 10 units in the first month, 20 in the second (when additional labour is being employed on each of the first two stages) and 30 in the third. After that, the additional output is ready; thus from this point there is no input which is not matched by output, and investment in working capital falls to zero.

The increase in the rate of investment during the period of production is of course not necessarily uniform; if the bulk of the inputs occur in the middle of the productive process the rate of increase will be most rapid at this point.

process, it will be twice as large. This can be seen in the following way. Suppose that demand has increased by one unit a month above the original level; then the total disinvestment in stocks at the end of three months will amount to 3 units. But the investment in working capital began at zero, and only worked up to a rate approximately equal to one unit of output a month, at the end of the three months; thus on the average of the three months, the rate of investment in working capital will have been equal to $\frac{1}{2}$ unit per month, and the total investment in working capital over the three months will have been $1\frac{1}{2}$ units.

Taking the two effects together, there will have been a net disinvestment over the period, beginning at a comparatively high rate (1 unit per month) and gradually falling to zero. This, so it seems, is the picture (with appropriate adjustments for irregularities) which we ought to have in our minds.

But now let us remember that we began by assuming that in the initial position the stock of liquid capital was adjusted to the output which had to be produced. We have got to the end of our three months, and we find that output is higher, while liquid capital is reduced (perhaps severely reduced). Evidently this is not a situation which can be maintained. It will be necessary for the dispersed stocks to be replaced; their replacement will require a positive investment equal to the previous disinvestment in stocks.

This process of replacement does not have any very determinate time-shape; it may be fast, or it may be slow. (It is characteristic of investment in liquid capital that it is less tied down by technical rigidities than is investment in fixed capital; so that there is less that we can say about it.[1]) The replacement could, theoretically, be so fast that it was actually simultaneous with the disinvestment; although this is wildly improbable, it is the limiting case, and it will be worth our while to consider it for a moment in order to fix our ideas. Suppose, in terms of our example, that demand increased by one unit a month from 1 January, and that the process of adapting output began on the same date. Then it is for the three months, January to

---

[1] Much more could be said if we allowed ourselves to attend to reactions through prices (cf. Keynes, *Treatise on Money*, ch. 29). But we are obliged, by our present approach, to leave these matters rather on one side.

March, that one unit a month has to be taken from stock, making three units in all. These withdrawals cannot be replaced before April. If they are to be replaced at the first possible date—which is April—input will have to be increased in January, not only by the amount needed to produce one extra unit in April, but by the amount needed to produce four extra units: one to meet the April demand, and three to replace the withdrawals from stock. Thus there will have to be an extra investment in working capital during January, which will be more or less equivalent to the disinvestment of stock during January; and the same thing will happen in February and March. Thus there will be an extra investment in working capital during the period of production which will balance the disinvestment in stocks during the same period. At the end of the period of production this extra working capital will be in a form which can be used to fill the gap on the liquid capital side; at the same time other working capital will have been accumulated, sufficient to support the regular rate of output at the higher level.

Obviously, if this is to happen, the reactions of business men must be unbelievably quick. Normally, the replacement of stocks will be somewhat deferred—maybe it will not begin until 'April' or later. This means that there must be, first of all, a phase of disinvestment, and subsequently a phase of investment—the latter being the larger of the two. But the *rate* of investment during this later period is quite indeterminate. If businesses are content to replace their stocks slowly, the rate of investment will be low, but the phase of investment will be long-continued; if they are in more of a hurry, there will be a hump—short and sharp.

All this argument is valid, *mutatis mutandis*, for the case of a fall in demand. There is no necessary asymmetry between rises and falls, in their effects on working capital and stocks, as there is in their effects on fixed capital. A fall in demand will induce, first of all, a phase of positive investment (the 'accumulation of unwanted stocks', of which we have heard so much); and a subsequent phase of disinvestment in which the stocks are worked off. In so far as it is easier to carry surplus stocks than to make do with a shortage of stocks, there is perhaps some tendency for the whole adjustment to take longer in the case of a fall than in the case of a rise. But this point should not be pressed; from the producer's own point of view a condition of surplus stocks is more alarming than a condition of deficiency, and he may well react more quickly in his attempts to remedy it.[1]

8. To sum up. The characteristic effect on investment of a rise in the demand for output seems to be capable of division into three phases. In the first phase there is a tendency to disinvestment; the additional output is not yet forthcoming, and the additional demand is satisfied (so far as it can be satisfied) out of stocks. Towards the end of this phase the rate of disinvestment diminishes, because the decumulation of stocks is offset by accumulation of working capital. Thus the first phase passes, not sharply but gradually, into the second, in which the main part of the induced investment takes place. This has to include (1) investment in stocks, to make up for the raiding of stocks in the first phase; (2) investment in fixed capital, needed to adjust equipment to the production of the larger output. The positive net investment which is needed in this phase may be very large indeed. Finally, there is a third phase, stretching into the remoter future, which is troubled by oscillations in investment due to the alternate building up and running down of depreciation reserves in the process of replacement. This last is purely a problem of fixed capital; there seems to be nothing corresponding to it on the working capital side.

The characteristic effects of a fall in the demand for output can be classified in a similar way. Here again there is a first phase in which the effect goes in the 'wrong' direction—the fall in demand leads to positive investment in stocks, 'surplus stocks' as they will become. It is followed by a second phase, in which disinvestment occurs; the surplus stocks are gradually disposed of, and fixed equipment is gradually reduced by cessation of replacement. But although the total amount of disinvestment which has to occur in this phase is comparable (for an equal change in demand) to the total amount of investment which has to occur in the corresponding phase of the other movement, it is likely to be much more spread out in time. Because of this

[1] See below, Ch. IX.

spreading out, the third phase (the 'tail') is of negligible importance in this case.

If one rise in demand supervenes upon another, the induced investments to which they give rise can be added directly; thus if the second phase of the second rise begins before the second phase of the first rise is terminated, the humps in investment will intensify one another. But if one fall in demand supervenes upon another, such adding may not be possible; the disinvestment induced by the second fall will then prolong the disinvestment due to the first, but will not intensify it materially. If a rise supervenes upon a fall, the investment induced by the rise may be moderated, for the same reason. For if the capital stock has not yet gone far towards completing its adjustment to the lower level of output, what will happen is that the process of disinvestment can be suspended; much less positive investment will then be required than was necessary in the standard case which we previously discussed. But if a fall supervenes upon a rise, a similar cancelling-out can only occur if the fall follows the rise very speedily. Net investment normally follows a rise more rapidly than disinvestment follows a fall; thus if the engines are not reversed quickly, it will soon be too late to say 'as you were'. It is indeed only in the one case of the recovery after a fall that output is likely to be able to change appreciably without inducing a substantial amount of investment (or disinvestment); what really happens in this case is that disinvestment which was due to occur, but had not yet had time to happen, is called off.

It is no doubt the existence of this exceptional case which was responsible for the neglect of Induced Investment in the *General Theory*. It is easy to see why Keynes was so interested in this case, when one considers the time at which he was writing. But in a really general theory it would not appear as anything more than an exception—the one case in which the rule does not work.

9. Before concluding this already long chapter there is another point which needs to be made. It might have been convenient if we could have made it before this, but we were not yet in a position to do so properly. The reader will probably have noticed that when discussing induced investment in working capital, we had to make it depend upon the *demand* for output, not upon the actual volume of output; and we came to see that these were not the same thing. Induced investment in fixed capital can generally be thought of as depending upon changes in *actual* output; for the output which can be produced from a given equipment is capable of some variation within the Marshallian short period. But even in the case of fixed capital this is not exactly right; and in the case of working capital it will not do at all. For the induced investment in working capital (as well as the induced disinvestment in stocks) comes before the actual rate of output changes; it occurs in response to a change in demand, and is part of the process whereby supply adjusts itself to demand. How are we going to fit this consideration into our structure? The conventional way of doing so (I think it can now be said) is to introduce a concept of *ex ante* income which is distinguished from current income or output; but although this is quite a useful device if we are adopting the quasi-static 'supply and demand' interpretation of savings-investment analysis, it will not fit at all conveniently into our present technique. How then are we to overcome the difficulty?

Let us remember that our generalization of the multiplier theory has left us with a 'unit period' which is quite arbitrary in length. And let us also remember that we are not obliged to regard our various dated quantities (outputs, or volumes of investment) as the average rates over successive periods; they may quite well be interpreted as the rates ruling at a certain specified date within each period. (Thus, if the period is one month, the output figure may be that ruling at the end of the month, or during the last week in each month.) Adopting this interpretation, our period analysis gives us a series of snapshots of the process we are examining, snapshots which are too far apart in time to form a continuous cinematic film, but which (if there are no systematic fluctuations within the periods) suffice to give us a general idea of the process.

Now let us suppose that one period is precisely the normal time taken for output to adjust itself to a change in demand, so that at the end of one period induced investment in working capital and induced disinvestment in stocks are just about balancing. (It is a drastic simplification to suppose that the *period*, in this sense, would be even approximately constant; but it is a simplification which we may allow ourselves to use until we have reason to abandon it.)

If we interpret the regular multiplier analysis in terms of this convention, it comes out as follows.

In period 0, we should say, there is an increase in *planned* investment; but actual investment does not materialize in this period, for any positive investment which occurs is offset by decumulation of stocks. Thus we pay no explicit attention to the planned investment in the 0 period. The actual investment appears in period 1, when output rises by the amount of the planned investment. In this same period 1 some of the consequential earnings may be spent; but these spendings do not give rise to extra output in period 1, being themselves offset in period 1 by decumulation of stocks. The extra output due to the spendings of period 1 only begins to appear in period 2. And so on.

If we adopt this convention the multiplier analysis of Chapters II and III can be kept fully valid; but we have a new reason for consumption lags (a reason which applies even to the spending-out of wages), and must therefore expect the whole process to be slower than we might otherwise have thought it to be. The arguments against the static interpretation of the multiplier, which we have previously advanced, thereby gain in force. It also has to be noticed that the time-shape of the consumption relation (the lengths of time taken for consumption—in the sense of consumption out of output—to react to changes in income) now depends in part upon the characteristics of production technique; it is not entirely a matter of consumer habits.

With this convention we need not pay much attention to the initial phase of adjustment in stocks which accompanies a change in income; the only sorts of induced investment which do concern us are the later stages—the re-building of stocks after the preliminary depletion (in the case of an expansion in output), the working off of surplus stocks (in the case of a contraction), and all the long story of the induced investment in fixed capital. That is what we shall have to try to deal with—as far as we can.[1]

[1] In his paper 'Three Lags in the Circular Flow of Income' (*Income, Employment and Public Policy, Essays in honour of Alvin Hansen*), Lloyd Metzler makes essentially the same classification of what I call consumption lags as I do here. His 'household expenditure lag' explains itself; his 'earnings lag' is the lag through undistributed profits; and his 'output lag' is that which we have just been discussing. In the American data for 1929–38, which he examines, using Barger's quarterly figures, the output lag appears to be by far the easiest to distinguish. This is interesting; nevertheless, for the reasons explained on pp. 34–5 above, it would be rash to conclude that the other lags are generally negligible.

V

THE ACCELERATOR IN ACTION

(I) THE POSSIBILITY OF EQUILIBRIUM

1. IF the theory of the Multiplier offers in itself no explanation of the tendency to fluctuate, the position is quite otherwise as soon as we take account of Induced Investment. We have seen that any simple change in the level of output is likely to induce a stream of investment which is not constant in time but has a systematic tendency to vary; and some of these variations are suspiciously cyclical in character. Without going any farther, we can see that here is a force with considerable potentialities as a cycle-maker; but it remains to be seen whether the cycles which are likely to arise from these technical properties of investment are naturally to be identified with the major business cycles, or whether they are more likely to reveal themselves in practice in the form of relatively minor disturbances.

What we now have to study are the interactions of the Accelerator and the multiplier; it seems almost inevitable that in the course of these interactions some oscillations will arise. It is, however, of interest (and it will prove convenient) if we begin by asking whether it is possible for an economy, in which Investment is *induced* by changes in output, to avoid fluctuations: is there any possibility of steady 'equilibrium' with reference to which fluctuations might subsequently be defined? Let us try to answer this question before we go any farther.

One possibility of *equilibrium* presents itself at once; it is our old friend, the stationary state. In the stationary state, since output is always constant, there can be no induced investment; the possibilities of fluctuation due to induced investment are therefore annihilated. But before we accept this *equilibrium* as a possible answer to our query, a word must be said about its consistency with the multiplier theory. In a stationary state it is not merely true that induced investment must be nil; total net investment must be nil, gross investment being equal to depreciation. If the system is to remain in equilibrium, net investment must equal saving; therefore saving must be nil. If, in static equilibrium, saving is a constant proportion of income (as at an earlier stage in our discussion we were inclined to think it might be) then zero saving means zero income—which effectively blows up the stationary state as a useful concept! Now there are many purposes for which this argument has to be taken very seriously; but in the present context we are justified in brushing it aside. For though we shall make much use of the stationary state in our further discussions, we shall only use it as an expository device. And for that purpose we can restore its self-consistency quite sufficiently if we suppose, when we are using it, that the S-curve is of the form which is represented in Figs. 1–4 above, so that saving falls to zero before income falls to zero. With this qualification the stationary state becomes a possible state of affairs; it gives us one *equilibrium* which we can use as a standard of reference in our further work.[1]

2. The other possibility of equilibrium is much more interesting. It is the Regularly Progressive Economy, the discovery of which (as an instrument of this sort of analysis) must be attributed to Mr. Harrod.[2] In the regularly progressive economy, output is not constant, but grows at a constant rate; thus output in period $n+1$ is always $(1+g)$ of output in period n, where g is a positive constant. (If the period was one year, and g was 0·03, we should have the trend rate of growth which seems to have been characteristic of the nineteenth century.)

A steady growth, so defined, will call forth induced investment; but if the growth has been maintained at the same rate in the past as it is in the present, the induced investment will tend to be in a constant proportion to output. This can be seen in the following way. Output p periods before (Y_{n-p}) will bear a constant proportion to current output (Y_n)—constant, that is, in the sense that it does not depend on n though it does on p. And the change in output between that period and one pre-

---

[1] Of course this Stationary State does not necessarily, or even probably, possess the additional characteristic of Full Employment.

[2] Op. cit., p. 76. I do not mean to say that Mr. Harrod is the first who has perceived the usefulness of a progressive equilibrium as a tool in the analysis of fluctuations. (See, for instance, Cassel, *Theory of Social Economy*, Part IV.) But it is Mr. Harrod who has emphasized the essential part which it must play in a theory based on the acceleration principle.

ceding it $(Y_{n-p} - Y_{n-p-1})$ will also bear a constant proportion to Y_n in the same sense. Now if we can assume that a given change in output calls forth induced investment (positive or negative) p periods later which is a constant proportion of that change in output,[1] it will follow that the induced investment in period n, which is due to the change in output $Y_{n-p} - Y_{n-p-1}$, is a constant proportion of that change in output, and therefore a constant proportion of Y_n itself. The same will hold for each previous period (that is to say, for each value of p). Adding up, we see that total induced investment must be in a constant proportion to Y_n.

We can argue in the same way[2] that saving will be a constant proportion of Y_n. For though consumption is taken to depend upon previous incomes, as well as on current income, these previous incomes will be proportionate to Y_n, so that the consumption depending on them will also be proportionate to Y_n, as soon as the rate of growth is given. Therefore, since consumption is a constant proportion of income, saving will be so also.

Now both the ratio of current induced investment to current income, and the ratio of current saving to current income, though they will be constant over time, will depend upon the rate of growth g. Thus if the rate of growth is such that these ratios are equal, induced investment will be kept equal to saving, and the system can remain in equilibrium so long as the induced investment is the only investment there is. It follows that provided the rate of growth is properly chosen, the regularly progressive economy can remain in equilibrium without fluctuation.

3. It thus appears that the regularly progressive economy does provide us with an alternative variety of equilibrium; and it is undoubtedly true that it takes us one step nearer than we are taken by the Stationary State towards a concept which could be of use in the practical analysis of the cycle. But there is one

---

[1] A doubtful assumption, certainly, for it implies a kind of *constant* returns which cannot be generally valid. But it is a good rule in economic theory to stick to constant returns until you have some reason for giving it up! See Math. App., p. 170.

[2] As we have done above, on p. 28. We here return to the assumption that static saving is a constant proportion of income, which we had to abandon when dealing with the Stationary State.

further amendment to it which can be made, and which improves it very considerably. It is not necessary to assume that all investment is induced investment. While there can be little doubt that quite a large proportion of the net investment which goes on in normal conditions has been called forth, directly or indirectly, by past changes in the level of output, there is certainly some investment for which this effect is so small as to be insignificant. Public investment, investment which occurs in direct response to inventions, and much of the 'long-range' investment (as Mr. Harrod calls it) which is only expected to pay for itself over a long period, all of these can be regarded as *Autonomous Investment* for our purposes. Naturally the distinction is not in practice a sharp one; but it is sufficiently clearly marked to serve for the articulation of a theory. When we allow for the existence of autonomous investment, we have to think of the equilibrium condition as taking the form:

Autonomous Investment+Induced Investment = Saving.

Now we have seen that if the regularly progressive economy is to remain in equilibrium, both saving and induced investment must continue to bear a constant proportion to output. It follows that autonomous investment must bear a constant proportion to output. Thus autonomous investment itself will have to increase at a constant rate of growth if equilibrium is to be maintained. Subject to that condition, there is no reason why the existence of autonomous investment should be inconsistent with progressive equilibrium.

At this point the reader may very naturally ask: how is it, if autonomous investment has to be so completely tied down, both in its size and in its rate of growth, that it can be described with any justice as autonomous? This is a question which deserves an answer. By introducing autonomous investment into our model we have in fact made a bigger difference than appears at first sight. It is a difference which has important consequences.[1]

In the regularly progressive economy without autonomous investment Saving will equal investment so long as the *rate of*

[1] Mr. Harrod's failure to perceive these consequences is, in my view, responsible for most of the weaker points in his otherwise very suggestive analysis.

growth of the economy is appropriate. For both the ratio of saving to output and the ratio of investment to output depend upon the rate of growth;[1] thus if the rate of growth is such as to make these two ratios equal, the system is bound to be in equilibrium, and can remain in equilibrium. Further, it can be in equilibrium whatever is the level of output which is attained at any particular time. If the level of output which was attained at all dates was 10 per cent. higher, so that the rate of growth remained the same, the system could still be in equilibrium. It is only the rate of growth which is determinate; the level of output (in this sense) is quite indeterminate.

But as soon as we allow for the existence of autonomous investment the ratio of saving to output, and the ratio of induced investment to output (both of which depend on the rate of growth) are no longer equal. What we learn from the equality of investment and saving is that the difference between these ratios must equal the ratio of autonomous investment to output. Thus for a given rate of growth, this latter ratio must be constant over time. It follows that if the rate of growth of output is given, autonomous investment must have the same rate of growth. But if we now turn round and suppose that the rate of growth of output is not yet determined, all that will follow is that autonomous investment must have a *constant* rate of growth. Autonomous investment must expand uniformly if the economy is to remain in progressive equilibrium. And this is certainly not a condition that need surprise us.

Suppose that we have a system in which autonomous investment is expanding uniformly at a constant rate of growth, and that this rate of growth is given. Suppose that the *level* of autonomous investment is also given, so that there is to be a given amount of autonomous investment at each particular date. We can conclude straight off that the only equilibrium possible will be one in which output has the same rate of growth, while saving and induced investment will then also have the same rate of growth. Further, the rate of growth of output having been determined, the ratio of saving to output is determined; and also the ratio of induced investment to output. Hence, by sub-

---

[1] In Mr. Harrod's model it is only the ratio of induced investment to output which depends upon the rate of growth.

traction, the ratio of autonomous investment to output is determined. But since the *level* of output has not previously been determined, we are now free to determine it from the level of autonomous investment. The level of output (in each period, and therefore in all periods) must be such as will engender an amount of saving, and an amount of induced investment, which are just sufficient to keep total investment equal to saving when the given autonomous investment is taken into account. Thus the larger the amount of autonomous investment, the higher the level of output will have to be.

In the light of this argument (which of course belongs to the same family as the conjuring trick with which Keynes produced the multiplier) it appears that autonomous investment really is autonomous after all. The only condition which it must satisfy in order for the regularly progressive equilibrium to be possible, is that it must expand at a constant rate. Subject to that condition, its rate of growth and its 'level' are both of them independent variables. It is the rate of growth of autonomous investment which determines the equilibrium rate of growth of the whole system; and it is its level which determines the equilibrium level of output.

4. It thus appears that conditions of progressive equilibrium are possible at different levels of autonomous investment, and with different rates of growth of autonomous investment; and that this is so even when the relations which express the dependence of consumption on past and present income, and the dependence of induced investment upon past and present changes in income, are taken to be given. It is natural to ask whether, once these relations are given, *any* level of autonomous investment, and any rate of growth of autonomous investment, could be consistent with equilibrium. I think it can be shown that in an economy where output of consumption goods and of investment goods was indefinitely expansible in response to demand, the answer would be in the affirmative. In fact, of course, output is not indefinitely expansible at any given time. There are limits, of the kind which Keynes expressed in his concept of Full Employment. We shall be discussing these limits at length in Chapters VIII–X below, but for the time being let us neglect them. Then it follows from our preceding argument that with a given rate of growth the ratio between autonomous investment and equilibrium output is determinate. This provides a kind of 'Super-Multiplier' which can be applied to any given level of autonomous investment in order to discover the equilibrium level of output which corresponds with it. The higher the level of autonomous investment, the higher (in this fixed proportion) the equilibrium level of output must be. That is all that there is to be said.

Now let us start with the equilibrium corresponding to a given rate of growth, and ask what would be the character of the equilibrium corresponding to a different rate of growth—say a higher rate. It is evident (it follows from our discussion in Chapter III) that with a higher rate of growth the proportion of saving to output would be higher. What about the proportion of induced investment to current output? It seems almost inevitable that this proportion will also increase, and even that it will increase more than the proportion of saving to output.[1] I think we can assume that this will happen. Then it follows that the proportion of autonomous investment to output must be diminished, so that the 'super-multiplier' must be increased. Thus if we are comparing the development of two economies with the same consumption and investment relations, but different rates of growth, A's rate of growth being higher than B's; it will follow that at a date in which the volume of autonomous investment in A was the same as the volume of autonomous investment in B, A's equilibrium output would be higher than B's. For this is what the 'super-multiplier' must be taken to mean.

5. In this way a theory of equilibrium with induced investment can be constructed. But what is the significance of such a theory? It does not show us what will actually happen under the given conditions. As we shall see in what follows, it is perfectly possible for autonomous investment to go on expanding

[1] The induced investment due to the increase in income p periods earlier is proportional to this increase in income; and the ratio of this increase in income to Y_n is $g/(1+g)^p$. This expression inevitably increases with g unless $p-1 > 1/g$; and it is impossible that a significant part of induced investment should satisfy this condition unless the average lag is fabulously great or g is remarkably large.

for a long time at a constant rate, and yet equilibrium may fail to be achieved. Further, it is evident that in the real world autonomous investment does not expand steadily. It is itself liable to develop 'humps' of the same sort as those which characterize induced investment, and for much the same reasons. Though it is possible (just as it is in the case of induced investment) for these humps to add up to a steady progress, there is not much reason in practice why they should do so. The best that is in fact likely to happen is that autonomous investment should have a clear trend rate of expansion, with fairly considerable oscillations about its trend.

One type of oscillation has a political origin—wars and revolutions; but the oscillations which can be ascribed to major inventions, such as the railway and the automobile, are strictly economic in their causes. In our progressive equilibrium we put all these things on one side; but there is a perfectly clear justification for doing so.

No one can doubt that the economic system must react in some way to 'exogenous' disturbances; a fluctuation in autonomous investment must cause fluctuations in output unless steps are taken to counteract it. The crucial question which a theory of the cycle has to ask is whether fluctuations are possible, and if so, how they are possible, in the absence of exogenous disturbances. This is the question with which we are at present concerned.[1] But in order to phrase that question sharply—sharply enough for us to have a chance of answering it—we have got to define the meaning of an 'absence of disturbances'. The Stationary State does not give us an adequate definition. One of the things which the regularly progressive economy does for us is to help us to define this question adequately.

But it does more than that. It does not merely show us that a condition is definable in which economic progress could go on, and yet there would be no fluctuations. It shows how stringent the conditions are which have to be fulfilled in order for this to happen. The system will not remain in progressive equilibrium unless it is *completely adjusted* to it. For this is not a static equilibrium like that with which we are familiar in elementary

[1] We shall return to the question of exogenous disturbances in Ch. IX.

supply and demand analysis—a condition which, if it is once taken up (even for a moment), can be maintained. A system is unlikely to be completely adjusted to a progressive equilibrium until it has been in approximate equilibrium for a long time. It is not sufficient that the capital stock should be adjusted to current output; it is also necessary that it should fall due for replacement at the right dates. The induced investment of the future which is already preconditioned (to a considerable extent) by past changes in output, the effects of which are embodied in existing equipment, must be such as to be consistent with steady development. It must not engender peaks and troughs which will cause divergences from the equilibrium path. Any such divergence will upset the equilibrium; and once the equilibrium has been upset we do not know that it will be possible to get back.

If *equilibrium* has to be defined so rigidly as this, how is it ever to be attained? Even if the underlying determinants (the consumption and investment relations, and the course of autonomous investment) are such that equilibrium is possible, can it ever be reached? Suppose that we take an actual economy with a capital stock whose composition reflects the innumerable vicissitudes of the past; and say that from now on it is to be submitted to a perfectly regular progress of autonomous investment, while its saving and induced investment relations can be relied on to remain unchanged—so that it could stay in progressive equilibrium if it had the right capital structure—what will happen? Will it converge to its equilibrium? Or will it diverge from it? Or is it possible that it will oscillate about it? If we can show that an economy, tied down by these very stringent assumptions, would in fact fail to find its equilibrium, but would have a tendency to oscillate, we should have got very near to the root of the matter. For we should then be on the way to showing that a cycle can be generated, and almost necessarily must be generated, even in the absence of exogenous disturbances; these disturbances can then be introduced, in their right place, to explain the differences between the behaviour of the system during one cycle and its behaviour during another.

This is what I hope to be able to show in the following chapters.

VI

THE ACCELERATOR IN ACTION

(II) THE INSTABILITY OF EQUILIBRIUM

1. THE next thing which we have to do is to make a rather formal inquiry into the consequences of a displacement from the equilibrium path. It is at this point that our analysis begins to get into touch with the 'macro-dynamics' of the econometrists; we shall have to draw heavily upon the results which they have attained. Since this borrowing has to be done, it is best done quite openly; I shall therefore put this chapter into a form which will make it something of a break in the general argument. Metaphorically speaking, we have a river to cross; while we are thinking about building a bridge on the stretch in front of us, we notice that our neighbours have already built a bridge somewhere upstream; it seems only sensible to make a detour in order to use it.

This chapter falls accordingly into three parts. First of all, we have to cross over from our own on to the other track; then we have to make our way across by the bridge; and finally, we have to work back towards our own route—on the other side of the stream. Or, speaking less metaphorically, we have first to break down our own problem so as to make it substantially identical with that which has already been solved; then we have to summarize the solution; and then we have to generalize the solution in order to be able to use it for the purposes which we have in mind. Of these three stages the first is quite straightforward. With the second it is easy to summarize the results and illustrate them by examples, but not so easy to prove them without the use of mathematics. The third stage is really difficult, and has cost me more pains than anything else in this book. I still feel dissatisfied with what I am going to say about it. I think, however, that the main results which we shall need can be sufficiently well established, even if the argument on which they rest is not as tidy or as conclusive as one would like to make it.

2. The first stage of this procedure is one of drastic simplification. We will begin with two simplifications which I shall maintain throughout this chapter—the process of clambering back from them being postponed to the chapter which follows.

1. We shall confine ourselves, in the present chapter, to the simpler (but less interesting) of the two potential equilibrium conditions with which we are now familiar: the case of the Stationary Economy, in which (it will be remembered) autonomous investment is nil. In order to make the Stationary State into a possible equilibrium we shall assume that output is not zero when (equilibrium) saving is zero.[1] The generalization to the Progressive Economy will be our first task in Chapter VII.

2. We saw in Chapter IV that the disinvestment, induced by a *fall* in output, must be expected to have a time-shape which is radically different from the time-shape of the investment, induced by a *rise* in output. The expansion in investment, induced by a rise in output, can be as large as it likes, provided that the necessary resources are available; but the corresponding contraction is slowed up by the condition that Gross Investment in fixed capital cannot be negative. This is a difference to which we shall later attach much importance; but for the present we shall leave it out of account. In this chapter we shall follow the usual practice of the mathematicians in assuming that the effects of rises and falls in output are symmetrical.

These two simplifications are such as to affect the whole character of the problem. As long as they are retained the results we get will have little direct significance; they do not become useful until they are transformed (as we shall transform them) into more meaningful results later on. The other simplifications which we must make are of a more ordinary type; they are just the regular sort of simplification which one has to make when cutting down a complicated problem into a simple 'model'. The pattern of induced investment which, in our study of the subject, we decided to be typical, is much too complicated to be worked into a theory of the course of output all at once; it can only be reached, if at all, by a series of steps. It will be remembered that a rise in output appeared to have its main

[1] See above, pp. 56–7.

effect on investment in the form of a Hump in investment, coming some time after the rise in output has occurred—a hump which includes some investment in working capital as well as in fixed. Here we shall provisionally assume that this hump is all that has to be taken into account. This assumption does not cause us to lose anything on the side of the initial decumulation of stocks (for we have decided to look after that by an elaboration in our concept of the 'period'); what we do leave out are the remoter effects through the accumulation and the spending of depreciation allowances. These remoter effects (which we called the Tail) look like being a matter of minor importance as compared with the hump; we must try to take them into account before we have done, but it seems quite justifiable to start by neglecting them.

Having simplified so far, it is natural to simplify one step further, and to assume that the hump in investment takes the simplest possible shape. This would mean that all of the induced investment corresponding to a particular change in output is concentrated in a single period; the simplest period to take would be that which follows immediately after the period in which the change in output has occurred.[1] If we also make the 'Kahn' assumption—that all consumption is lagged one period behind income—we have got the maximum possible amount of simplification. When all these simplifications have been performed, we shall say that the problem is reduced to its *elementary* case. This is the case which is most convenient for mathematical analysis; its properties have been thoroughly explored already and are quite well established.[2]

3. But let us phrase the problem in our own way. What we want to find out is whether a stationary equilibrium, with the possibility of induced investment of this type, is *stable*. Thus we start from an economy which is such that it can exist in

---

[1] It is theoretically conceivable, bearing in mind our assumptions, that the induced investment should be concentrated in the same period as the increase in output; but it involves the same sort of 'split-second' adjustment as we considered on pp. 49–50 above, and dismissed as unrealistic.

[2] Cf. P. A. Samuelson, 'Interactions between the Multiplier Analysis and the Principle of Acceleration' (*Review of Economic Statistics*, 1939); A. Smithies, op. cit.

stationary equilibrium. In the *past*, it has actually been in stationary equilibrium. Net investment was zero, and saving zero, but output was not zero, for we are assuming that the relation between income and saving (the S-curve) is such that saving becomes zero at a non-zero income. In a certain period, which we call period o, the economy suffers a single simple displacement. The easiest form in which to express this displacement is to say that there is an autonomous investment of amount A, which takes place in that period, and is not repeated. (We can visualize this by supposing that some asset, previously supposed indestructible, is destroyed by an earthquake, and has to be replaced.) After period o, autonomous investment returns to zero. The economy could therefore return to stationary equilibrium, if it were not for this disturbance in its past. Can it work the disturbance out of its system? That is what we have to find out.

In period o, consumption will remain at its equilibrium level (for the *previous period* was one of equilibrium). Investment is equal to A, instead of being equal to o, as it would be in equilibrium. Income (or output) therefore exceeds its equilibrium value by A; we may write it as $+A$, if we take the equilibrium level as a basis of measurement.

In period 1, consumption will exceed its equilibrium level by $+(1-s)A$, s being the marginal propensity to save; for previous income is now $+A$. There is no autonomous investment; but induced investment equals vA, if v is the investment coefficient —the ratio of the induced investment to the change in output which called it forth.[1] In this case the change in output (in the previous period) is the change from the equilibrium level of the past to the output of period o, and we have seen that this change equals $+A$. Output in period 1 is therefore equal to

$$+(1-s)A+vA, \quad \text{or} \quad +(1-s+v)A.$$

Applying the same procedure to period 2, we find that consumption comes to $+(1-s)(1-s+v)A$; while the rise in output between periods o and 1 was $+(v-s)A$. Induced investment is therefore equal to $v(v-s)A$; and output in period 2 is

$$+[(1-s+v)^2-v]A.$$

---

[1] v is assumed to be constant; see above, p. 58.

Thus we may continue. The general rule by which the output of each successive period is calculated can easily be put down. Let us write y_n for the excess of output (in the nth period) over the equilibrium level of output; if output falls below the equilibrium level (as it may do) y_n will be negative. Then consumption in the nth period will exceed its equilibrium level by $(1-s)y_{n-1}$; and there will be an induced investment in the same period of $v(y_{n-1}-y_{n-2})$. Adding up, we get

$$y_n = (1-s+v)y_{n-1} - vy_{n-2}.$$

We know that $y_0 = A$ and $y_{-1} = 0$; thus by repeated applications of this formula the whole sequence can be worked out.

4. To work out the sequence for different values of s and v is a mere matter of arithmetic; the results, for certain selected values, are shown in Fig. 7. But in this case, with all the simplifications which we have made, a complete description of the possible forms of the sequence can be attained by fairly simple mathematical methods. The mathematical argument is summarized in the Appendix, but the results must be given here. There are in principle four things which can happen; the four alternatives are readily distinguishable according to the values of the investment coefficient v. If v is lower than a certain critical magnitude, which we will call the Lower Point, output may go on increasing for a few periods, but it must soon turn down; and when it does so, it will decline steadily until it reaches the equilibrium level, where it will stay. Thus in this case the presence of induced investment makes no really essential difference to the ordinary multiplier mechanism. We get the same sort of regular convergence as in the Kahn multiplier theory (which is, of course, the case where $v = 0$). As long as v remains below the lower point, there is just the possibility of the initial kick-up; otherwise nothing unfamiliar can happen.

If v is above the lower point, but below the Middle Point, the first phase will be the same (though of course the kick-up will be larger). But instead of there being a steady approach to equilibrium, once the path has turned in that direction, the equilibrium level (when it is reached) will be overshot. Output will then oscillate about the equilibrium level: but the swings

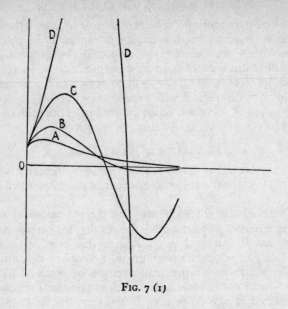

FIG. 7 (1)

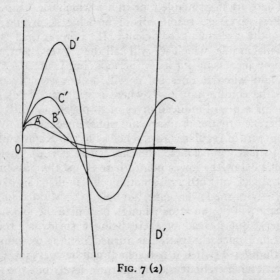

FIG. 7 (2)

will gradually diminish, so that equilibrium will be approached in the end, though only after a series of diminishing fluctuations.

If v is above the middle point, but below the Upper Point, there will be similar fluctuations, but the swings will now increase in amplitude, instead of diminishing. Thus there will be an oscillation about the equilibrium position, and no tendency to settle at it. All the while, as v increases, the initial swing is getting larger and larger.

If v is above the upper point, the initial upward movement becomes so large that it fails to turn round at all; thus the system moves relentlessly away from equilibrium.

The points which distinguish these four alternatives are readily definable in terms of the value of s (the marginal propensity to save). Under the assumptions we have made, the middle point is always to be found where $v = 1$. The lower point occurs where $v = (1-\sqrt{s})^2$, and the upper point where $v = (1+\sqrt{s})^2$. The positions of the three Points, for different values of s, are shown in the following table.

Critical values of v

s	Lower	Middle	Upper
0·05	0·60	1·00	1·50
0·10	0·47	1·00	1·73
0·15	0·38	1·00	1·93
0·20	0·31	1·00	2·09

The specimen curves shown in Fig. 7[1] can easily be interpreted in the light of these figures. The curve A (and, as far as the eye can see, A') are of the first type, showing the regular convergence. B and B' are of the second type, with the damped fluctuations. C and C' are at the middle point; the fluctuations are therefore steady, having no tendency to expand or to contract. D and D' are of the third type, with the 'explosive'

[1] Arrangement of graphs in Fig. 7:

s	$v = 0·50$	0·75	1·00	1·25
0·05	A	B	C	D
0·10	A′	B′	C′	D′

Each curve starts with a given autonomous investment in period o, which necessarily corresponds to the amount by which output in period o exceeds its equilibrium value.

fluctuations; the completely explosive type is not drawn, but it will evidently rise even more steeply, and run right off the paper at an early stage of its course.

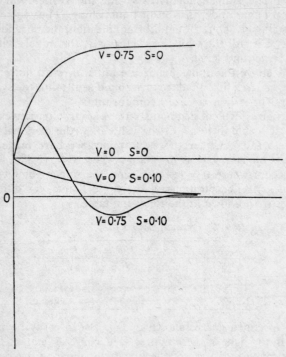

Fig. 8

5. I expect that the reader will probably be prepared to accept the statement that some such classification as this must be possible, even under less restrictive assumptions than have been made in the elementary case which has just been studied. As soon as the accelerator is at work as well as the multiplier, in a lagged process, steady convergence (stability) and steady divergence (instability) are not the only alternatives that are open. There are cyclical possibilities which come in between. It looks as if this should hold fairly generally. Under less restrictive

assumptions the cycles may be less regular; evidently we have to be prepared for that. But the oscillatory alternative will remain; and the further distinction should also remain, between cycles which are damped, so that they are steps on the way to an ultimate equilibrium, and cycles which fail to converge, even in the end.

What we are going on to say will not disturb this general impression; nevertheless, it is unsatisfactory to leave things like that. There are several questions which we ought to ask in the way of generalization. What difference does it make if the hump of induced investment, instead of being concentrated in the single period after the change in output, as we have hitherto assumed it to be, is postponed or is spread out over a number of periods? What difference does it make if some consumption is lagged for more than one period? Is there anything which can be said about the effect of the tail? As soon as we start asking questions of this sort, our concept of the Investment Coefficient loses precision. Is there anything which can be put in its place?

All these, as it turns out, are very difficult questions, which cannot readily be answered in a simple and satisfactory manner. They are discussed at some length in the Mathematical Appendix; though the mathematical analysis gives us a good idea of what the answers are, I have not been able to make it quite complete, and it is not at all easy. All I can do here is to peer round the corner a little with the aid of a few general considerations, which give us an inkling of what to expect in the more complicated cases, though they stop short of giving us a firm guidance.

6. The first of these considerations is reached rather indirectly. Consider what would happen in the model we have just worked out if s (the marginal propensity to save) were actually zero. In the first place, notice what would happen if v also were zero. We should then have a Kahn model with zero saving; such a model (as is well known) is in 'neutral equilibrium'. A single act of investment permanently changes the level of output. Output would increase by A in period 0; in period 1 consumption would increase by A, while investment relapsed to its old level; income would therefore remain at $+A$, and it would remain at $+A$ until there was some new outside disturbance. This is what happens in the absence of saving; a positive saving coefficient may be looked upon as pulling the output path below this ceiling at $+A$, so that it returns to equilibrium in the familiar manner. (See Fig. 8, on which are drawn the 'ceiling' at $+A$, which is the path where $v = 0$ and $s = 0$, and also the Kahn path which is followed when $v = 0$ and $s = 0.10$.)

Now go on to the case in which $s = 0$ but v is not 0. In period 1 there is now an induced investment equal to vA, even though autonomous investment has returned to its old level. Consumption is $+A$, so that output is $+(1+v)A$. In period 2 consumption is $+(1+v)A$; induced investment is $v(1+v-1)A$, or v^2A. Thus output is $+(1+v+v^2)A$. And so on. In the nth period, output will have become $+(1+v+v^2+...+v^n)A$. This is the familiar geometrical progression, so that provided $v < 1$, the expansion will converge to a limit, even in the absence of saving. There will be a ceiling, provided $v < 1$, beyond which output cannot pass.

We now get an inkling of why it is that the point where $v = 1$ (the middle point) is of such importance. For we have now shown that the system cannot run away altogether, so long as $v < 1$, even in the absence of saving; and saving, we may reasonably expect, will be a braking factor, moderating divergences from equilibrium, and therefore checking explosions. (This tendency is illustrated on Fig. 8, which also shows the limiting path for $s = 0$, $v = 0.75$, and, for comparison, the path for $s = 0.10$, $v = 0.75$ with which we are already familiar.) Thus it is not surprising that the system cannot run away altogether as long as $v < 1$.

7. Having got so far, it is tempting to suppose that we may learn something about the behaviour of the system under more complicated assumptions about induced investment by looking into the case where $s = 0$. It turns out that even when the induced investment is 'distributed' (so that the hump is spread over several periods) or 'postponed' (so that it is concentrated in one period, but a later period than that which we have been assuming for the elementary case), the special case where $s = 0$

remains quite manageable. For if $s = 0$, the increase in output in the current period (over the output of the preceding period) is equal to the induced investment of the current period; and that current induced investment always depends, in some way or other, on past changes in output. We therefore get a simple relation (for the case where $s = 0$) between the current change in output and past changes in output. If we assume (as we did in the corresponding place in the multiplier theory) that this relation can be sufficiently represented by treating it as linear, then it could be expressed as

$$d_n = v_1 d_{n-1} + v_2 d_{n-2} + ... + v_p d_{n-p},$$

where d_n is the *increase* in the output of period (n) over the output of period $(n-1)$, and $v_1, v_2, ..., v_p$ are the *partial investment coefficients* (so that v_r is the part of the induced investment which materializes r periods later as the result of a change in output of one unit in some particular period).

Now this relation between changes in output is exactly the same as the relation between successive outputs (or incomes) which we met when we were generalizing the Kahn theory of the multiplier, at the end of Chapter II. It can be treated in exactly the same way. The sum of the partial investment coefficients $(v_1 + v_2 + ... + v_p)$ plays the same role as the (total) marginal propensity to consume. We know that the generalized Kahn model will settle down to equilibrium if outright saving is positive—that is to say, if the (total) marginal propensity to consume is less than 1. Here the same reasoning tells us that the change in output will settle down to zero if the sum of the v's is less than 1. It follows that if the *total investment coefficient* (as we may call it) is less than unity, the expansion in output will have a ceiling on it, at least in the case where $s = 0$. Thus it looks as if it is the total investment coefficient (so defined) which takes the place of the simple investment coefficient v, when we go over to the more general case.

8. This is simple and satisfactory; but it only gives us a guide for use in the cases where we need to use it, if we can show that this damping effect of saving still persists even when we are dealing with a Distributed or Postponed Hump. Until this has

been shown, we cannot affirm that explosion is impossible in cases where the Investment Coefficient is less than unity. Unfortunately it turns out, on examination, that the damping effect of saving is not a universal rule. But it is a good rule, being valid in almost all cases, apart from a definable class of

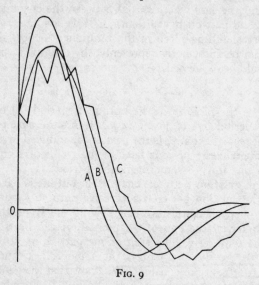

FIG. 9

exceptions; the nature of these exceptions is capable of being explained fairly simply.

Let us begin by looking at some particular examples. Fig. 9 shows the paths followed in three cases, in all of which $s = 0.10$ and in all of which the *total* investment coefficient is 0.75. Case A is the elementary case, with a path (exhibiting damped fluctuations) which has already been twice represented. All the induced investment is here concentrated in the period following the change in output. Case B shows the case of a distributed hump. The induced investment is now divided equally between the following period and the period which follows that. Case C is the case of a postponed hump. There is now no induced investment in the period immediately following the change in output; all the induced investment is concentrated in the *second* period following. Since the total investment coefficient is less than unity, we should expect that all these paths would be decidedly damped. They should converge to equilibrium in the end, though possibly after fluctuations.

The calculated paths seem to bear out this expectation. The paths are all of them damped; the distributed hump gives a path which is very similar to that found in the elementary case. But in Case C there is a noticeable difference. Though the path does ultimately converge, it has some adventures on the way. It first exhibits a number of short oscillations, up in one period and down in the next; then these short oscillations begin to fade out, chiefly showing themselves in the form of pauses and plunges, short oscillations about a path which begins to take on the familiar character. Gradually the familiar form becomes dominant. What are the causes of these short oscillations?

They are a general phenomenon of postponed humps, or of humps which approximate to the postponed type. If there is an appreciable interval between the time at which a rise in output occurs and the time at which its induced investment materializes, there will be a sag in output during the interval (from the effect of saving), and the fall in output which then occurs will induce (according to our present hypotheses) a negative investment which will only materialize after the positive investment due to the first rise in output is over. An initial disturbance will therefore provoke an alternation of phases, in direct accordance with the investment time-lag; the even phases get the stimulus of the rises in output and the odd phases the checks due to the falls. In the case shown in Fig. 9, this short oscillation is damped, like the major oscillation; in fact it damps out sooner than the major oscillation does. So convenient a result is, however, not at all necessary.

For let us go on to consider what will evidently be a more critical case, that in which the total investment coefficient is equal to 1. Fig. 10 shows three paths, constructed under exactly the same assumptions as those in Fig. 9, excepting that the total investment coefficient has been made equal to unity, not 0·75. Case A (the elementary case) shows the regular cycle, undamped and unexplosive, which we know to be appropriate to a unit value of v. Case B (the distributed hump) is, we are not surprised to find, slightly damped, but otherwise quite well-behaved. But Case C (the postponed hump) is not at all well-behaved. It develops a short oscillation, of great violence, and which does not diminish in violence. If one smoothes out this short oscillation, averaging the periods in pairs (0 with 1, 2 with 3, and so on) then one does get the slightly damped *major* oscillation, which we might have expected. But the short oscillation is not damped; it actually gets a little larger as the process goes on. This is the kind of case which upsets our rule.

If the system has a strong underlying tendency to short oscillation, which must mean that induced investment has a time-shape something like that which we have given to the postponed hump, an increase in the saving coefficient will accentuate the sag in output during the *interval*, and will therefore accentuate the short oscillation. In order for this to happen, to a significant extent, it is necessary for the induced investment to be much concentrated in a period which comes some time after the change in output has occurred, and it is necessary that the investment coefficient should be rather large. These are the conditions which facilitate the dominance of short oscillations.

In the absence of such special conditions, our rule—that a rise in the saving coefficient tends to damp down oscillations—seems to be a perfectly good one. Thus, unless the tendency to short oscillation is serious, it is possible to carry through the argument on which we have embarked. If the total investment coefficient is less than unity, a single autonomous disturbance will have a limited effect, even if $s = 0$; this will hold *a fortiori* if s is positive. We can thus expect that the size of the total investment coefficient will give us a rough means of distinguishing between damped and explosive cases. It is not a refined test, but it gives us a good general idea of what to expect—in all cases other than the exceptional case which we have discovered.

How important is this exceptional case? The violent short oscillations do not look realistic, and our analysis of the process of induced investment does not make it look very probable that we should commonly find humps which approximate to the postponed type. That there should be an interval before much induced investment sets in is not at all unlikely; but it seems much less likely that the induced investment would be highly concentrated in time.[1] *Both* of these conditions are necessary before the short oscillations can become of dominating importance. I think that we can set the exceptional case on one side, at least so long as we are discussing the effects of the initial hump (not the tail), and so long as we neglect consumption lags,

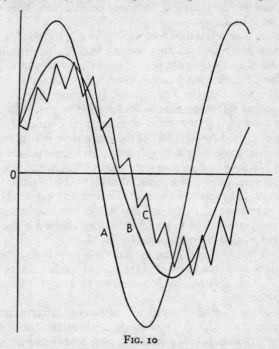

Fig. 10

in the way we have neglected them hitherto. We must conclude this chapter by giving some attention to these further complications. They will give us relatively little trouble, but they do make the exceptional case of rather greater potential importance.

9. We begin with the question of consumption lags. So far, in this chapter, we have maintained the assumption that con-

[1] It is, of course, extraordinarily easy, when one is constructing artificial examples of sequences, to fall upon assumptions which do eventuate in a postponed hump, and which do therefore show strong short oscillations.

sumption depends on the income of the preceding period, and
on that alone. What happens if some part of consumption is
further lagged, as we have learned to expect it to be? Such
further lags can be dealt with in a very simple way. The effect
of a consumption lag is exactly the same as the effect of a reduction in one of the partial investment coefficients. This can be
proved as follows.

Suppose that a fraction b of each period's income (or rather
of the amount by which that income exceeds the equilibrium
level), instead of being consumed in the next period following
(as we have hitherto supposed it to be, if it is not saved outright)
is actually saved in the next period following, but consumed
in the period following that. Consumption in period n is thus
increased by by_{n-2}, the extra consumption coming from the
income of period $(n-2)$; but at the same time it is diminished
by by_{n-1}, the temporary saving from the income of period $(n-1)$.
The net result is to diminish the consumption of the nth period
by $b(y_{n-1}-y_{n-2})$. But the induced investment in period n also
depends (to the extent of the partial coefficient v_1) on this same
change in income $y_{n-1}-y_{n-2}$. Thus output in period n is affected
in just the same way as it would have been affected if the partial
coefficient v_1 had been replaced by v_1-b.

If the fraction b had been lagged for two periods, the effect
would have been the same as if the partial coefficients v_1 and v_2
had *both* been reduced by b. A simple rule of this kind holds
quite generally.

Now if the partial investment coefficients, after adjustment
for consumption lags by this method, all remain positive, our
previous argument holds without any amendment. All that
happens is that there is a reduction (which may easily be a quite
considerable reduction) in the total investment coefficient; and
such a reduction must, in accordance with our arguments, have
a strongly damping effect. We saw in Chapter III that consumption lags have a damping effect upon fluctuations in output
which arise out of fluctuations in autonomous investment without any investment being induced; we now see indications that
the same kind of thing will hold even when induced investment
is present.

But there is one snag. Some of the partial coefficients, after adjustment, may go negative; and it is the 'early' coefficients, the first in the series, which are most likely to do this. For v_1 is reduced by a fraction which corresponds to the whole of the temporary saving; whether the consumption is being deferred until the second, or the third, or the twenty-third period after the income has been earned, the temporary saving is always at the expense of consumption in the first period after, and will therefore tend to reduce the first coefficient. Later coefficients will only be reduced by such temporary saving as persists beyond their time. Thus v_1 will be reduced more than v_2, v_2 more than v_3, and so on. Now with a pattern of induced investment which takes the hump form (which we have assumed it to take) v_1 may be quite small, even before adjustment; the heavy adjustment which falls upon it may therefore quite easily push it over to the negative side. What then happens?

It is not hard to see that the main trouble which arises is an increase in the danger of short oscillations. It was by reducing v_1 relatively to the later v's that we got our case of the postponed hump; if we reduce it so far as to make it negative, we are increasing the chance of this happening. But it is still true that the short oscillations only become dominant if the negative coefficient is followed by coefficients which are *large* and positive. Since even the later coefficients are being damped down somewhat, we get some help on that side. The final result is that consumption lags have some tendency to push the sequence in the direction of the dangerous postponed form; but excepting in cases which are such that the pattern of induced investment was already inclined in that direction, before adjustment, it does not look as if the short oscillations would become very marked as a result.

The main effect of consumption lags seems still likely to be damping. They may increase the danger of short oscillations, but for our purposes this can be treated as subsidiary to their main effect.

10. Finally, to complete the list of these awkward problems, is there anything which can be said about the tail? The mathematical skeleton, round which this chapter has been built, here almost fails us; one simple thing can, however, be said, which

needs no mathematical apparatus to justify it. One can think of main fluctuations being set up by the hump; and the reinvestment echoes which follow behind it in the tail may then aggravate the original fluctuations, or may alleviate them. The worst aggravation will occur if the periodicity of the fluctuations set up by the hump gets into step with the periodicity of the replacements.[1] Suppose that in the absence of the replacement echoes, there would be a fluctuation in which there were upswings in alternate decades—output rising from periods 1 to 10, falling from 10 to 20, rising from 20 to 30, and so on. Now if the capital invested in the first decade fell due for replacement in the third decade, it would aggravate the upswing in the third decade; if this happened, the gap in investment in the second decade would probably be echoed by a gap in replacements in the fourth decade, thus aggravating the downswing in the fourth decade. We have, however, seen that there is a tendency for replacements to spread themselves out over time;[2] such exact reinforcement is therefore unlikely. In practice, some of the replacement echoes will be aggravating, some alleviating. But the aggravating effects, when they occur, are a very serious matter. There can be little doubt that they are recognizable in practice. After the mathematical tricks which we have had to play on this part of our course, a point like this may be accepted by the reader as a breath of realism.

[1] What this means is that the long, or major, cycles set up by the hump have just about the same periodicity as the short oscillations set up by the little, very much postponed, humps in the tail. Just because these little humps are so very much postponed, their short oscillations are likely to be much more important than their longer oscillations, which would be negligible. This is the kind of way in which we could fit the above remarks into our previous analysis.

[2] See above, p. 42.

VII

FREE OR CONSTRAINED CYCLES?

1. The theory which we have just set out is a necessary preliminary to the theory of the cycle, but it is no more than that. It cannot even be a first sketch of the true theory. It has shown us some reasons why the economic system may be liable to cyclical fluctuations, but it has not shown that these causes are actually those which are the most important in practice. In fact, the theory which I am going to present here is not a mere elaboration of the cyclical tendencies which we have been discussing. It puts its main weight not on them, but on other matters not yet examined. But these main causes (as I believe them to be) cannot readily be found except along the road which we have been following. The formal theory of the accelerator (which is what we have been discussing) has to be mastered before the true character of its operation in the economic process can be clearly seen.

The next stages of our inquiry will thus bring about a striking transformation. The transformation will be effected as soon as we have taken account of three simple points, each of which is unquestionably valid, and unquestionably important. They have often been mentioned in what precedes, but we have not yet worked them into our cycle theory. The first of them is the necessity of converting our analysis from its stationary background into terms of a progressive economy. The second is the fact that, at any given time, output is not indefinitely extensible against an increase in effective demand. There is a Ceiling which Keynes called full employment. The third is the fact that falls in output cannot induce disinvestment in the same way as rises in output induce investment. We were impressed by the importance of this consideration when we made our first study of induced investment (in Chapter IV) but have deliberately left it out when constructing the formal model of the last chapter.

In carrying through this programme we shall not usually need to pay much attention to the complexities about distributed

lags which have just been giving us so much trouble. For one
broad result of these investigations has been to show that the
elementary case, which is so much the easiest to manage, does in
fact provide a better approximation to what happens in the
more complex cases than we might have expected. So long as
the short oscillations are mild (and in most of the cases with
which we shall be concerned they may be taken to be quite
mild), it will be the major cycle, already apparent in the elementary case, which will dominate the rest. It will therefore be
sufficient, in what follows, if we keep the elementary case in the
front of our minds; we shall only have to remind ourselves, now
and then, of the consequences which may follow from more
complex lag-patterns.

2. The first thing we now have to do is to drop the assumption
of the stationary state. This gives little trouble. It was simpler
to set out the theory against a stationary background, in the first
place; but it does not depend on that background in the least.
We can simply read off the more general application.

Consider the application to the regularly progressive economy,
in which autonomous investment is present. We have previously
discovered that for progressive equilibrium to be possible, this
autonomous investment must be increasing at a constant (geometrical) rate. Suppose that it is increasing in this way.[1] Then,
as we have seen, there will be a moving equilibrium path along
which output increases at a constant rate, and which is such
that the system can move along it if it is not disturbed. But what
happens if it is disturbed? *The answer is just the same as in the
Stationary theory.* If the investment coefficient[2] is very small,
there may, at first, be some continued divergence from the equilibrium track in the direction of the displacement, but it must
soon turn round and come back to its equilibrium path. If the
investment coefficient is rather larger, there will be fluctuations

[1] In the present chapter we shall maintain the assumption of a *regular*
increase in autonomous investment, because we want to show that a cycle
will be developed, in an expanding economy, even if there are no exogenous
causes making for fluctuations. But this assumption is not necessary. We
shall in fact abandon it in Chapter IX.

[2] In strictness, *total* investment coefficient. But the *total* will often be
omitted when we are not specially interested in the time-distribution of the
hump, and when misunderstanding seems unlikely to arise from the omission.

about the equilibrium path; damped fluctuations if the investment coefficient is below its middle point;[1] explosive fluctuations if it is above its middle point. Finally, if the investment coefficient is very large, there will be a movement away from the equilibrium path as the result of any disturbance.

These rules are to be taken as subject to all the qualifications which were set out at length in the last chapter—identically the same qualifications, for we are still dealing with what, in formal terms, is identically the same theory. The identity can be readily proved in the following way.

Current output is the sum of current autonomous investment, current induced investment, and current consumption. Each of these two latter magnitudes depends upon the outputs of previous periods in such a way that it can be regarded as a weighted sum of these previous outputs. (In the case of the induced investment some of the weights will be negative.) Current output is therefore equal to autonomous investment plus a weighted sum of previous outputs.

There is a relation of this kind between the actual output of the current period and the actual outputs of preceding periods. But there is also exactly the same relation between the *equilibrium* output of the current period and the equilibrium outputs of the preceding periods. (For the equilibrium outputs are the outputs which the system would produce, under the same pressures as exist in the actual case, if it had started on a suitable track.) Thus we have two identically similar relations, one connecting actual outputs, the other connecting equilibrium outputs. The same figure for autonomous investment appears in both. For the autonomous investment is given; the equilibrium path is the path which the system would follow if output was always in adjustment to the given movement of autonomous investment.

Now subtract one of these two relations from the other. The autonomous investment will cancel out. The difference between actual current output and the current equilibrium output will appear as a weighted sum of the differences between the actual outputs of previous periods and the corresponding equilibrium

[1] It is only in the *elementary* case that the middle point is necessarily at unity. Lags in consumption, in particular, may make it much higher.

outputs. In this relation no autonomous investment will figure. This is precisely the relation which we have been studying in the stationary theory. The same theory of deviations from equilibrium which is valid when the equilibrium is stationary (as we have hitherto assumed it to be), is also valid when the equilibrium is of any other type.

This principle, which is important, may be sufficiently illustrated from the elementary case. If current consumption only depends upon the income of the preceding period, and current induced investment only depends upon the immediately preceding change in output, current output (Y_n) will be determined by

$$Y_n = A_n + (1-s)Y_{n-1} + v(Y_{n-1} - Y_{n-2}),$$

where A_n is the current level of autonomous investment, which we now suppose to be increasing from period to period. The equilibrium output of the current period (E_n) is determined by an exactly similar relation

$$E_n = A_n + (1-s)E_{n-1} + v(E_{n-1} - E_{n-2}).$$

Subtracting one of these equations from the other, the autonomous investment cancels out. If we write y_n for $Y_n - E_n$ (the deviation from the equilibrium output), we get

$$y_n = (1-s)y_{n-1} + v(y_{n-1} - y_{n-2}),$$

which is precisely the relation with which we were concerned in the stationary theory.

3. It thus appears that the deviations of actual output from equilibrium output have exactly the same properties, whether we are studying an economy which has a stationary equilibrium, or whether the course of autonomous investment is such that the equilibrium is moving in some definite way. The conditions for stability, semi-stability, or instability (expressed in terms of investment and saving coefficients) are exactly the same. It is, however, important to notice that the deviations for which this is true are the simple differences between actual output and equilibrium output—the absolute deviations, as we may call them. In a regularly progressive economy, it is conceivable that the absolute deviation from equilibrium might be tending to

increase (in the course of oscillations), so that there was a cyclical movement which was slightly explosive; yet, when the steady expansion of the equilibrium output was taken into account, the *relative* deviation from the equilibrium output might be tending (in the course of oscillations) to diminish, so that its cyclical movement was slightly damped. If we define the relative deviation as the proportional excess (or, if negative, deficiency) of actual output over equilibrium output, then the relative deviation will itself be determined by a relation of the same sort as determines the absolute deviation—but the investment coefficient, which figures in the determination of the relative deviation, will be somewhat diminished.

In the regularly progressive economy, $E_n = E_0(1+g)^n$, where g is the rate of growth, and E_0 is the equilibrium output in period o. If r_n is the relative deviation,

$$y_n \text{ (as defined above)} = r_n E_n = r_n E_0(1+g)^n.$$

Substituting this value for y_n in the last equation, we get

$$r_n = \frac{1-s+v}{1+g} r_{n-1} - \frac{v}{(1+g)^2} r_{n-2},$$

an equation which is just the same as the equation for the absolute deviation, except for an adjustment in the constants.

When we look at the relative deviation the system appears, as it should, a little more stable than it does when we are looking at the absolute deviation. The absolute deviation reaches its middle point (above which fluctuations become explosive) when $v = 1$; the relative deviation reaches its middle point when $v/(1+g)^2 = 1$, which is when $v = (1+g)^2$. Thus the middle point is slightly raised, but it can be shown that the upper and lower points are (as we should expect) unaffected.

One of the great advantages of working in terms of relative deviations is that they help us to construct a convenient method of graphical representation—which the reader has probably felt to have been badly missing in our discussion of the progressive economy hitherto. In Fig. 11 we measure time along the horizontal axis, and on the vertical axis we measure the logarithm of output. By this device we are enabled to represent steady (geometrical) growth by a straight line. The line E thus represents the equilibrium path, along which output increases by a uniform percentage from period to period. The line slopes upwards more steeply the greater is the rate of growth (g).

When there is a deviation from equilibrium output, actual output will be represented by a point which lies above or below

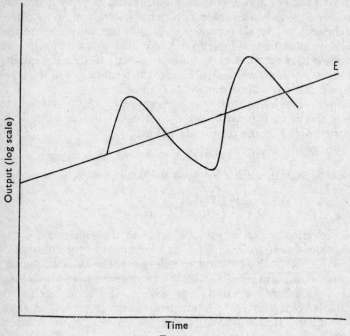

FIG. 11

the E-line. The vertical distance between the actual position and the E-line represents the *relative* deviation. Thus what we have learned up to the present can be summed up in terms of the four alternatives with which we are familiar. When there is a displacement from the equilibrium path, one or other of these four things may happen. Either (a) there is a return to the equilibrium path, after the initial kick-up; or (b) there are damped oscillations; or (c) there are explosive oscillations; or (d) there is a relentless divergence. (The case of the steady fluctuation, intermediate between (b) and (c), is shown in the diagram.) The larger (other things being equal) is the investment coefficient, the more explosive is the alternative which is likely to be taken. Although this classification may be subject to some qualification on account of the distributed lags, which we studied in the last chapter, it does not look as if the qualification will seriously disturb the general picture of the alternatives which are open.

4. This being so, it is time for us to consider which of these alternatives is most likely to correspond with actual experience, and which of them could be an element in the explanation of a cycle such as we find in reality. When we do so, it is at first sight natural to take particular interest in the case which marks the borderline between (b) and (c), the case where the investment coefficient is actually at its middle point. In this case, any initial disturbance will produce a regular fluctuation about the equilibrium path—a fluctuation which is not damped nor has it any tendency to explode. Here we seem to have found something which is extraordinarily like the cyclical oscillation for which we are looking. But it would be quite wrong to conclude that this case can, in itself, have anything to do with the actual cycle. For these regular fluctuations only occur with a very special value of the investment coefficient;[1] it would be an extraordinary thing if we lived in a world which had got stuck for two centuries with an investment coefficient which was always equal to this precise value! The chances against a hypothesis of this sort are quite overwhelming.

A much more promising alternative, which has sometimes been thought to provide an adequate theory of the cycle, almost without further ado, is the case (b) where the investment coefficient lies *between* the lower and middle points. In this case a single disturbance will produce a damped oscillation. There will be one or two considerable oscillations, but as time goes on the swings will tend to fade out. Evidently, then, a single disturbance cannot produce the fairly regular cycle which has been experienced. But why should we assume no more than a single

---

[1] It should be remembered that, in general, the middle point is not found where the investment coefficient is unity. Several other factors, of which the consumption lags are the most important, have also to be allowed for.

disturbance? An actual economy, it can reasonably be maintained, will not be subject to rare occasional disturbances, so far apart in time that the consequences of each are played out before its successor comes on the scene. The disturbances will follow one another thickly. If the disturbances followed some regular law, it might be possible to absorb them into some re-definition of the equilibrium path;[1] but if they are wholly random, this will not be possible. Thus if the investment coefficient lies between the lower and middle points, each of the disturbances will set up a wave motion; and since these waves are likely to have much the same period,[2] they will reinforce one another to some extent. A single disturbance would lead to a damped fluctuation with the amplitude of the oscillations steadily diminishing; but the cycle will be prevented from dying out if new disturbances keep on recurring.

This is the theory which Frisch has called the theory of *erratic shocks*;[3] it is capable of considerable elaboration in terms of modern probability theory. It certainly is an interesting theory; it is quite likely that a 'stochastic' hypothesis of this sort has some part to play in the explanation of what happens. But this particular hypothesis will not do. It does not represent any considerable progress over the simple-minded idea that the investment coefficient might have got stuck at its middle point—the idea which it is meant to supersede.

If the investment coefficient is close to its middle point, but a little below it, then it may readily be admitted that erratic shocks will set up a regular cycle; but this condition would ensure that a regular cycle (with only a slight damping) would follow even from a single disturbance. If, on the other hand, the investment coefficient is quite low, so that a single shock would set up a fluctuation which was decidedly damped, then

[1] As we did with fluctuations in investment, when we were studying the pure multiplier theory in Chapter III above.
[2] The period of the oscillation depends upon the investment and saving coefficients, not on the amount of the initial disturbance. This is fairly evident from the diagrams in Fig. 7. A mathematical proof is given, p. 186.
[3] 'Propagation Problems in Dynamic Economics' in *Cassel* Essays. The first idea of this theory is attributed by Frisch to Wicksell, the reference being to a paper given by Wicksell at Oslo in 1907. It was Wicksell who gave the admirable analogy: 'If you hit a rocking-horse with a stick, the movement of the horse will be very different from that of the stick.'

the damping will affect the stochastic mechanism. For the current level of output will then be affected appreciably by the recent shocks; the effects of the earlier shocks must have been damped out. There is then a very limited room for the averaging, on which the theory depends; the current level of output will be mainly a matter of what the recent shocks have happened to be—that is to say, it will be mainly a matter of chance.

The actual level of output, on this theory, has two components, one of which is systematic, having a tendency to cyclical fluctuation, while the other is random. The smaller the damping, the larger is the systematic component; so that in cases where the middle point is nearly approached, the systematic component will be dominant. In such cases, the stochastic theory would have great explanatory force; but to assume that the real situation is (always is) of this type is as difficult as it is to make the cruder assumption which we have rejected. As the degree of damping becomes larger, the systematic component diminishes rapidly in relation to the random component. A quite moderate reduction in the investment coefficient leaves us with fluctuations which are mainly random—with fluctuations, that is, which remain unexplained.[1]

5. Thus the theory of damped fluctuations and erratic shocks proves unacceptable; but if we reject it, what is the alternative? There is an alternative; it is possible that the investment coefficient may lie, at least as a rule, *above* its middle point.

At first sight, this alternative looks quite ridiculous; one's first reaction is to reject it out of hand. For if the investment coefficient lies above the middle point, the cycles produced by a single shock will be explosive. The oscillations may be small to begin with, but they will get larger and larger, until they result in complete chaos. Some recent fluctuations have looked like behaving in this manner, but is it really possible to explain the

[1] It is interesting, in this connexion, to take a look at Frisch's own diagram (op. cit., p. 202). The amount of damping assumed in this example is not stated; but the graph shows exactly what we should expect to happen in cases when the damping is not very small. The systematic part of the fluctuation is perceptible to a statistician, but to the ordinary mind it seems quite small in comparison with the erratic part. Certainly we do not want a theory of the cycle which clamps the facts into a vice; but this theory (so it seems to me) does not explain *enough*.

long sequence of nineteenth-century cycles in these terms? Clearly not in these terms alone. But suppose that there is some constraint which prevents the fluctuations from passing outside certain limits; the system might then continue periodically breaking its head against these limits without running away altogether. If the cycle is 'free' or unconstrained, then certainly it is nonsense to suppose that the actual cycle can be, or can have been, explosive; but it is not nonsense to suppose that a constrained cycle may be explosive in itself, if the constraints prevent the 'explosions' from passing outside certain bounds.

6. I have become more and more convinced, as I have worked on this subject, that this latter hypothesis is the one which really fits the facts. My main reason for preferring it to its rival, the theory of erratic shocks, is that when worked out it seems much more convincing. I shall hope to show this in the following chapters. But in the meantime some attempt should be made to show that the explosive hypothesis is consistent with elementary statistical facts. There are several ways in which this could possibly be checked up; the following seems to be the simplest.

Whichever theory is adopted, the cycle remains (in a broad and general way) an oscillation about the equilibrium path. Thus the trend of advance, taken right across the cycle, should not differ too much from something which could be an equilibrium development. This is not to say that the system, if it could keep on the line of its trend, would remain in equilibrium; I do not believe that that is at all necessarily so. All that can be said is that a very large divergence between the actual trend rate of growth, and the rate which could be consistent with equilibrium, in the sense in which equilibrium is used here, would cast doubt upon both theories—both on the theory of constrained explosion and on the theory of erratic shocks.

Now if the trend rate of growth could be an equilibrium rate of growth, some information about the investment coefficient can be read off directly. We will begin by working the argument through in the 'elementary' case; the distributed lags can be allowed for afterwards. If all the induced investment is concentrated in the following period, the increase in output which is responsible for the induced investment of period n is $Y_{n-1}-Y_{n-2}$. In progressive equilibrium, this equals

$$\frac{Y_n}{(1+g)}-\frac{Y_n}{(1+g)^2}=\frac{gY_n}{(1+g)^2}.$$

Thus the induced investment equals $\dfrac{vgY_n}{(1+g)^2}$. Total investment equals autonomous investment *plus* induced investment. Thus if we write i for the ratio of total current investment to current income, and a for the ratio of current autonomous investment to current income, we have $i = a+g\cdot\dfrac{v}{(1+g)^2}$. Now we know[1] that in this *elementary* case the cycles are explosive (in terms of relative deviations) if $v > (1+g)^2$. We now see that this condition implies (under all the assumptions we have just made) that $i > a+g$. Is this inequality likely to hold?

Of these three ratios, i and g are statistically traceable; but a can only be guessed. The critical question is therefore whether i exceeds g by a sufficient margin to give a decent allowance for autonomous investment, or whether it does not. If there is an ample margin, it will provide prima facie evidence that the system is explosive. If the margin is small, or non-existent, the test would have come out in favour of the damping hypothesis.

The only statistics available which enable us to make a comparison of this sort for long periods are Kuznets's figures for the United States,[2] which cover the whole period 1869–1938. There was, over the whole of this period, a diminution in the proportion of net investment to income (i), but up to 1914 it was never under 12 per cent. for any length of time. The corresponding growth-rate (g) would be about 4 per cent. This seems to leave an ample margin. But it is unwise to apply the test in this crude fashion, without taking a further complication into account. The growth-rate (g) depends upon the length of the period which is being taken; i and a do not. Thus if we compare an *annual* rate of growth with an i and an a which are independent of time, we are implicitly assuming that the *period* on which the analysis is based is a period of one year. Now if we remember

[1] See p. 87.
[2] S. Kuznets, *National Income; A survey of Findings*, pp. 53, 63.

the definition of the period—the length of time which is necessary before the accumulation of working capital, induced by an increase in demand, just offsets the induced decumulation of stocks—it becomes very hard to believe that it should normally be taken to be as long as a year. But this *widens* the margin available. If we cut the period down to six months, g is reduced to 2 per cent., not 4 per cent. There seems, on these American figures, to be ample room for an adequate rate of autonomous investment, and for an investment coefficient quite large enough to generate explosive cycles, or even outright explosions.

With a period of six months or less it becomes important to pay attention to the time-distribution of the investment hump, and still more important to attend to the consumption lags. But the shortening of the period to an extent which seems realistically quite proper can easily look after such damping as may arise from these causes. Take, for instance, the consumption lags, which probably form the main part of the correction. If (taking Tinbergen's estimate) non-wage consumption is lagged for a whole year, this would be a lag of two periods. The investment coefficient would then need to exceed $(1+g)^2$ by twice the ratio of lagged consumption to income, if the system was to be explosive.[1] Introducing this correction into our test, we shall require $i > a+g(1+2t)$, where t is the ratio of lagged consumption to income. Evidently even this will leave the balance of probability on the explosive side.

7. I must repeat, in concluding this chapter, that I put little stress on such rough calculations as this, as means of deciding between the 'erratic shock' and the 'constrained explosion' hypotheses. Better econometrists than myself could doubtless improve upon these calculations, and I hope that they will do so. My only reason for making such tests here is to show that the explosive hypothesis is not ruled out on simple statistical grounds. The substantial argument in its favour lies in its direct power to explain what happens. That argument will be developed, as we go on, in the course of the next two chapters.

[1] See Math. App., Section 26.

VIII

THE CYCLE IN OUTLINE

1. I NOW come to the centre of my argument. The theory of
the cycle, which it is the main object of this book to present,
has required a great deal of preparation before it could be set
out properly. That preparation is now completed, and we are
ready for the positive statement.

I begin with the following assumptions. (1) I assume that the
investment and saving coefficients are such—and they are distributed in time in such a way—that an upward displacement
from the equilibrium path will tend to cause a movement away
from equilibrium. The divergent movement may not set in
immediately; it may be considerably lagged. It may itself have
a cyclic character, so that it shows itself in the form of explosive
cycles; or it may take the simple (and more explosive) form of
a direct movement away from equilibrium without fluctuation.
This is what would happen in the absence of constraints. But
I assume (2) that there is a direct restraint upon upward expansion in the form of a scarcity of employable resources. Thus
it is impossible for output to expand without limit. (3) There
is no such direct limit on contraction. But the working of the
accelerator on the downswing is different from its working on
the upswing; this difference in mechanism, though it does not
provide a direct check, provides an indirect check which is
practically certain, sooner or later, to be effective.

In order to set out the consequences of these assumptions,
I shall begin by assuming that autonomous investment is increasing at a regular rate, so that the system is one which could
remain in progressive equilibrium if it were not disturbed from
its equilibrium path. It is not implied that autonomous investment does really behave like this. Doubtless, in practice, it has
an irregular course, with independent fluctuations of its own.
But from our point of view these fluctuations are exogenous.
For the present, what we want to show is how a system of this
kind will fluctuate in the absence of exogenous causes. Exogenous causes of fluctuation can be allowed for later on.

2. The exact nature of the 'Full Employment' Ceiling is another matter which we shall be considering later. In this chapter I shall follow Keynes in assuming that there is some point at which output becomes 'inelastic in response to an increase in effective demand'—and just leave it at that. I do not myself believe that the ceiling (and the behaviour of the economy as it reaches the ceiling) can be at all adequately analysed in these terms; but the assumption of a rigid barrier is a convenient simplification which will serve our turn until we are ready to replace it with something better.

It will be remembered that we are always measuring output in real terms. Thus in a progressive economy, in which equilibrium output has an upward trend, the ceiling itself must be expected to have an upward trend. Whether the rate at which the ceiling is rising can be the same as that at which equilibrium output is rising is a matter which deserves further discussion; but for the present it will be convenient to assume that the two rates are the same.[1]

Our assumptions can then be expressed diagrammatically, as in Fig. 12 (which is an elaboration of Fig. 11). As before, we use a semi-logarithmic scale, with time measured horizontally, and output (or investment) measured vertically by its logarithm. The line AA shows the course of autonomous investment, increasing at the constant rate g. The line EE is the Equilibrium Path of output, which depends upon AA, being deduced from AA by applying the 'super-multiplier' to it. The line FF is the full employment ceiling, which we suppose to be above the equilibrium path. (As we shall see later, it is not absolutely necessary that this should be so, but we shall begin by studying the case in which it is.) The line LL will come into the story later on.

3. We start from a position of equilibrium at P_0. It is not necessary to do this, and it has some unrealistic consequences; certainly I do not suppose that any actual economy has ever experienced a condition of 'equilibrium' in this sense. But since

---

[1] There is little doubt that the rates can be approximately the same when population is increasing; in cases of constant (or declining) population the possibility of such parallelism is not at all clear.

we want to show how the cycle arises, it is natural to begin from a state of affairs in which there is no cycle. Thus we will suppose that in the past, before it reached P_0, the system had been proceeding on the equilibrium path. At P_0, however, there is

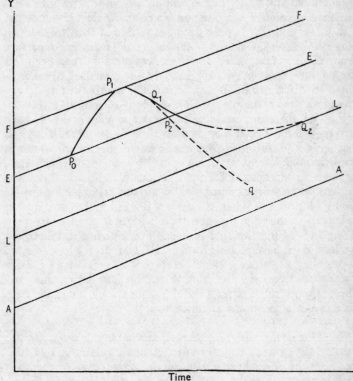

FIG. 12

a disturbance which takes the form of an upward displacement. The nature of this disturbance matters very little for the subsequent argument; we are starting from an unrealistic 'equilibrium' and it would not much matter if we got out of it in an unrealistic manner. But let us say that there is an invention which induces a little burst of autonomous investment. After the burst is over autonomous investment reverts to its old track. But, on our 'explosive' assumption, the same will not happen to induced investment, nor (in consequence) to output itself. Output will diverge from its equilibrium path—perhaps after a certain lag; the divergence will take the form, either of oscillations which increase in amplitude, or of a relentless expansion. (We shall see later on that this distinction does not matter very much. It only becomes visible at this 'theoretical' stage in the story when the system is making its initial departure from equilibrium. Later on, when 'equilibrium' has been left far behind—as it must have been in any practical situation—the distinction will disappear, or will take another form.) I have therefore drawn the path with a steady rise from P_0 to P_1.

Let us therefore pass on to the stage where the upward divergence has become large. It will be remembered that it is not only the absolute, but the relative, deviation which is capable of indefinite expansion, in the absence of constraints, as soon as the system becomes seriously explosive. Thus the expansion in output must finally hit the ceiling FF at some point such as P_1. When it does so, it cannot rise any farther relatively to the equilibrium path. The most it can do is to creep along the ceiling. But that is not a thing which it is able to do, so long as it is operating under the pressures which we are describing; or rather it cannot keep to this track, along FF, for more than a very limited time. When the path has encountered the ceiling, it must (after a little) bounce off from it, and begin to move in a *downward* direction.

4. This downward movement is inevitable, for the following reason. The initial burst of autonomous investment was supposed to be short-lived; thus on the upper part of the path $P_0 P_1$ no more than the normal amount of autonomous investment is taking place. Thus at this stage output is diverging from its equilibrium path purely because of the induced investment, which has been induced by the previous rise in output. Output in (say) period 6 is above its equilibrium level purely because of the expansions in output (in excess of the equilibrium expansion) which have taken place in periods 2, 3, 4, and 5; some of the investment due to these expansions in output is taking place in period 6, and it is this induced investment which

keeps total investment above its equilibrium level. We are supposing (and we have seen that it is a thing which can happen)
that the induced investment is so great that it enables the *boom*
to continue, with the relative deviation of output from its equilibrium level continuing to increase. This is the process by
which the path rises until it hits the ceiling. But when it hits
the ceiling, the relative deviation cannot increase any further.
It is impossible for output to expand at a faster rate than that
at which the ceiling itself is rising. Now the induced investment,
which is induced by an increase in output at this rate, is not
sufficient to support a growth of output along the path *FF*; it
is only enough to support an output which expands along the
equilibrium path *EE*. Output will therefore rebound from *FF*
back towards *EE*.

This conclusion[1] is perfectly general, in the sense that it does
not depend upon 'elementary' assumptions about the accelerator.
We can allow the hump of investment to be distributed over a
considerable time, and the argument is unaffected. Suppose, for
instance, that a large part of the induced investment is lagged
for 3 or 4 periods. Then, in the period after the ceiling has been
reached, induced investment will remain large, because it mostly
depends upon the change in output 3 or 4 periods back, and at
that time the relative deviation was still increasing. In this
period, then, there can be no flagging in the expansionary
forces; the path would still go on upwards, if it could, and as
it is, it will follow the most expansionary alternative open. That

[1] It may perhaps be argued that it is the increase in demand, rather than
the increase in output, which is ultimately responsible for the stimulation
of investment; and therefore that a retardation in the growth of output,
solely due to supply difficulties, need have no adverse effect on investment.
So far as the industries in which the supply difficulties first appear are concerned, this may be granted. The fact that the effective demand for their
products has shot up above the ceiling means that investment in these
industries is stimulated to a greater extent than would appear from an
examination of their actual output. But it remains true that the retardation
in the growth of output in these industries slows up the demand for the
products of other industries; this is the effective way in which the existence
of the ceiling imposes a check.

The credit for isolating this particular factor as the crucial reason for the
down-turn belongs chiefly to Mr. Harrod (*The Trade Cycle*, 1936, especially
p. 165; *Towards a Dynamic Economics*, p. 89). There is an illuminating
discussion of the same point in Haberler, *Prosperity and Depression* (1941),
pp. 368–9.

is, it will keep along the ceiling. The same situation may be reproduced in the next period, and perhaps again in the next. But, however much weight we give to this possibility, it remains impossible to escape the ultimate turn-down. A time must come when *all* the past changes in output, which are relevant to the induced investment of the current period, refer to that part of the path which runs along the ceiling.[1] When this happens, we have to argue as before. With a rate of growth in output, which is no larger than that which is permitted by the ceiling, no more induced investment will be generated than is sufficient to support an output running at the equilibrium level *EE*. The path must therefore turn downwards towards *EE*.

This argument, it should be understood, sets the outside possibility. It is almost inevitable that the path should turn downwards *before* the stage has been reached when all the past changes in output, which are directly responsible for positive induced investment in the current period, are changes which run along the ceiling. Thus there must be a fall in output, at least relatively to the equilibrium path. And once the fall has started, it must continue. There is nothing to stop it before it reaches *EE*, and our whole argument tends to show that the fall will not stop at this equilibrium level, but will go farther.

Let us, however, check over why this is. At P_2, when output has (momentarily) returned to equilibrium, all those past periods, the changes in output in which are directly affecting current investment, are either (1) periods along the stretch P_1P_2, when output was falling relatively to its equilibrium rate of growth, or (2) any periods in which output was creeping along the ceiling, so that it was expanding at no more than its equilibrium rate of growth, or (3) periods belonging to the stretch P_0P_1, in which output was rising relatively to its equilibrium rate. The induced investment resulting from (2) is in principle sufficient to play its part in maintaining output at the P_2 level. But the induced investment resulting from (1) is insufficient; and it is obviously unlikely that this deficiency would

---

[1] In this statement, the tail of the induced investment is left out of account. Much of the tail takes the form of disinvestment, which is depressing in any case. The case when all the periods relevant to the hump are running along the ceiling is the most favourable position—if it can be reached.

be made up by the more than sufficient investment coming from (3). Suppose, however, that this did happen; the result could be nothing more than a temporary halt in the decline. For in the following period the favourable effect of (3) would have become weaker, while the unfavourable effect of (1) would be no weaker; thus the decline would continue after—at the most—a short pause.

All that this argument has shown is that there must be a decline in output relative to the equilibrium rate of growth. It has not shown that the decline must be absolute. But unless the rate of growth is quite unrealistically large, the scope for a relative decline which is not absolute must be a narrow one. Mild 'cycles' in which nothing happens, which is worse than a slackening of the rate of progress, are not impossible; it is, however, much more interesting to inquire what happens when there is an absolute fall. Since the 'free' cycle has been assumed to be explosive, a contraction which went according to the same rule as held during the upswing could not end (if at all) until output had reached a very low level—the path followed being such as is shown by P_1q in Fig. 12. (Output would have to fall *below EE* to a larger, perhaps considerably larger, extent than it was above it at P_1.) But this assumes that the same forces are at work in the downswing as were at work in the upswing; and that is what we must not assume.

5. We have learned[1] that falls in output (absolute falls, that is) do not induce disinvestment in the same way as rises in output induce investment. There is a marked lack of symmetry. Disinvestment in fixed capital can only take place by a cessation of gross investment; thus the adjustment of fixed capital to a decline in the level of output can only take place by a slow process of wearing-out, which must take a considerable time. Once this condition has been reached, further falls in output can induce no further disinvestment in fixed capital—at least not immediately. The disinvestment is, indeed, due to occur in the end; but it will be added on to the end of the contractionary process. The prospect of an end to the process becomes more remote, but the disinvestment which occurs at any particular

[1] See above, p. 45.

time does not become any larger. (The same rule does not apply in the case of working capital and stocks; but it will make for clarity if we postpone the consideration of this part of the problem, and assume that the rule about disinvestment in fixed capital has a general application.)

Suppose then that output has started falling (in absolute magnitude) at such a rate that it shortly brings the gross investment, which is dependent upon changes in output, to a stop; *net* induced investment (what we have been calling induced investment without qualification) is therefore a negative quantity, equal to the depreciation on the corresponding part of the capital stock. From this point onwards, so long as the fall in output continues, induced investment ceases to depend on changes in output. Formally, therefore, it ceases to behave as we have been supposing induced investment to behave. The place of the accelerator is taken by something which behaves quite differently—something which can best be treated as a downward adjustment in autonomous investment. For total investment is now equal to autonomous investment *minus* a constant; and this is a condition which can best be represented on our diagram by shifting the AA line into a parallel position somewhat lower down.[1] (I have not shown this adjustment on the diagram.)

It seems, therefore, that the Slump, to which we have now come, is expressible as a situation in which autonomous investment is reduced a little below its normal level, while induced investment is zero. The mechanics of a situation such as this are quite familiar to us. It is the case of the simple multiplier theory without an accelerator which we generalized from the Kahn process in the opening chapters of this book. There will be an equilibrium path determined by applying the multiplier (with corrections for lags) to the (adjusted) course of autonomous investment. The system now has a perfectly stable relation to that path; it approaches its equilibrium quite steadily without any tendency to oscillation.

[1] Strictly speaking, the new AA line is not parallel to the old, but will rise a little more steeply. For the disinvestment is an absolute constant, depending on the 'induced' capital stock at the time when gross investment in it ceased; it is not a constant proportion of the autonomous investment. But the correction to be made on this score does not seem to have any significance.

The equilibrium path in the slump situation is the Lower Equilibrium marked in Fig. 12 by the line LL. It must lie below EE, for two reasons. One of them is the downward adjustment in the AA line, which we have just noted. The investment to which the multiplier is applied is lower. The other is the change in the multiplier itself. When constructing the upper equilibrium line EE from the autonomous investment line AA, we had to take account of the induced investment due to the rise in output along the equilibrium line; it was this which transformed the simple multiplier into a super-multiplier, as we called it. In the case of the slump there is no induced investment to be allowed for in this way. Such induced investment (or disinvestment) as there is has been otherwise accounted for. Thus it is only a simple multiplier which has to be applied in order to get LL. Both of these factors reduced LL below EE.

The course of the slump is thus to be interpreted as a *steady* movement from the point Q_1, just after P_1, when output turns downward in absolute magnitude, towards the slump equilibrium line LL, which it would tend to reach at a point such as Q_2. It will be noticed that the path $Q_1 Q_2$ must lie above $Q_1 q$ (the path which would have been followed if there had been no change in the working of the accelerator). The limitation of the induced disinvestment must retard the decline in output. Thus, though $Q_1 q$ might plunge downwards indefinitely, $Q_1 Q_2$ cannot plunge in the same way. The slump must have a bottom.

6. This conclusion is slightly, but not substantially, modified when we allow for the disinvestment in working capital and stocks. Here there is no technical limit to the magnitude of the disinvestment, so that the accelerator remains in operation, even on the downswing, so far as this part of the capital stock is concerned. Thus we have not been quite right in saying that the situation is characterized by a complete absence of the accelerator—by an investment coefficient of zero. Even after the disinvestment in fixed capital has reached its limit, further falls in output can still induce some additional disinvestment. But this disinvestment must evidently be much smaller than it would have been if the old accelerator had been at work. The

investment coefficient is much reduced. It seems quite safe to
conclude that any possibility of 'explosion' will be eliminated. It
is possible that the 'free' path, corresponding to a weakened
accelerator of this sort, might be overshot, to some small extent,
before recovery occurred. But it is just possible—and perhaps
more likely—that in spite of the existence of this weak accelerator, there will be a steady convergence to the Slump Equilibrium.
We have seen that this can happen with low values of the investment coefficient, and we seem here to have a case to which that
theory applies.[1]

One is fortified in this presumption by a further consideration. There is not the same pressure to restore stocks to a normal
level when they are redundant as there is when they are
deficient. The holding of surplus stocks may be a serious
burden, but it does not endanger the continuance of the productive process as a deficiency of stocks below the normal
level is likely to do. Hasty disposal of surpluses may entail
greater financial sacrifices than their retention. As far as their
finances permit, the holders of surpluses will hold on to them
and only dispose of them gradually. This well-known tendency
to avoid 'spoiling the market' means that the distinction between
the character of disinvestment in fixed capital and that of disinvestment in stocks is less sharp than we at first indicated.
Something of the same tendency to convert the disinvestment
from a variable (depending on changes in output) into a constant (free of such dependence) is present here also. The point
should not be over-stressed. It is certainly not true that the
acceleration principle ceases altogether to operate in the slump
—so that further falls in output induce no additional disinvestment. It does, however, seem safe to conclude that the
accelerator, in the form in which it persists into the slump, is
a mere ghost of what it was in the Boom.

7. We now come to the Recovery. Just as a bottom to the
slump is inevitable, so (provided that autonomous investment
maintains its upward trend) recovery is inevitable. Suppose that
the system has already reached its slump equilibrium at Q_2.

---

[1] Since, at Q_1, the system is already moving *towards* its (slump) equilibrium, there is no 'initial kick-up'.

What happens next? It will start moving along the lower equilibrium line LL. This line is geared to the autonomous investment line AA, and rises with it. Thus at this stage output will again have started to *rise*, and the rise should bring the old accelerator back into action. With the old accelerator at work, the equilibrium line is EE, not LL; thus the system cannot continue along LL, but (since it is now subject to a positive induced investment) it must sheer away from LL in an upwards direction. When once this happens, recovery has begun.

The exact point at which recovery will begin is, however, influenced by another factor. If the movement from Q_1 to Q_2 has been fairly rapid (the length of time which this movement will take depends mainly upon the consumption lags),[1] the economy will reach Q_2 with a capital (including both fixed capital and stocks) which is still in excess of requirements. A rise in output (along $Q_2 L$) can thus proceed for some distance without there being any appreciable stimulus for positive induced investment. But the mere efflux of time (which gradually reduces the capital stock through lack of replacement) will remedy this; and the upward trend of the autonomous investment will hasten the date at which this adjustment is completed. As soon as it is completed, the recovery can proceed.[2]

8. We are now almost back where we started. When the new upswing reaches the upper equilibrium EE, it cannot possibly stop there because output is necessarily expanding more rapidly than it would do along EE. The boom will therefore continue, apparently until it reaches the ceiling. After that the whole Cycle goes on being repeated.

The story—in this its first draft—is now told; there is, however, just one more thing of considerable importance which

---

[1] So far as we can see at present. It will, however, appear later that there is another factor of great importance which is likely to affect the *speed* of the slump. See below, pp. 115–18.

[2] This argument should perhaps be given a slight (very theoretical) qualification. Strictly speaking, the path $Q_1 Q_2$ is asymptotic to the LL line (since it reaches it by a Kahn convergent process); so that the point Q_2 is not actually reached until after an infinite time! But since LL is upward sloping, the path turns upward long before that! Once it has done so, and once the redundant capital has been worked off, the stage is set for the recovery.

in this place needs to be added. We started off, it will be remembered, with an arbitrary upward divergence from the equilibrium path; since the 'free' cycle was assumed to be explosive, it was natural to conclude that any such divergence would cause a motion which would hit the ceiling sooner or later. But if the system was only slightly explosive (the investment coefficient being only just above its middle point), and if the initial divergence was a small one, the first effect of the shock would consist in a series of small 'free' cycles of increasing amplitude. Only when the amplitude had increased beyond a certain point would the ceiling be reached. That, effectively, was where our story began.

It is, however, natural to ask what would happen if, on one of the earlier swings before the ceiling was struck, there was a sufficient absolute fall in output (on the downswing) to cause the accelerator to be transformed into its alternative shape. The downswing would then develop the characteristics which we have been analysing. The system would move, quickly or slowly, into its Slump Equilibrium, and from that slump equilibrium the next recovery would begin. Is there any reason why this next recovery, when it develops into its boom, should hit the ceiling? Clearly there is none. The fact that the 'free' cycle is explosive means that the peak output will exceed the upper equilibrium output by a larger proportion than the lower equilibrium output (from which the recovery began) falls short of the upper equilibrium output; but if the ceiling is high enough, even this peak may lie below the ceiling. The path may therefore turn round once more and pass into a downswing with the accelerator transformed as before. Once more it returns to the lower equilibrium, and once more it rises away from it by the usual mechanism. But now, in the new cycle which is being generated, the recovery starts from LL just as it did in the last, and the boom is generated by exactly the same forces as it was in the last; is there any reason why the exact course of the last cycle should not be repeated? I do not think that there is. The new upswing starts from a position where the relative divergence from the upper equilibrium is just the same as it was in the previous upswing; the relative divergence at the corresponding peak will therefore be exactly the same. We seem, therefore, to have identified the possibility of a self-generating and self-repeating cycle which does not require the investment co-efficient to be at its middle point (the condition which would be necessary if the cycle was 'free' or homogeneous), and without the constraint of the ceiling being operative. It is the transformation of the accelerator on the downswing which is the fundamental reason why the cycle repeats itself without damping or explosion.

When this qualification is admitted, it becomes natural to ask whether a self-repeating cycle would not be possible even if the character of the coefficients was such that a free cycle would be damped. It is tempting, at first sight, to suppose that this is a possibility; but reflection shows that in these conditions the transformation of the accelerator would not suffice to maintain the cycle by itself. The change in the character of the accelerator always has a damping effect; it causes the trough to be shallower than it would have been otherwise. Thus it can prevent explosive cycles from running away, but it cannot prevent a damped cycle from damping itself out.

The only way in which a cycle can be maintained in the damped case is by exogenous disturbances (erratic shocks). We have seen that such disturbances will maintain a fairly regular cycle *if the degree of damping is moderate*; this still holds, though with still greater emphasis on the proviso, when the transformation of the accelerator is allowed for. The theory of erratic shocks can be allowed to play a part in our theory, as showing what happens in the case of a weak accelerator. I do not rule it out; I only claim that the stronger cases analysed in this chapter look more important and (on the whole) more realistic.

The distinction which we have made in this chapter between booms which die of their own accord and booms which are killed by hitting the ceiling is very important. Some qualifications which we shall introduce later on will render it a little less clear-cut; but it retains its validity, and it is not at all an empty distinction when applied to the real world.

IX

PERIODICITY AND REGULARITY

1. WE have now shown that under certain rather strict conditions of uniformity in the course of economic development, a perfectly regular cycle will be induced. So long as these uniformities remain, each fluctuation will be exactly like the one which preceded it in all respects save one: there must be an absolute expansion in the volume of output (from one cycle to another), for it is the expansion of the volume of output which gives us the trend rate of growth on which the whole mechanism depends. In all other respects successive cycles will be exactly similar. The proportionate fall in the slump below capacity output will be the same in each cycle; the proportionate rate of expansion during the upswing and of contraction during the downswing will be the same; and the length of the cycle will be the same. All relative magnitudes will be the same; it is only the absolute scale of output which will be altered.

But in order to get such perfect regularity, such perfect repetitiveness, very strict uniformity in underlying conditions is needed. It is necessary, in the first place, that a constant basic rate of growth should be maintained; this constancy must manifest itself in two ways—in a constant rate of growth of autonomous investment, and in a constant rate of growth in the 'ceiling' of full employment output. Secondly, it is necessary that the accelerator (including in this term both the intensity of induced investment and its time-shape), though it changes in the way we have considered between upswings and downswings, should remain the same in every upswing, and the same in every downswing. Thirdly, it is necessary that the multiplier (including here also its lag-pattern) should remain constant. It is only when all these constancies are maintained that the cycles will repeat each other with precision.

In the real world we shall not expect to find such uniformity; and in consequence we ought not to expect that actual cycles will repeat each other at all closely. Certainly the cycles of reality do not repeat each other; they have, at the most, a family likeness. Thus, in order to explain the facts, we do not want to assume uniformity in conditions; what we want is a theory which allows variation in conditions, but still leaves us with a cycle of the same basic character. Our theory does seem to meet this need. It has already been shown that the investment coefficient can be changed very considerably without affecting the main character of the cyclical mechanism; one of the things which give different cycles their different histories may thus be found in a change in the investment coefficient. It looks very likely that variations in others of the fundamental conditions may explain other varieties of cyclical experience.

2. The study of these varieties is made more tractable by one special characteristic of our theory, to which attention should now be drawn. We have seen that it is highly probable that the system will have to get settled on its lower equilibrium level, and more or less adjusted to it, before recovery can begin. It looks, therefore, as if we can take this particular position, from which recovery commences, as the starting-point from which each cycle can most conveniently be measured. For although it is true of our theory (as of any theory which depends on the acceleration principle) that output at each date depends upon the course which output has followed up to that date, so that the whole process is causally interknit; nevertheless there is this particular point (the start of recovery) at which the dependence on the past is at a minimum. Even at this point such dependence still exists; the actual make-up of the capital equipment of the economy will still depend to a considerable extent upon the route by which the economy has reached the recovery point. But the recovery point is much better, as a starting-point, than any which we find elsewhere. No similar basis can be provided by any stage in the upper part of the fluctuation. As we have seen, output may turn down because it has hit the ceiling, or it may turn down without doing so. In the latter case we get no 'firm' point from which to begin; and even in the former case the course of events in the neighbourhood of the upper turning-point is very intimately tied up with the particular course which has been followed in the immediate past.

It is, on the other hand, a fairly good rule that each recovery must start from a point on the lower equilibrium line; this does seem to give us a determinate initial position from which each cycle can be measured. Having adopted this convention, we must, of course, regard the cycle as complete when the system has come back to the corresponding recovery point.

A single cycle having been defined in this way, we can look upon it as a unit, and consider how its course would be affected if the fundamental conditions were changed in any way. The theory which can thus be envisaged is possibly quite extensive, but I shall make no attempt to set it out systematically here. Some parts have already been covered, by implication, in the preceding chapter. What I shall do is to illustrate by the consideration of a problem which falls within the field of this theory, but which we have rather neglected up to this point— the question of the duration of the cycle.

3. It must not, of course, be expected that a theoretical argument will tell us anything about the length of the cycle in calendar time—in years, months, and days. All that we can hope to identify, on particular hypotheses, is the length in 'periods'; and though we have tried to give a definition[1] of our 'period', that definition is a fragile basis on which to build any firm propositions about duration. It is quite possible that the period will itself expand and contract during the cycle; so that when we measure time in periods, we are using a clock which may not keep time at all reliably.

This dependability can be tested, at least to some extent, if we consider, not the total duration of the cycle, but the relative durations of the various phases. There are some things which do follow from our theory about the relative lengths of the phases in terms of 'periods'; we can see how far these results look reasonable. If they do seem reasonable, it will give us a check on the dependability of the 'period'; if they do not, we may have to contemplate some transformation of the 'period' in the different phases of the cycle, just as we have allowed a transformation of the accelerator itself when the system passes from rising to falling output.

How is it best to define the phases of the cycle? In the light

[1] See Ch. IV, above.

of our analysis it seems natural to distinguish four phases, which were clearly articulated in the standard model which we worked out in the last chapter. The first phase is the Upswing, which runs from the starting-point at the commencement of recovery, to the point at which the ceiling is encountered. The second is the Full Boom, in which the path is creeping along the ceiling. The third is the Downswing, marked by falling output—a fall which begins by being no more than relative to the equilibrium path, but soon becomes absolute. The fourth is the Depression, in which output has ceased to fall absolutely, and will soon be rising absolutely, but in which it has, as yet, no tendency to rise relatively to the equilibrium level. Once that rise does begin, the depression is over, and we are back at the starting-point of the next cycle.

In the standard model all four of these phases are represented; but we recognized the possibility of 'weak' cycles in which the ceiling is not reached, so that the second of the above phases is missing. In order to take account of this possibility, and to be able to compare it with the standard case, it is often convenient to fix our attention on the total length of the two first phases taken together, which we may reckon as the total length of the boom. In the standard case the upswing is cut short by the encounter with the ceiling, but the boom continues until the downswing begins. In the weak case the upswing continues until it has exhausted itself, so that it passes at once into the downswing; thus the whole boom is included in the first phase.

4. It will be convenient to begin with the weak case. In this case the upswing is the complete upswing of a 'free' cycle, and the question of its duration can be discussed in the same terms as we used when analysing the theory of free cycles in Chapter VI, above. We can begin, as we did there, with the 'elementary' assumption, according to which all induced investment is lagged for one period. The duration of the upswing is then easily calculated by a simple formula.[1] The duration depends entirely upon the saving coefficient s and the investment coefficient v; it does

---

[1] See Math. App., section 21. The geometrical rule given at the end of that section will probably be found useful by other than mathematical readers.

not depend upon the extent of the expansion needed from the starting-point until the equilibrium line is reached.

The number of periods taken by the upswing for various representative values of v and s are shown in the following table:[1]

v	$s =$	0.03	0.04	0.05	0.06	0.07	0.08	0.09	0.10
0.80		22	18	15	13	12	11	11	10
0.90		19	16	14	13	12	11	10	10
1.00		18	16	14	13	12	11	10	10
1.10		19	17	15	13	12	11	11	10
1.20		22	19	16	15	13	12	12	11

It will be seen at once that duration is distinctly insensitive to changes in the coefficients. Once the savings coefficient becomes fairly large, it can vary considerably, and the investment coefficient can vary a great deal without the length of the upswing varying outside the range of 10–12 periods. Durations much shorter than this can only occur if the savings coefficient is very large indeed. But with a low savings coefficient we do get distinctly longer durations, and in these cases (on the left of the table) the duration becomes a little more sensitive to changes in v than it is on the right.

So much for the weak case, which shows a good deal of stability in the length of the upswing except when the savings coefficient is low. But when the savings coefficient is low it is not very likely that the boom will be weak. A low value of s gives us a large multiplier; with a given height of the autonomous investment line, reductions in s raise the equilibrium path EE very rapidly as soon as s becomes small. But if the equilibrium path is high, expansion will not be able to go very far without encountering the ceiling. The upswing will therefore be cut short. Now, on the 'elementary' assumption, the full boom cannot last for more than two periods. In the third period after an encounter the downswing must begin. Thus it is practically inevitable that the whole duration of the boom (up-

---

[1] This table is calculated from the formula

$$y_n = (1-s)y_{n-1} + v(y_{n-1} - y_{n-2}).$$

Thus the s's and v's are supposed to be already adjusted for the growth factor. The number of periods is given in every case to the nearest whole number.

swing and full boom together) will be cut short by an encounter. We can thus conclude that long booms, of the kind shown on the left-hand part of the table, are, in fact, improbable; a boom of this sort is likely to die a violent death before it has a chance to put its potential longevity to the test.

It is, of course, possible that a boom may be cut short even though the savings coefficient is high. But the extent to which this would reduce the length of a short boom must not be exaggerated. Approximately half of the duration shown will always be occupied in passing from the starting-point to the equilibrium line. Thus if we assume (as seems justifiable) that the ceiling is normally above the equilibrium line, the whole length of a short boom (such as those shown on the right of the table) could not be greatly reduced by an encounter. The 10 periods shown might be reduced to 8, or thereabouts; that is all.

Discussion in terms of the elementary assumption does thus seem to indicate a significant degree of stability in the total length of the boom in terms of periods. If the 'period' can be relied on to keep time, something has therefore been done towards explaining the observed time-periodicity. We are at liberty to allow considerable variations in the coefficients, and the length of the boom will not be affected so very much. But how far does this interesting result remain valid when we drop the elementary assumption and allow for lags in the response of investment (and in that of consumption)?

5. This is a matter on which I am unable to say anything very conclusive. The possibilities which ought to be examined are extremely numerous, and we lose the help of the mathematical formula by which durations can be calculated in the elementary case. I have spent a good deal of time working out examples by arithmetic, and I find that these examples do suggest certain hypotheses, which are distinctly encouraging (in the scientific sense) so that they are perhaps worth setting down in case it is possible for them to be verified. At present they have no more than a suggestive value.

A relatively simple case, which seemed worth examining, is that in which induced investment, instead of depending on the increase in output in the preceding period, depends on the average increase in the preceding r periods.[1] (Consumption is assumed to be lagged one period, as before.[2]) Experiment shows that on this assumption we get no short cycles; there are clearly marked *lower* and *upper points*, between which the system behaves in a regular cyclical manner, at least so far as its first upswing (which is all that interests us) is concerned. An increase in r obviously has a damping effect, so that weak booms are possible with larger values of v than in the elementary case (where $r = 1$). But a fall in the value of s still raises the equilibrium line in the same way; so that weak booms are still unlikely to occur with low values of s.

Let us look at some of the results which we get with a moderately high value for r, say, $r = 5$. I have not attempted to re-calculate the whole of the preceding table for this value of r, but the following figures are evidently symptomatic.

v	$s =$	0·05	0·10
0·80		23	15
1·00		22	15
1·20		24	17

When these figures are compared with the corresponding figures in the preceding table, it will be seen that each of them is increased in nearly the same proportion—between 50 and 60 per cent. Since our previous argument was based on the relative durations of the boom with different values of the coefficients, and these relative durations appear to be affected so little by the change in the value of r, it looks as if the conclusions which we reached for the elementary case have a much wider validity. It looks as if we can still say that the duration is rather insensitive to the coefficients, and can add that it will also be rather insensitive to moderate changes in the amount of lag.

There is, however, one qualification to this. Lags in the accelerator increase the number of periods during which the system can remain in full boom, after an encounter with the

---

[1] Thus the difference equation, from which the sequence is calculated, is $y_n = (1-s)y_{n-1} + \frac{v}{r}(y_{n-1} - y_{n-r-1})$. A mathematical discussion of this equation is given in Math. App., section 28.

[2] As explained in Math. App., section 26, consumption lags can formally be absorbed into investment lags, so that they do not need separate attention.

ceiling. If $r = 1$, the full boom cannot last for more than two periods; but if $r = 5$, the full boom can possibly last for as much as six periods, though the investment coefficient will have to be very high if the full boom is to last as long as that. This prolongation of the full boom means that an encounter with the ceiling may be rather less dangerous to the continuance of the boom than it appeared to be in the elementary case. Long booms, with a low savings coefficient, become rather more possible when induced investment reacts more slowly.

These are very tentative results; but they do seem to show (1) that the length of the boom (in periods) does not vary enormously with moderate changes in the coefficients and in the lags; (2) that it is particularly insensitive to changes in the investment coefficient excepting in so far as a high investment coefficient causes the boom to be cut short—a possibility which is less dangerous when the lags are long; (3) that it is more sensitive to changes in the savings coefficient, and this sensitivity is more effective when the lags are long; (4) that an increase in the lags, in the sense of a spreading-out of the response of induced investment, always tends to prolong the boom. These conclusions all refer to the length of the boom, expressed in periods. How far they still hold in terms of calendar time, is a matter of the reliability of the period itself—and that is a matter of periods of production, and of the speeds of reaction of entrepreneurs. It would not be surprising if the period were fairly reliable. The general intelligibility of our conclusions, when interpreted in calendar time—I think the reader will agree that they do not look at all unreasonable—does perhaps provide some slight evidence in this direction. There does not seem to be any reason why we should not take it, so far as the boom is concerned, as a working hypothesis.

6. What, however, of the downswing? Here at once we get into difficulties. One of the most striking characteristics of actual cycles is that output, once it has passed its peak, falls off rather rapidly. This does not happen invariably (and on our theory we do not expect that any particular property, such as this, of the actual cycle will be invariable); but it has happened sufficiently often for it to seem likely that a *rapid* downswing ought to be a feature of the theoretical cycle, if we are on the right lines.

On our theory we do not get a rapid downswing. In order to show this, let us begin by neglecting the transformation of the accelerator. If the same accelerator were at work in the downswing as in the upswing, approximately the same number of periods should elapse between the downturn and the point at which output again reaches the equilibrium line, as did elapse between the starting-point and the point at which output crossed the equilibrium line on its upward course. That this is so in the case of a weak boom can be illustrated by reference to the diagrams in Chapter VI. For when a weak boom is not followed by any transformation of the accelerator, we are effectively dealing with a free cycle, and the analysis of Chapter VI applies to the relative deviation without any qualification. It will be seen from those diagrams that in each type of sequence there represented, the passage from the top of each cycle back to equilibrium takes the same amount of 'time' as the passage from the bottom up to equilibrium. This duration varies, in the way we have just been examining, as we pass from one set of coefficients to another; but with a particular set of values for the coefficients, the number of periods taken over each of these phases should be nearly the same.

This result still holds, without qualification, when we pass to the case of a strong boom which has been broken by the ceiling. The downswing has then begun from a 'steady' position (along the ceiling) just as the upswing started from a 'steady' position (along the lower equilibrium line). Each of these starting positions is momentarily steady, with relative deviation approximately constant, but it is out of equilibrium, so that a movement back to equilibrium is ultimately inevitable. It is just the same sort of movement, apart from the difference in direction; so that if the accelerator is the same, the same number of periods will be occupied by the movement. There is no escaping from the symmetry along this track.

Now let us allow for the transformation of the accelerator. At the point in our argument which we have now reached, we have ceased to be committed to the symmetry of the free cycle; but the lack of symmetry, which we have so far introduced, does not help us here. It makes matters worse. For what we have said is that the induced disinvestment, which occurs on the downswing, can be expected to be *less* than it would have been if the accelerator had remained unaltered. Thus in every period, after the transformation has taken place, output will be *greater* than it would have been with an unchanged accelerator. Thus the number of periods which are occupied by the return to equilibrium is unlikely to be reduced by the transformation of the accelerator; it is likely to be increased. There is no doubt about it. Our downswing is too slow.

The difficulty is serious, but there is no need for us to feel much less confidence in our theory because we have come to a particular characteristic of the typical cycle which it does not explain. At the stage of elaboration which the theory has now reached, it does not oblige us to be narrow-minded. What we have been showing is that the cycle itself, regarded as a periodical fluctuation in output, can be explained in terms of simple reactions, by entrepreneurs and by consumers, which are not in any mysterious sense psychological, but are based upon the technical necessities of a capital-using economy. But we are not obliged to maintain that all aspects of the cycle can be explained in these terms. It would be surprising, for instance, if the price-mechanism and the monetary mechanism, about which we have said little or nothing, had no part to play in the story. I do think that they have less to do with it than is commonly supposed. But it is very possible that some important aspects of the actual cycle can only be explained by their aid. The problem to which we have now come seems to be a very likely candidate for such assistance.

I shall postpone the main part of what I have to say on these matters to the following chapters. Here it is only necessary to suggest that the same forces of 'liquidity preference', which are evidently responsible for the association of cyclical downturn with financial crisis, can very plausibly be invoked to explain the rapidity of the downswing—even in those cases when good monetary management keeps the financial crisis itself within narrow bounds. A fall in output—even a retardation in the expansion of output—will almost inevitably be accompanied by some financial troubles; it would be surprising if these did not have some influence on the particular form which the down-swing takes.

We should, I think, expect that financial difficulties would reveal themselves in a shortening of the 'period'. Technically speaking, it is easier to carry surplus stocks than to make do with deficient stocks. But surplus stocks require financing; if finance is difficult (and it is always likely that it will be difficult when there is a prospect of losses), surpluses will have to be avoided, or attempts will have to be made to avoid them. Thus when demand decreases, inputs are likely to be reduced very rapidly. But the mere reduction of input to the point where its prospective output will match the reduced demand will not prevent the surpluses from arising, and will hold out no prospect of working them off. In terms, therefore, of our previous dis-cussion,[1] we must think of the representative business (when it has got into financial difficulties) endeavouring to offset the unwanted accretion of stocks by a compensating reduction in goods in process—and reacting thus with a minimum of delay. This is what is meant by the shortening of the 'period' in terms of calendar time.

In some such way as this, the rapidity of the downswing can be explained—along lines which involve some extension of the theory we have been constructing, but which are not at bottom inconsistent with what has so far been said. All that does follow from our theory is that if there were no financial stringency the downswing could be expected to last at least as long as the upswing. This is an interesting proposition; but since it is difficult to conceive of institutions under which there would be a complete absence of financial stringency (in the broad sense in which we are using the term), it is a proposition which could not be tested directly, but would have to be tested by some indirect means.

7. Just as we measured the total length of the boom by taking upswing and full boom together (for it was this total length which turned out to be the more significant magnitude), so we should measure the total length of the slump by com-bining downswing and depression. Before recovery can begin,

[1] See above, Ch. IV.

certain things must have happened. These things begin to happen immediately after the downturn; they do not have to wait for the (rather arbitrary) date at which we reckon the downswing to have terminated. Thus it is the whole time (calendar time) from the downturn to the recovery point, about which something useful can be said. If the downswing is rapid, this only means (other things being equal) that the depression, in the narrow sense, will last longer; if the downswing is slow, it may hardly have finished its course before the time for the upturn has come.

The fall in output during the downswing means that the capital stock (or that part of it which is related to current output) has become in excess of requirements; the recovery cannot begin until this excess is removed. There are two forces at work which tend to remove it; one of them is the disinvestment, which is the response to the fall in output, and the other is the upward trend in autonomous investment, which we suppose to continue. Because of this upward trend, the *LL* line (which the economy follows during the depression) slopes upwards; once the downswing is finished, the depression itself is marked by rising output—rising in absolute terms, but not rising in relation to the capacity of the labour force. Thus, even apart from the disinvestment, a time must come when the volume of output is equal to what it was at its last peak, so that the capital stock is no longer excessive. Once this happens, recovery can begin. How soon it happens depends on the rate of growth in autonomous investment. If autonomous investment is expanding rapidly, the slump will in any case be short. If it is expanding very slowly, a sufficient recovery in output may be long delayed; the main hope for an end to the depression will then have to be based upon the other force, the disinvestment process. How long that will take to come to the rescue depends upon the nature of the capital equipment installed in the preceding boom. If the investment in that boom was mainly an investment in stocks, it is possible that they will be worked off fairly quickly;[1] if it consisted in the installation of a large amount of very durable equipment, the process of disinvestment may be very slow indeed.

[1] See above, Ch. VIII.

It thus appears that the length of the slump does not depend, like that of the boom, on a complicated balance between 'coefficients'; it is not to be explained in terms of 'periods'. This is a very important distinction; it is not, as the reader may at first be inclined to suspect, a mere result of the form in which we have chanced to express our arguments. The length of the slump cannot be affected, as that of the boom may conceivably be affected, by changes in the speeds of reaction of entrepreneurs. When once the depression has set in, the system has settled into an equilibrium; it is in a stable equilibrium, from which it cannot be deflected by a mere change in psychological atmosphere. It needs something substantial to lift it; otherwise recovery must await the appointed hour.

8. In this discussion of the length of the slump I have assumed, as I assumed in the last chapter, that autonomous investment continues throughout on a steady course, such as that which was represented by the line AA on Fig. 12. But this assumption may well be called into question. Our autonomous investment is only autonomous with respect to the multiplier and accelerator mechanism; when we introduce other influences, as we did in our discussion of the financial aspects of the downswing, have we any right to leave autonomous investment unaffected? It is not clear that we have. One of the most dangerous things that can happen (and on one occasion, at least, surely *has* happened) is that autonomous investment itself is severely checked by financial breakdown. I do not think that this need happen, but undoubtedly it can happen. This, however, is a matter which we are not yet ready to discuss. We shall come to it later—along another road.[1]

What does need to be said, in concluding the present chapter, is that while the cycles of reality should be thought of as occurring against the background of an upward trend in output, such as we have throughout assumed; and while that trend can fairly be regarded as being supported by an upward trend in autonomous investment; nevertheless, the actual course of autonomous investment cannot possibly be so very regular—it must experience autonomous fluctuations on its own account. These

[1] See below, Ch. XII.

fluctuations, and their consequences, are superimposed upon the cycle which we have been studying.

The formal analysis of this complication causes no particular difficulty. Fluctuations in autonomous investment will be reflected in corresponding fluctuations in the equilibrium lines—both in the upper equilibrium line *EE* and in the lower equi-

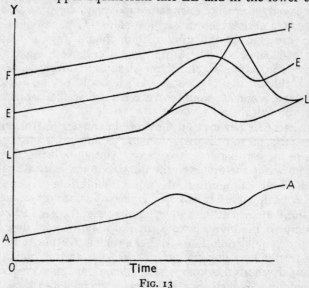

FIG. 13

librium line *LL*. With this amendment, the theory stands; it will still be true that the upper equilibrium is unstable, the lower stable—so that a cycle of the kind we have been describing can still be generated. But let us look at some of the possibilities more specifically.

It should first be noticed that the theory of the time-shape of investment, which we set out in Chapter IV, applies in principle to autonomous investment as well as to induced investment. The discovery of a new investment opportunity is itself likely to be followed by a stream of net investment with the characteristic time-shape of the hump and the tail. Thus, if such a discovery becomes effective in a period of depression, there will be a hump in the *AA* line, and a corresponding hump in the LL line, as shown in Fig. 13. Output is following along the LL line, and it will follow it up the hump. If the hump is large enough, or comes late enough, the mere following-over of the hump will raise output to such an extent that the accelerator will come back into action—and will do so at an earlier date than it would have done if no hump had occurred. But if the hump is only a small one, or comes too early, the expansion in output may never reach this critical point. Output would then fail to leave the LL line until after the hump was completed. What had happened would then look like a weak boom—an expansion in output which fell away again without reaching the ceiling. But theoretically considered, it would not be a boom at all; the economy would have remained in its depression equilibrium all the time.

But let us fix our eyes on the more interesting alternative— represented in the diagram—when the hump is sufficiently effective for it to kindle a true boom. Output will then begin to rise towards the upper equilibrium line; and since that line will also have a hump in it, the upper equilibrium may not be reached until a greater output has been attained than would have been attained at the corresponding point if there had been no hump. If the hump is very large, it may temporarily push the upper equilibrium line above the ceiling. Output can then remain on the ceiling for at least as long as this condition persists. Even if the hump is not large enough for this to happen, it is still likely that the boom will go on until the ceiling is encountered, and will then be broken by the ceiling in the usual manner. This is the case which I have chosen to illustrate.

What happens next? If the hump in investment is very pro-longed (so that it is in the nature of a semi-permanent rise in autonomous investment) the hump in the LL line will also be prolonged, and will be ready to arrest the downswing after the rebound from the ceiling. The subsequent depression will then be moderated. But if the downswing coincides with the relapse in autonomous investment (which may then be expected to fall to a lower level than it would have attained if there had been no hump) the depression will be by so much the deeper. Even if the relapse in autonomous investment is postponed to a later date than this, it may still occur before the depression is over.

There will then be an 'apparent' secondary slump, which of course postpones the date of recovery. If we allow for the possibility of 'apparent' booms, occurring in the midst of theoretical depression, which do not lift the economy out of its theoretical depression, we must allow also for the possibility of 'apparent' slumps. But since these 'apparent' booms and slumps do not induce investment (or disinvestment) on any considerable scale, they are likely to be in themselves of a mild order.

These are some of the possibilities which arise when we allow for fluctuations in autonomous investment. By their means many of the superficial irregularities, superimposed upon a fundamental regularity, which is what we seem to find in actual experience, may well be explicable.[1]

[1] A fuller discussion of the matters discussed in this last section ought undoubtedly to take into account the effects of a bulge in autonomous investment on the movement of the ceiling itself. If the investment is of a productive character, it must clearly have some effect on the ceiling, and this must have some influence on the course of developments, though it cannot (so far as I can see) make any decisive difference to the results obtained. It is, indeed, not only in this case, but in others also, that consequential movements of the ceiling ought to have been further considered than they have been here. But the field of inquiry which this opens up is considerable; and the investigation would have to be conducted in the light of the interpretation of the concept of the ceiling itself on which we shall embark in the following chapter. I have not felt able to do anything about it; this is one of the cases where the theory which I am offering poses questions without answering them.

It may be, also, that when this point is looked into, it will prove that the movement of the ceiling (that is to say, of the full-capacity output) has more effect upon actual output, when that is below the ceiling, than I have allowed it to have in the present formulation. I do not rule out this possibility; but I still think that the distinction with which we have worked is a useful one, and that although it may be somewhat blurred in practice by cross-effects of this kind, it does in the main give the right impression.

X

FURTHER INSPECTION OF THE CEILING

1. REGARDED as a constructional enterprise, our own investigation has now passed the top of its hump. The main building has been completed; what remains to be done is tidying-up and the strengthening of weak points. In the course of these supplementary operations we still have some very important matters to consider, but I shall not attempt to treat them with the fullness they deserve. They will be discussed here not in their own right but merely from the point of view of their relation with what has gone before.

It will be convenient to begin by examining an objection against the foregoing theory which is very likely to be brought up by readers who approach it from the full Keynesian position. I have argued that when the economy has reached the ceiling of full employment or full-capacity output, it may remain on the ceiling for a few periods (the duration of this full boom depending on the lags in the accelerator), but it must ultimately turn downwards towards the equilibrium line. When the process is analysed in real terms, as we have analysed it, this conclusion seems unescapable; but it may be questioned whether in this case the 'real' analysis is sufficient. Has not Keynes taught us that when an uncontrolled economy reaches a position of full employment, without the expansionary forces being exhausted, it will break into a boundless inflation of wages and prices, unless the inflation is counteracted by monetary restriction? In the light of this teaching of his, may we not have to admit that there is something wrong, or at least inadequate, about our treatment of the working of the full boom?

It might seem at first that our theory would not suffer very much if we had to have recourse to the monetary factor in order to explain why it is that in practice a strong boom does not necessarily result in inflation. After all, it is a matter of history that booms have in most cases been accompanied by a hardening of interest rates (especially of short-interest rates); a sufficient hardening could always be relied upon, even on Keynes's reasoning, to prevent the boom from running away. We could accept this Keynesian explanation of the price-phenomena, and still maintain that the process works out in real terms in very much the way we have described.

Nevertheless, I think it would have to be admitted that the adoption of this explanation would make a substantial difference. For there is no reason why the monetary check should operate at exactly the right level. It would most probably err on one side or the other. It is possible, on the one hand, that the monetary check might operate before the full employment ceiling was reached—in which case our theory would need substantial amendment, for it would not be a real ceiling, due to real limitation of resources, but a monetary ceiling, due to the inelasticity of the monetary system, which would break the boom. It is possible, on the other hand, that the monetary check would only come into operation after the real ceiling had been attained. The Keynesian argument then suggests that there would be a violent rise in wages and prices, abruptly cut short by monetary restriction. Although it is conceivable that the real boom might continue after it had received a monetary shock of this kind (and only meet its end, as we have supposed it to do, through a collapse in the accelerator), it is also conceivable that the sharp application of the monetary brake would induce a sharp revision of expectations in a downward direction; and that this revision would be sufficient in itself to cause output to turn downwards. Thus, in this direction also, it looks as if the operative ceiling may be a monetary ceiling; the real ceiling, on which we have relied for the explanation of the downswing, looks like being relatively ineffective.

I do not at all wish to deny that some weight has to be given to this argument. I would admit that one of the things which may happen to a boom is that it is cut short by monetary scarcity;[1] this is a possibility which has received too little atten-

---

[1] When I wrote *Value and Capital*, I still held the Keynesian view that a strong boom could only be checked by monetary restriction. The distinction between strong and weak booms which I there drew was between those which are 'killed by credit restriction' and those which 'die by working themselves out' (p. 297). It is only in the course of writing the present book that I have come to realize that a strong boom is in fact more likely to be killed in another way.

tion in the foregoing, and which must be explored, at least to some extent, before we conclude. I shall examine it, together with other monetary complications, in the following chapter. But before we pass on to these monetary problems, it is necessary to develop some further points which will help to keep the monetary factor in its place. It is not, I think, by any means inevitable that an encounter with the real ceiling should result in out-and-out inflation, even when there is no monetary scarcity. It may do so, but it may not. There is a fairly wide zone in which the expansion of output will be impeded by real scarcities, so that the effect on the accelerator, on which we have relied, will be operative; but in which, on the other hand, the rise in prices which occurs during the full boom will not be unlimited. It is within this zone that the theory advanced in the preceding chapters holds good with the minimum of qualification.

2. In order to show this we can, in the first place, get some assistance from lags. Once we have allowed that consumption responds to income, and investment to changes in income, only after the delay of one or more periods, why should we suppose that the reaction of employment—even full employment—on wage-rates is instantaneous? As soon as the question is posed, it becomes apparent that there are lags here too. The existence of wage-lags is one of the most elementary properties of the labour market.[1] They may be shortened by strong unionization, but even the most powerful unions do not prevent them altogether. Thus although, with the onset of the full boom, there must be a tendency towards wage-inflation, it does not follow that the inflation will become actual at once. We must expect that the full boom will be a time of rising wages and prices, and that the longer the boom continues the farther the rise will go. But if the duration of the boom is limited by other factors, it is understandable that there may not be time within that limit for the inflation to get altogether out of hand.

It involves no departure from Keynesian doctrine if we maintain that wage-inflation makes no difference to the *realities* of

[1] The older economists were well aware of these wage-lags; it was essentially on such lags that they built their concept of 'forced saving'.

the situation. Real output is still prevented from rising above the ceiling, so that the check to the expansion of output may still have a depressing effect on investment, even though wages and prices are tending to rise. In this way, the mere introduction of wage-lags may be sufficient to restore coherence to our theory. But I should not like to press this argument too far. It lays itself open to the rejoinder that the higher profits, which are a necessary consequence of the wage-lag, will stimulate investment in a way which we have not so far taken into account. Not everyone would agree that boom profits do have this effect;[1] but the contention that they do has a certain degree of plausibility. In order to counter it we shall probably be wise to open up a further line of defence.

3. The reader may perhaps remember a promise which was made to him at the very commencement of our discussions[2]—a promise which has remained unhonoured for many pages, but which cannot any longer be neglected altogether. When we first made our decision to work in real terms, we came up against the difficulty that the ratio between the price-level of consumption goods and that of investment goods might vary. We dealt with this difficulty in a way which may have been justifiable in Chapter II, but is not justifiable in Chapter X—by putting it on one side and promptly forgetting about it. It is now high time for it to be taken out of cold storage.

It will, however, hardly be expected that at this stage in our investigations we should embark upon the formidable task of reworking all our arguments in the light of the variability of relative prices. The matter will have to be treated rather cursorily. The kinds of adjustment which need to be made are fortunately fairly evident.

What type of change in relative price-levels should we expect to find over the course of the cycle? Since the variation in investment goods output over the cycle is greater than the variation in consumption goods output, we should expect to find investment goods prices rising more than consumption goods prices

---

[1] See, for instance, F. A. Hayek, *Prices and Production*, to whose theory our own has some striking resemblances—and some essential differences.
[2] See above, pp. 11–12.

in the boom, and falling more than consumption goods prices in the slump. With some particular exceptions due to deliberate price-stabilization (cartels, valorization schemes, and so on) this is on the whole what seems to happen. When we remember that investment includes investment in stocks of commodities (reckoned at wholesale prices) the greater variability of wholesale prices than of retail prices is itself a consideration which tends in the same direction. We may therefore take it as normal for a time of high activity to be marked by a rise in the ratio of investment goods prices to consumption goods prices, and for a period of low activity to be marked by a fall in that ratio.

Before considering the consequences of a change in this price-ratio, let us look more deeply into its causes. Investment goods prices rise in the boom because the resources needed for making such goods are becoming scarce; they rise relatively to consumption goods prices, because the resources needed for making investment goods are becoming scarcer than the resources needed for making consumption goods. So far in our discussion of the ceiling we have assumed that all sorts of resources become scarce at the same moment—at the same stage of the cycle. For only so would there be a particular point at which *the* ceiling was encountered. It now appears that we cannot discuss this question of price-changes at all adequately unless we begin by adjusting our previous argument to allow for differential scarcity. Let us therefore suppose (as is realistic) that different sorts of resources are specialized to the production of investment goods and consumption goods respectively; and consider what happens if the production of investment goods reaches its ceiling at a time when the production of consumption goods is still capable of further expansion in response to effective demand. And let us begin by discussing this question on the assumption that prices do not vary—an assumption which can be made sufficiently realistic if we suppose that prices are kept from rising by price-control regulations, with consequential rationing of supplies or deferment of deliveries.

We take it, then, that the economy is working under conditions in which there is a strong tendency to expansion (so that its 'free' path would be strongly upward); but that the further expansion of real investment is stopped by the encounter with a sectional 'Investment Ceiling'. There can then be no further expansion in the output of investment goods (except such as is permitted by an upward slope of the investment ceiling); but the rise in output of consumption goods is not yet stopped by its ceiling, so that an expansion relative to the ceiling is on that side still technically possible. But in view of the arrest in the expansion of investment, a further expansion in consumption goods production (relatively to trend) can only take place by the deferred multiplier effects of the previous increases in output; there must therefore be a sharp reduction in the rate of expansion, as compared with the rate of expansion in the previous stage when both accelerator and multiplier were at work. Besides, the increases in consumption goods output due to these multiplier effects must get less and less as time goes on; they are soon nothing more than the last stages of a Kahn convergent process, so that the increases in output due to this cause must get less and less from period to period, and must ultimately become negligible. Long before that happens the increases in output will become insufficient to induce (through the accelerator) a volume of investment which reaches the investment ceiling. Although it is possible that investment may now be maintained for a while by deliveries which had previously been deferred, this also is a source which must ultimately fail. When it does so, investment will turn downwards, and the downswing of the cycle will set in. All this will happen—will inevitably happen—merely because of the encounter with the investment ceiling. It is not necessary that the consumption ceiling should be reached, and it is distinctly unlikely (on these assumptions) that it would be.

4. We can now examine what difference is made to this picture when we admit a rise in the price-level of investment goods. In the first place, a rise in the ratio of investment goods prices to consumption goods prices will cause some resources to be transferred from the consumption goods to the investment goods industries; and this may be considered to have the effect of raising the investment ceiling, while lowering the consumption ceiling. Since it is the investment ceiling which is the impediment to the expansion of output, the transference is clearly a

favourable influence, which permits the boom to continue longer than it would otherwise have done. But the resources which are capable of being transferred from the one sort of production to the other within a short period will clearly be limited; and the transference will have to be speedy if it is to be effective. Belated transference will be useless, and even worse than useless; in practice we must surely expect that most of the transference induced by the price-change will be heavily lagged.

Not very much can therefore be expected from this source of relief; but there is another. If for the moment we leave transference out of account, the rise in prices cannot increase real investment in terms of investment goods; but the relative price-change does itself increase the value of that investment in terms of consumption goods. We are assuming, it will be remembered, that the consumption function is given in real terms; that is to say, the demand for consumption goods is taken to depend upon real income in terms of consumption goods. Real saving is therefore measured in terms of consumption goods; and it is real investment, measured in terms of its consumption goods equivalent, which tends to equality with real saving. The value of real investment in terms of consumption goods is the Multiplicand, to which the multiplier has to be applied. Thus, without any expansion in real investment in terms of investment goods, there will be an expansion in consumption, due to the multiplier effect, merely as a result of the price-rise. And the farther the price-rise continues, the greater the expansion in consumption goods output from this cause may potentially be.

When this multiplier effect is taken together with the transference effect, it becomes clear that the further possibilities of expansion, which are opened up by the relative rise in investment goods prices, are very considerable. Thus the chances of an encounter with the consumption ceiling, as well as with the investment ceiling, are much enhanced. But it is still not inevitable that the consumption ceiling will be reached before the downswing occurs. If the prices of investment goods rise sharply, while the effects of the rise (both in the transference direction and in the multiplier direction) are large and rapid, then consumption goods output will expand rapidly, and there will also

be a fall in the consumption ceiling; an encounter with that
ceiling will then be inevitable. But if the price-rise is moderate,
or is slow to take effect in these two directions, we may get some
effect of the sort described, and yet it may be insufficient to
prevent the boom from working out in the same way as it would
do if there had been no change in relative prices. There will be
a downturn without all-round inflation. It is true that in all
cases a relative rise in investment goods prices will cause the
consumption ceiling to be approached more nearly; but it may
be approached more nearly without any actual encounter taking
place.

The extent of the rise in investment goods prices, at a stage
in the process when the investment ceiling has been reached
but the consumption ceiling has not been reached, is determined
in the ordinary supply-and-demand manner. We can admit that
institutional price-rigidities and deliberate price-stabilization
policies may retard the price-rise, so that the actual rise in prices
at each moment is less than the rise which would be required
to restore equilibrium between the demand and supply for the
investment goods; nevertheless it is clear that the elasticities of
demand and supply set a maximum on the price-rise which can
take place. If the supply of investment goods is very elastic,
there will only be a small rise in the prices of these goods; if the
increase in supply comes about by a transference of resources
from consumption goods production, that must mean, as we
saw, that the consumption ceiling is lowered. It is, however,
very possible that the prices of investment goods may be kept
down by a high demand-elasticity, even though there is a low
elasticity on the supply side; a high demand-elasticity has an
unambiguously anti-inflationary influence.

We are supposing, it will be remembered, that the prices of
investment goods are rising, but that the prices of consumption
goods have not yet risen to any important extent. Thus even if
the rise in investment goods prices were expected to be permanent, the profitability of investment would be severely reduced
by the rise in price; it follows that the extent of the price-
rise needed to bring about a given reduction in demand may be
quite limited. If we also allow for the fact that the things which
have risen in price are likely to be things which are known to

be liable to price-fluctuations, we have a further factor making for a fairly high degree of elasticity. For a rise in 'sensitive' prices will usually be assumed to be temporary, not permanent; and on this interpretation there will be a strong case for *post-poning* any investment which can at all readily be postponed. A quite moderate rise in prices will then reduce investment demand very appreciably; and no more than a moderate rise will be needed to restore demand-and-supply equilibrium. When the rise in investment goods prices is no more than moderate, the course of the boom is not substantially affected by the price-rise; it will come to an end in much the same way as it would have done if prices had remained stable, as in the case with which we began.

5. The reader will doubtless have noticed that while we have made some advance towards realism by distinguishing between consumption and investment ceilings, we could easily have made a further advance by splitting up these ceilings, and allowing a sectional ceiling for every product, or (perhaps better) for any group of products which are strong substitutes for each other. Such elaboration is obviously possible, but I do not think that it would make much difference to the argument. It would still be the case that the arrival at each successive bottleneck would itself tend to slow up the boom *in real terms*; and these successive retardations would gradually accumulate a pressure which would ultimately tend to arrest the expansion. It would still be true that the rises in prices, at the successive bottlenecks, would themselves tend to relieve this pressure; but if the bottlenecks were mainly on the investment goods side, rises in price would imply reductions in the profitability of investment, and reductions in profitability would be tending to moderate the rises in price.

It is understandable that the accumulating real pressures will usually precipitate a downturn before the general shortage has become so acute as to induce a general inflation. It must be remembered that institutional price-rigidities are at least as important on the side of consumption goods as on that of investment goods; it is in consequence not necessary that there should be any large amount of unemployed resources in the consumption goods trades at the height of the boom, in order to prevent a general rise in the prices of consumption goods. It is very possible that a point may be reached at the peak when the general scarcity is sufficient to lead to a general inflation, or would be sufficient to do so if it were maintained for any great length of time; but if, at that point, the pressures making for a downswing have already become powerful, the chances are that the boom will not endure long enough for the potential inflation to become actual.

When the argument is extended in this way, some of the distinctions we have been making get a little blurred at the edges; but that is the common fate of theoretical distinctions when they are transplanted out of their 'models'—it need cause us no undue concern. The sharp line which we once drew between the upswing (before the ceiling is encountered) and the full boom (after the encounter with the ceiling) had already begun to soften in the previous chapter; we found, even in our discussions of periodicity, that this particular distinction did not stand a great deal of emphasis. We must now admit that some sectional ceilings may be encountered at an early stage of the upswing, while the downturn (even of a strong boom) may well occur before the economy has reached a position which could be described, according to the strictest Keynesian definition, as one of full employment.

The distinction between strong and weak booms has itself to be modified, though it is certainly not to be abandoned. Its importance remains, though it becomes a matter of degree rather than of kind. We must now admit that even the weakest boom will encounter some sectional ceilings, and will be somewhat slowed up by the encounter. But it will be characteristic of a weak boom that these encounters are only incidental. The main reason for the collapse of a weak boom is the insufficiency of its accelerator; the main reason for the collapse of a strong boom is the insufficiency of real resources to sustain it. In this sense the distinction is as important as ever.

6. We have now dealt with the main problem which has concerned us in the present chapter. We have shown how it is that a boom may be broken by the ceiling (or ceilings) without being much affected by monetary stringency, and without there being any phase of general inflation. Of course, it does not follow that this is what has usually happened in fact; all that can be claimed is that it is an hypothesis which seems to fit the more obvious facts. But our confidence in it may be strengthened by a negative check. For if the theory offers an explanation of the absence of general inflation in the ordinary commercial boom, it also points to conditions in which the danger of general inflation would be much greater. And it looks as if occasions could be identified in which these conditions would be realized in practice.

Our argument has been based on the supposition that the boom is marked by a relative shortage of investment goods (and of the factors to make them) so that the prices of investment goods are tending to rise even while those of consumption goods remain fairly steady. The greater variability (over the cycle) in the demand for investment goods seems to be a good reason why things should work out in this way. But it is not inevitable that a boom should take this form. Cases can arise in which the primary shortage is a shortage of consumption goods. If expansion runs into the consumption ceiling before it runs into the investment ceiling, the rise in consumption goods prices has an immediate effect in stimulating investment; this effect will tend to offset the depressive effect from the check to the expansion of consumption goods output. In the phase (it must, I think, be a brief one) when the consumption ceiling has been reached but the investment ceiling has not yet been reached, there will be some transference of resources from the investment to the consumption goods trades, thus lowering the investment ceiling; but there will at the same time be a stimulus to investment goods production, and the combined effect of these tendencies must soon cause the investment goods trades to reach their ceiling also. Thus the inflationary pressure is likely to become general at an early stage in the full boom, and may well lead to a general rise in prices and wages before the check to the growth of real output has had time to exercise its customary effect in retarding investment.

For the reasons which we have stated, a development of this kind is unlikely to occur in the case of the ordinary commercial boom; but one can recognize something of this sort as one element in the inflationary boom which often succeeds a destructive war. The destruction of real capital in war-time, and the non-replacement which is one of the most convenient methods of liberating resources for war purposes, are reflected, when the war is over, in a shortage of consumption goods—a shortage which cannot adequately be remedied (at least for the time being) by any absorption of additional labour into the consumption goods trades. But the shortage does itself provide an immense stimulus to investment; thus the shortage of consumption goods is almost at once reflected in a shortage of investment goods, leading to an all-round pressure. It is certainly not to be denied that the inflationary pressure, which occurs in such situations, is aggravated by autonomous expansion in investment, and by the contemporary difficulty of contracting government expenditure. But the shortage of consumption goods is itself a powerful inflationary force, which is a basic factor in post-war inflations; there is nothing parallel to it in the peace-time boom, or nothing (at least) of any comparable significance.[1]

[1] Some further developments of this last point will be found in my articles, 'World Recovery after War' (*Econ. Jour.*, 1947) and 'Full Employment in a Period of Reconstruction' (*Nationalokonomisk Tidsskrift*, 1947).

XI

THE MONETARY FACTOR

1. THE theory of the cycle which has so far been put forward in this book is almost entirely non-monetary; it is at the opposite extreme from that of a writer such as Mr. Hawtrey, who has held that the cycle is 'a purely monetary phenomenon'. We have, of course, not denied that the cycle has monetary repercussions; but we have only invoked those repercussions to explain one single characteristic of the *real* cycle—the rapidity of the downswing. Excepting in this one connexion, the monetary aspect has been kept firmly in the background; the monetary system has been given nothing more than a passive role.

This emphasis on the *real* (non-monetary) character of the cyclical process has of course been entirely deliberate; it has been one of the main objects of this work to show that the main features of the cycle can be adequately explained in real terms. But now that our *real* analysis is substantially complete, it is natural to turn round and inquire whether the part played by money has not been underrated. Even if the factors we have been considering are the main causes of the cycle, may it not be that there are some subsidiary monetary causes, which should not be left entirely on one side? This is a possibility which we have in no way excluded; one of the supplementary tasks which seems to be incumbent on us at this point is to give it some examination.

2. There is one special form of the monetary explanation of the cycle which suggests itself very readily when one reflects upon the monetary side of Keynes's *General Theory*. In substance, I think, it is all the same explanation, whether we develop it out of Keynes or take it direct from Wicksell or even from Hawtrey. The differences are secondary. But modern readers will probably find it easiest to recognize when it is given its Keynesian dress; and in that dress it is readily comparable with the real theory which we have been elaborating.

In the real theory it is the accelerator which is ultimately responsible for producing the cycle. Since we now want to discover whether there may not be some independent cycle-maker on the monetary side, it will be proper to begin by leaving the accelerator out of account. We can therefore follow Keynes in making the volume of investment depend upon the rate of interest, while neglecting the effect on investment of changes in the volume of output. We can in fact go back, for the present, to the regular Keynesian model.

The ideas which we now want to get out of the Keynes theory emerge very easily if that theory itself is put into a particular form—a form which I myself suggested in an article[1] written a few months after the publication of Keynes's book. I still feel that the diagram which was worked out in that article gives the most convenient summary of the Keynesian theory of Interest and Money which has yet been produced. In itself the diagram is nothing more than an expository device; but since more use can be made of it than has yet been made, it will not be out of place to reintroduce it here.

3. We begin with the provisional assumption that rates of money wages are constant. Subject to this assumption, values in Keynesian wage-units are the same as money values. Thus the Marginal Efficiency of Capital schedule shows the money value of investment as a function of the rate of interest. With the accelerator neglected, it is not unreasonable to regard the schedule of the marginal efficiency of capital as independently determined. Other things being equal, the value of investment depends upon the rate of interest, rising when the rate of interest falls. (Just what is meant, or can be meant, by the rate of interest in this connexion is a matter which we shall consider later.)

If, like Keynes, we neglect any direct influence of interest on saving, we can go on to say that with a given value of investment (at constant money wages) the equilibrium value of money income will be determined by the multiplier. Thus, with a given rate of interest, the value of investment is determined from the marginal efficiency of capital schedule; and further, once the value of investment has been determined, the total

[1] 'Mr. Keynes and the Classics', *Econometrica*, 1937.

value of money income is determined by the consumption function. Taking both of these steps together, we can say that with a given marginal efficiency of capital schedule, and a given consumption function, there is a determinate money income corresponding to each rate of interest. If we now construct a diagram with income (Y) on the horizontal axis, and interest (r) on the vertical, the relation between interest and income can be drawn out as a curve, the SI-curve of Fig. 14. This curve can

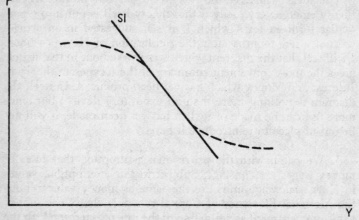

FIG. 14

be defined as showing the level of income which keeps equilibrium saving equal to equilibrium investment at each rate of interest. Since a fall in interest increases investment, and an increase in investment increases income, the SI-curve can be relied upon to slope downwards from left to right.

This simple argument gives us the basic generation of the SI-curve. But, having got so far, it is obviously possible to relax the assumptions a good deal, without the character of the curve being substantially affected. We can, in the first place, take account of a possible direct effect of the rate of interest on saving. If a fall in the rate of interest affects the volume of saving forthcoming out of a given income, the multiplier itself becomes a function of the rate of interest. But with a given rate of interest there will still be a determinate multiplier, so that income is still a function of interest, as before. If a fall in the rate of interest makes the representative individual save less out of a given income, the multiplier will be increased by a fall in interest, so that the SI-curve is made more elastic; if a fall in the rate of interest makes the representative individual save more, the SI-curve will become less elastic. We can, I think, be confident that this latter effect will never be large enough to disturb the general rule that the SI-curve slopes downwards.[1]

Secondly, we can go some way towards relaxing the assumption of given money wages. Suppose that money wage-rates are fixed in some trades, but are flexible in others. Then a high level of income (in terms of wage-units) is likely to lead to a rise in wages in the flexible trades, so that money income will rise more than it would have done if all wage-rates had been rigid. In the same way a low income in wage-units may be associated with a fall in wages in the flexible trades, so that money income will fall more than it would have done if all wage-rates had been fixed. Thus the assumption of partial wage-flexibility has the effect of making the SI-curve more elastic, particularly at its extremities. It is, indeed, not impossible that the lowest conceivable rate of interest might fail to stimulate a rise in employment which was sufficient to call forth an upward movement of wage-rates, so that the elastic stretch on the right would fail to operate. But the characteristic shape of the curve, on the assumption of partial wage-flexibility, is that shown by the dotted line on the diagram.[2]

[1] I may refer to *Value and Capital*, pp. 232–6, for a general argument which seems to show that the tendency of a fall in interest to increase consumption, in the economy as a whole, is more reliable than might appear at first sight.

[2] It is tempting to ask whether the assumption of given money wage-rates could not be relaxed altogether by a further application of this method. As the flexible sector increases in size relatively to the fixed, the elastic stretches of the dotted curve will become more elastic, and the range over which the rate of interest can vary without upsetting the wage-structure will be diminished, so that the elastic stretches will draw together. The curve as a whole will go on flattening out, so that in the limit, when all wages are flexible, it should apparently be replaced by a horizontal straight line.

I think that there is some sense in this construction, and it is useful for some purposes. It is essentially the case of Wicksell's *Interest and Prices*; the height of the horizontal line is Wicksell's 'natural rate of interest'; there is cumulative inflation if the actual rate goes below the natural rate, cumulative deflation if there is a discrepancy in the other direction. Wicksell's theory

4. Thus the equation of saving and investment can be regarded as giving us one relation between income and interest; a second relation can be derived from the theory of Liquidity Preference. The demand for money, Keynes held, can be divided into two parts: in the first place there is a demand for money to finance current transactions, and in the second place there is a demand for money to act as a liquid reserve. The amount of money required for the first purpose will depend, in the main, upon the volume of transactions in money terms, and this will vary closely with money income (the Y of our diagram). The amount of money required for the second purpose will be a matter of the relative advantage, at the margin, of holding money (considered as a non-income-yielding asset) as against the holding of an asset which does yield interest or profit. The exact nature of this liquidity advantage (on which much might be said) does not greatly signify for our purposes.

Now let us make the provisional assumption that the supply of money is fixed. This fixed supply of money will have to be divided between the above two purposes; the more that is absorbed in one, the less will be available for the other. A rise in money income (Y) will increase the amount of money

is the correct theory for a world of completely flexible wages (and prices). The essential difference between Keynes and Wicksell lies in Keynes's assumption of wage-rigidity (at least in a downwards direction).

Where our diagram gets into difficulties is precisely over this last possibility—that wages may be flexible upwards but not downwards. If all wages behave in this way, a sufficient fall in interest will produce a state of full employment, and an indefinite rise in money income; at that point, therefore, the SI-curve becomes horizontal. Since (ex hypothesi) wages do not fall at a low level of employment, there will be no horizontal stretch on the left; the curve will consist of (1) a relatively inelastic stretch, on which employment is less than full, and (2) a horizontal stretch corresponding to full employment. But if the curve is drawn in this way, a static interpretation of it (such as we shall require) breaks down. Once interest had fallen to the full employment level, wages would rise indefinitely; if interest were subsequently raised, the rise in wages would be checked, and unemployment would appear. But wages would not fall to the old level, so that money income would not contract along the old 'inelastic' curve, but along a new curve to the right of it. The curve, in fact, would not stay put.

Under the assumption which we have made in the text—that some wages are flexible, and flex in both directions, while other wages are absolutely rigid, the curve will stay put, so that we can use it without danger of displacement. These assumptions seem to me to be sufficient for the purposes of our present inquiry.

required for the transactions purpose; if the total supply of
money is fixed, this additional demand can only be satisfied if
money is drawn away from the other use. If the 'liquidity preference schedule' remains the same, the liquid reserves can only
be reduced by giving people an incentive to hold their assets in
another form—that is to say, by a rise in the rate of interest.

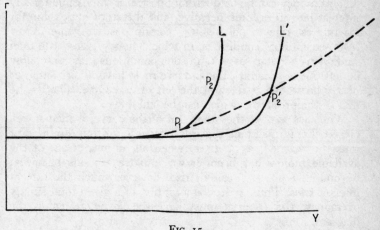

FIG. 15

Supposing, on the other hand, that money is released from the
transactions balances (by a fall in Y); then more money will be
available for holding in liquid reserves than people will desire
to hold at the ruling rate of interest. They will therefore increase
their demands for income-yielding assets, which will raise the
prices of such assets, and the rise in price is equivalent to a fall
in the rate of interest.

It follows, then, that under the assumption of a given quantity
of money, and given liquidity preference, the rate of interest is
a function of money income (Y). This relation can be expressed
as a curve on the same income-interest diagram as we have just
been using. Since interest rises as income increases, this liquidity
curve L (Fig. 15) will slope upwards to the right.

What can be said about the shape of the L-curve? It is an
essential part of Keynes's argument that an increase in the

supply of money, available to satisfy the demand for liquid balances, cannot reduce the rate of interest indefinitely; there must be a minimum below which it cannot fall. The exact position of the minimum depends on the method we adopt of choosing a single rate of interest to represent the whole interest-structure. But whatever method is adopted, it is clear that so long as money can be held without cost, it is impossible for any interest rate to become negative, and therefore impossible for *the* interest rate to fall below a certain positive value. Apart from exceptional conditions, in which money is less safe than some non-monetary asset (and such conditions may reasonably be left out of account), the L-curve must have a horizontal, or nearly horizontal, stretch at the left of its course. That is the first of the properties which can be laid down.

When we look at the other end of the curve, it seems even clearer that it must tend towards a vertical position. For a point must be reached, as Y rises, when all, or nearly all, of the available money has been drawn into transactions balances; beyond that point Y cannot rise, however much the rate of interest rises. Thus, on the assumption of a given total supply of money, the L-curve must have the shape drawn in the diagram.

If the supply of money increases, the L-curve will be moved to the right. The maximum Y which can be financed with the available money will clearly be increased, so that there is an undoubted rightward movement of the curve on the vertical stretch. But the increase in the supply of money is unlikely to have much effect on the minimum to which the rate of interest can fall; thus the left end of the curve will be little affected. There will be a shift into some such position as L'.

Further, having got so far, we can easily abandon the assumption of a given supply of money. And it is fortunate that we can do so, for the exact meaning of the 'supply of money' in Keynes's theory is one of the things about it which can cause trouble. If, for example, money means bank deposits, then it can be argued that there are bank deposits which do bear interest; and (what is more important) it can be objected that the supply of bank deposits is not fixed, but is to some extent responsive to the same forces of interest and income on which the demand has been made to depend. At the point we have now reached, these complications need cause no difficulty. We can allow for some elasticity in the supply of money—or, more generally still, some elasticity in the monetary system—without changing the essentials of our construction. If the monetary system is elastic, in the sense that a rise in the rate of interest increases the supply of money, a suitable rise in r will allow an expansion, not from P_1 to P_2 on curve L, but from P_1 on curve L to P_2' on curve L'. By joining P_1 to P_2' and continuing to the corresponding points on other curves, we can draw an 'L' curve (dotted in the diagram) which shows the relation of income and interest, not with a given 'supply of money' but with a given monetary system—and the curve will be more or less elastic according as the monetary system is more or less elastic. If the supply of money is responsive to changes in Y, we get substantially the same effect. A perfectly elastic monetary system would enable Y to expand without any rise in r—so that the adjusted (dotted) curve would become horizontal; an imperfectly elastic system would be represented by a curve of less elasticity in its upper reaches. We can express the principle of the liquidity minimum by saying that even a monetary system which is in general inelastic behaves elastically when the rate of interest falls to a low level.

5. Having now constructed the savings-investment curve (SI) and the liquidity curve (L) let us superimpose them on the same diagram (Fig. 16). Suppose that the curves intersect at a point P. Then at P both the savings-investment and the liquidity relations between income and interest are satisfied. With given marginal efficiency of capital schedule, given consumption function, given liquidity preference schedule, and given monetary system, money income (which we are supposing—in spite of the limited allowance we have made for wage-flexibility—to be correlated with employment) and the rate of interest are simultaneously determined. It is this simultaneous determination at P which effectively sums up the Keynesian system.

Many of the possibilities to which Keynes has, explicitly or implicitly, drawn our attention can now be read off directly from the diagram. If the curves are in the position drawn, intersecting at a level of *r* which is above the liquidity minimum, and at a level of *Y* which is apparently well short of full employment, expansion can come about either by an upward movement of the *SI*-curve (a rise in the marginal efficiency of capital, or in the propensity to consume) or by a rightward movement of the *L*-curve (fall in liquidity preference, or greater willingness on the part of the monetary authority to create money).

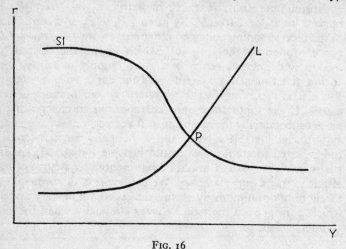

FIG. 16

If, however, the *SI*-curve was farther to the left, so that *P* lay on the horizontal part of the *L*-curve, monetary action (represented by a rightward movement of the *L*-curve) would be ineffective; for monetary action would only affect the upward-sloping part of the *L*-curve, leaving the horizontal part substantially unaffected. And so on; but I may leave the reader to work out the rest of these (mostly familiar) possibilities for himself.

This is as far as Keynes's argument takes us; but, having reached this point, it clearly becomes necessary to reconsider the argument in the light of some of the things which have been said in the earlier chapters of this book. By this I do not mean that we should introduce the accelerator—for we are deliberately leaving the accelerator out of account; but even apart from its neglect of the accelerator the preceding argument is unsatisfactory. For it takes no account of lags.

6. We saw in the early chapters of this book that it is incorrect to think of income as being *determined* by the equation of saving and investment; all that is determined by that equation is the equilibrium position, to which actual income tends. Applying that principle to the present construction, we must conclude that the *SI*-curve does not show an actual position which will be established automatically and immediately as soon as the rate of interest is fixed at some particular level; all it can show is the equilibrium Y corresponding to a given r. This must be so, merely because of the lags in the multiplier; but we have learned enough about the inducement of investment (whether the investment is induced by the acceleration principle, or by some other cause) to be sure that there must be lags on the side of the marginal efficiency of capital schedule also. A change in the rate of interest will never exercise its full effect upon the volume of investment excepting after some delay—often after a very considerable delay. Thus there are two sorts of lags which affect the working of the *SI*-curve. When it is properly understood, that curve cannot be taken to indicate anything more than an equilibrium relation.

Before considering the consequences of this reinterpretation, we must ask whether anything of the same sort has to be said of the *L*-curve. At first sight, it would appear that this curve represents a much more quick-acting effect. The financial markets, which are the main haunts of liquidity preference, are notoriously sensitive parts of the economy. The speed with which the liquidity effect can therefore be supposed to act is no doubt one of the reasons why it has become customary, since the appearance of Keynes's book, to think of the rate of interest as being *determined* on the monetary side, instead of being governed by the interaction of real and monetary factors, as equilibrium analysis shows it to be. The rapidity of the speculative reactions must of course be accepted; but the *L*-curve, as we have defined it, is not solely a matter of the behaviour of speculators. It is in part a reflection of another monetary reaction, through the transactions balances, by which changes in income (Y) affect the demand for money. It is not at all evident that this latter reaction must be instantaneous. The first effect of a rise in income may well be a fall in the ratio of transactions balances to turnover, at the cost of some inconvenience which is tolerable for the moment but becomes less tolerable as time goes on. Similarly for the case of a fall. But not much can be said about this process in general terms; it is very dependent upon particular monetary institutions, on the kinds of money used for particular purposes, and on the ways those kinds of money are provided. In any special application, the matter would have to be considered in detail; here we need only notice that some lag under this head ought to be taken into account.

Much more important than this is the corresponding lag on the supply side of money itself—a lag which enters into our L-curve as soon as we interpret the curve to represent the relation holding with a *given monetary system*, rather than with a given supply of money in the sense of bank credit. It is generally accepted that a banking system ought to have a certain amount of 'play' in it, so that the supply of credit will adjust itself to temporary expansions of demand—such as those due to seasonal disturbances, the exigencies of public finance, and similar causes. It must be admitted that when the disturbance is essentially temporary, so that it can be relied upon to come to an end of its own accord, a rise in interest rates cannot possibly serve any useful purpose. But since it is difficult to distinguish, at first, between changes that are essentially temporary and those which are potentially permanent (if they are not checked), it has to be taken as a rule that any change is liable to be treated as a temporary change *in the first place*.[1] Thus the full response of the banking system to a change in the demand for money will only reveal itself after a lag. The supply of bank money is normally more elastic in the short run than it is in the long run. This, then, is another and more important reason why the actual

[1] In behaving like this, bankers are doing nothing else but behaving as we have assumed the ordinary entrepreneur to behave. Lags of this sort are a characteristic of normal human conduct in a world of imperfect foreknowledge.

position of the economy, when it is not in monetary equilibrium, may lie elsewhere than on the *L*-curve.

7. We must now ask what happens to our theoretical construction when we allow for these lags. Formally, the effect is very simple. The formal, or mechanical, relation between our *SI*- and *L*-curves is the same as that between an ordinary

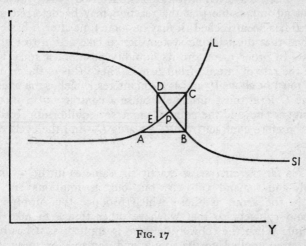

FIG. 17

demand curve and supply curve. It is well known that the effect of lags on the supply-and-demand mechanism is to produce a tendency to cyclical fluctuation, which is conventionally expressed in the well-known 'cobweb theorem'. So it is here. The monetary cycle is the Savings-Investment-Liquidity Cobweb.

Let us look at this on our diagram (Fig. 17). We must now suppose that the economy is starting from a point which is not one of monetary equilibrium. In order to put this assumption in a readily intelligible form, let us begin by assuming that the *SI*-curve has recently shifted from a position in which monetary equilibrium was at *A*, into the position shown which is such that monetary equilibrium is at *P*. If the rate of interest remains for a while unchanged, because the increased demand for money takes time to show itself, and because the supply of money begins by adjusting itself to the demand with a high short-run elasticity, income will begin by increasing along the path AB. There will, of course, be no immediate movement from A to B; the expansion will take a considerable time. As the economy moves from A towards B, the demand for money for transactions purposes increases, though with a lag; the banking position accordingly becomes increasingly difficult, and sooner or later there must be a reaction towards the L-curve. It is, however, not at all impossible that the reaction may be deferred until after B has been reached; it may be some time after B has been reached that the banking system has to take action to restrict credit. In order to restore its liquidity position, it must then raise the rate of interest from B to C. Since B is to the right of P, C must be above P; and a rate of interest which is maintained at the C level must ultimately cause a contraction in income which goes beyond the point of monetary equilibrium. Income will therefore contract from C towards D—and the cycle continues.

8. So far the analysis is exactly the same as in the ordinary supply-and-demand cobweb; but our assumptions are not exactly the same as those which produce the supply-and-demand cobweb, so that we have other things to take into account. When the cobweb theorem is applied, as it has been most often applied, to the supply and demand for an agricultural commodity, demand is assumed to react immediately, while supply only reacts after a definite lag, the length of the lag depending on technical conditions of production.[1] Under these assumptions, the amplitude of the cycle depends entirely upon the static properties of the system—the initial displacement, and the elasticities of the curves. If the supply reaction took place more slowly (the length of the lag was increased), the only result would be to slow up the whole process; the form of the cobweb would not be changed, it would merely take more time.

In our application, the position is quite different. The static properties retain some importance, it is true. An increase in the elasticity of the SI-curve will generally tend to increase the

[1] Thus in Schultz's work on annual crops, supply depends on the price of the year before. For the study of the pig cycle, a lag of three or four years is assumed.

amplitude of the cycle, and a reduction in the elasticity of the L-curve (causing more violent oscillations in interest rates) will have a similar effect. But this is not the whole story. For in our case neither reaction is immediate. The liquidity reaction has a definite lag, not dissimilar to that of the supply reaction in the supply-and-demand case; but the savings-investment reaction does not take place at once, nor does it take effect after a single definite lag. It is gradual; part of the reaction is quick, part slower, and part slower still. This means that we have to pay a good deal more attention to the lengths of the lags than is necessary when dealing with the supply-and-demand cobweb. If all the lags were diminished (or increased) in the same proportion, then the effect would be the same as in the supply-and-demand case. There would be a change in the time-unit, but the character of the cycle would be unaffected. Relative changes in the lengths of the lags do, however, affect the character of the cycle.

Suppose, first of all, that the lags on the savings-investment side are given, and consider the effects of changes in the length of the liquidity lag. We have seen that if the rate of interest is temporarily maintained at a level which is lower than the equilibrium level, an expansion will set in (going in the direction AB). If the liquidity reaction is delayed until the point B has been reached, there will then be a sharp rise in interest, from B to C. But if the liquidity reaction had come at an earlier stage in the process, the full expansion from A to B would not have been completed before the rise in interest occurred. The necessary rise in interest would then be less, and it appears that the cobweb would be damped down.

Arguing in the same way, it appears that a sufficiently rapid reaction on the liquidity side would eliminate the cobweb altogether. For if the rise in interest took place early enough, the point C would lie to the left of P; the rise in interest would then do no more than check the expansion, without causing it to be reversed. Thus (possibly, it is true, by a series of steps) there would be a regular movement to equilibrium. It is the slowness of the liquidity reaction which is the villain of the piece.

Let us, however, look at the matter a little more closely. Suppose that the liquidity reaction takes place at a point B' (before B) and the rate of interest accordingly rises to C'

(Fig. 18). From the moment when C' is reached, new invest-ment plans will begin to be affected by the new high rate of interest; but the old investment projects induced by the old low rate are not yet fully developed, and their multiplier effects are unexhausted. Thus the situation is not the same as it would have been if the rise in interest had occurred at a point when the system had already adjusted itself completely to the low rate of interest. The rate of interest which is current at C' has itself

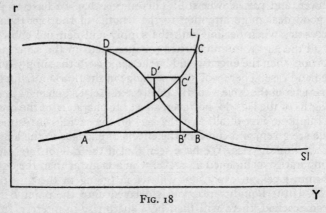

Fig. 18

a contractionary effect; but if the contractionary effect is lagged, it is possible that there may be a stage in which the contrac-tionary effect of the current rate is offset by the still unexhausted expansionary effects of the lower rate which existed previously. Thus income may not begin to contract as soon as the rate of interest is raised to C'; there may be a phase in which income remains constant at C', or even continues to expand beyond that level. It is conceivable that this further rise in income may call forth a further rise in interest; thus although the first rise would have been sufficient, after a time, to convert expansion into con-traction, the delay in its operation leaves room for a further rise in interest, which must, after a time, have an additional effect in a contractionary direction.

The damped cobweb $AB'C'D'$ may therefore give too favour-able an impression of the effect of an early rise in the interest rate. The actual damping may be less than that which appears on the diagram. But there must be some damping. Income cannot expand, after the rate of interest has been raised to C', as much as it would have done if the initial expansion had been allowed to go to its full length without any rise in interest at all. We are therefore fully justified in concluding that a more rapid response on the part of the monetary system will damp down the cobweb; but serious lags in the response of business to changes to interest may still leave the system with some tendency to fluctuate, even if the monetary response is fairly rapid.

9. It would probably not be useful to follow out this construction in greater detail; enough has been said to show that a monetary theory of the cycle, quite independent of the real theory which we have elaborated in previous chapters, can in principle be constructed and can be set out in fairly comparable terms. The Keynesian dress which we have given to the theory is not at all essential. Modifications, which do not affect the essence of the theory, would give it a distinctly different look; but the monetary theory of the cycle is at bottom always one and the same.

One important source of variation in the details of the theory concerns the interest-rate structure, which we have throughout assumed to be capable of representation by some one *rate of interest*. In fact, of course, there is not one rate of interest, but many; different rates of interest can coexist because of differences in risk, differences in maturity and perhaps because of market imperfections. But there is usually some degree of interrelation between these various rates; although all rates do not move together, the particular forces of monetary ease and monetary stringency (with which we are concerned) tend to move them in the same direction. This is the justification for treating one single rate as representative of the whole system.

Although the different rates tend to move in the same direction, their sensitivity is very different. The same monetary forces which move short rates much and quickly will move long rates to a smaller extent and more slowly. Thus it makes a good deal of difference to the look of the theory according as we decide to select as our representative rate of interest a short rate or a long rate. But in spite of the lesser sensitivity of the long rate, the long rate is the more powerful influence on business decisions. A small movement in the long rate gives as powerful a stimulus to investment, or as powerful a deterrent, as a large movement in the short rate. Essentially the same sequence of cause and effect can therefore be expressed in terms of the movement of either rate. If the representative rate is a long rate, its movements will be relatively small, but these small movements will be relatively powerful. Thus both the L-curve and the SI-curve will appear more elastic on the 'long' than on the 'short' interpretation. But the relation between the curves, which is the thing which matters, may in either case be much the same.

I am inclined to think that our decision whether to interpret *the* rate of interest as a short rate or as a long rate (our decision, that is, whether to give our construction a Hawtreyan or a Keynesian colour) should depend, not on any theoretical considerations, but on the empirical facts of the economy with which we are dealing. In a predominantly commercial economy, such as that which existed in the early nineteenth century, the widespread use of bills of exchange made the whole system extremely sensitive to fluctuations in short interest rates; in such conditions there can be little doubt that it was the short rate which was the cutting-edge of the whole interest structure. It may, indeed, be maintained that it was because the system was so sensitive to fluctuations in the short rate that the long rate was so steady as it usually appears to have been in those days. But with the change in the relative importance of industrial and commercial business, and with the corresponding changes in methods of business finance, the long rate has inevitably grown in importance; already (I should guess) by the beginning of the twentieth century, the long rate was having to do a good deal more of the work. To change from a formulation which emphasized movements in the short rate to one which emphasized movements in the long rate was then nothing more than a quite proper adaptation of theory to the course of events.

One consequence of this change (not in the theory, but in the facts) should, however, be noticed. It has been remarked that the effects of monetary policy on the long rate are not only smaller, but *slower*, than its effects on the short rate. It could further be added that the effects of changes in the long rate on the actual volume of investment are slower than the effects of changes in the short rate. A change in the short rate affects, almost at once, the profitability of the whole of that part of investment which is financed short; but a change in the long rate only affects directly the profitability of that part of the investment, financed long, which actually comes to be financed within the relevant period. Thus a shift over from short financing to long greatly diminishes the control over the volume of income exercised by the monetary system. Purely monetary cycles, arising under a system of short financing, can largely (though even then not wholly) be ascribed to deficiencies in banking policy; but under a system of predominantly long financing, there may be a strong tendency to monetary instability, which the most ideally alert banking policy could not conceivably do much to prevent.

10. If the trade cycle is a 'purely monetary phenomenon' it must, I think, be at bottom something of the kind which I have been describing. That cycles have occurred which have been mainly of this type does not seem to be at all improbable. Nevertheless, I find it hard to believe that the monetary explanation can often have been the whole explanation. It is hard to believe that the accelerator can often have played so negligible a role as we have assumed it to play when setting out the monetary theory. A more general, and more convincing, approach would be to assume that both sources of instability are, at least potentially, at work—that monetary instability, of the kind we have just considered, is superimposed upon the real instability which we analysed in the earlier chapters of this book. The final hypothesis, to which our whole argument tends, is a combined hypothesis of this character. It is a very complex hypothesis, which could hardly be approached directly; I could not see any way of setting it out except by the separate elaboration of the two wings which constitute it. At this point, if we sought to set it out formally, we should mainly have to go over the same ground again. I shall not do that; but I shall devote some part of my last chapter to a consideration of the interactions between the two instabilities. I cannot pretend to treat that matter at all completely; but there are some important conclusions on the subject which one can now begin to see, and which evidently need to be set down.[1]

[1] The monetary theory, set out in this chapter, may be very incomplete as a theory of the cycle; but it does by itself throw a good deal of light on a number of dark places, both in theory and in the interpretation of history. As an example of the latter, we may take the 'Rostow paradox' (W. W. Rostow, *British Economy in the Nineteenth Century*, pp. 145–60.

Professor Rostow points out that in the 1850s and 1860s, when the supply of gold was increasing rapidly, interest rates generally ruled higher than they did in the 'Great Depression' of the 1870s and 1880s when the British Economy (at least) was supposed to be suffering from a shortage of gold. Arguing on Keynesian lines, that an ample supply of gold ought to have lowered interest rates, if the marginal efficiency of capital remained unchanged, he concludes that the gold supply had nothing to do with the 'depression', which must have been due to real causes. I do not wish to disparage his real causes, the importance of which I accept; but our development of the Keynesian analysis seems to show that he is quite unjustified in excluding the monetary factor. Properly considered, the monetary factor behaved as one would expect it to behave.

We have always, I think, when dealing with nineteenth-century conditions, to assume an L-curve (for the international economy) which is decidedly inelastic in its upper reaches. But one has to distinguish between elasticity and speed of reaction; and when one is dealing with a long-run historical movement, of Professor Rostow's type, one has to allow for movements of the curves. In the 'fifties and 'sixties, when the gold supply was increasing, the L-curve would be moving to the right, but would remain inelastic. The rightward movement would nevertheless facilitate short-run expansion of credit; with the new gold coming so frequently to their rescue banks would be inclined to take risks. A strongly marked monetary cobweb, with high interest rates at the top of the boom, would be then what we should expect. Later on, when the supply of gold ceased to expand, relatively to the normal demand for it, expansions away from the L-curve would be more difficult. The monetary booms would therefore be weaker, and the interest rate would rise much less.

This argument applies, in the first place, to short-term rates of interest, which were still of great importance; but in view of the known relation between short and long rates, we should expect to find that the occasionally very high short rates in the first period would keep up the long rate in that period; while the disappearance of these acute stringencies in the second period would result in a gradual fall of the long rate. If one looks at the movements of the two rates, this is what does in fact seem to have happened. Some part of the movement is almost certainly to be ascribed to real causes (shifts in the SI-curve); the point is that the monetary causes can be expected to operate in the same direction.

XII

THE PLACE OF THE MONETARY FACTOR

1. BEFORE going on to the main subject of this concluding chapter—the interactions between monetary instability and the real cycle—there is one further observation on the monetary theory, as so far set out, which needs to be made. In our presentation of the monetary theory we have followed Keynes in assuming that we are dealing with a closed economy. Of course we did the same when presenting the real theory in earlier chapters; but the closed economy assumption is more defensible when one is dealing with the accelerator than it is when we pass over to the monetary side. After all, the world as a whole is a closed economy; and the processes which the real theory studies are not made different in character by the fact that they extend across national frontiers. Doubtless there is a job to be done in re-working the real theory so as to put it in 'international' terms; since economic statistics are compiled on a national basis, a more explicitly 'international' formulation would be convenient for purposes of application. But such reformulation of the real theory could not affect the principle of the argument. As our purpose has been to clarify principles, we can claim ample justification on that side for making the simplification of the closed economy.

When, however, we turn to the monetary aspect, the position is different. A monetary theory, which assumes a closed economy, can only be applied to the world as a whole in conditions when the whole world uses the same money. Otherwise we have many 'monetary systems', not one; the unity of our *L*-curve, in particular, is liable to be disrupted. This is a serious complication, which can easily cause the monetary theory, in the form we have given it, to make a misleading impression. For when the theory is set out in this form (and the same is true of the form which Keynes gave it), it becomes tempting to think of the 'monetary system' of the theory as being analogous to a national monetary system, and therefore to be such as to be readily controllable by policy. It is then an easy step to ascribe the whole trouble to an institutional deficiency, which could easily be removed by political reform. All that seems to be needed is that the monetary system should be made as elastic in the long period as it is in the short period; once that had been done, the tendency to a cobweb would disappear.

But this is a misapprehension. The only conditions, so far known, and so far likely to exist, in which nearly the whole world does (in a fundamental sense) use the same money, are conditions in which national currencies are tied to a metallic standard. These conditions did exist for the greater part of the historical period in which cyclical fluctuations have been noticed; there is therefore much justification for using the closed economy assumption in a theory which seeks to interpret the *history* of fluctuations. But it was an essential feature of this international arrangement that the basic money was limited in supply; imperfect elasticity of the L-curve, at its rightward end, was a thing which was needed to make the international standard possible. A managed international standard, which is what would be needed in order to produce the situation represented by an elastic L-curve in a closed economy, is a thing which is hardly consistent with national political independence. A prior condition for its establishment would be the formation of some effective nucleus of world government.

The practical alternative to an inelastic international standard, as the experience of the last twenty years has shown, is not an elastic international standard, but separate national systems of greater elasticity. Now it has not been shown that on this alternative the difficulty disappears. If economic nationalism went so far as to cut off international trade altogether, or to reduce it to a basis of contemporaneous exchanges (barter without credit), then the national monetary systems could be made completely elastic, and the monetary cobweb could be abolished. But for most countries the costs of such complete autarky are too formidable to be faced. What, in fact, occurs is a compromise; and under that compromise something analogous to the monetary cobweb is by no means entirely absent.

In this mixed system, expansion in one country still tends to facilitate expansion in others; simultaneous expansions (and contractions) are therefore by no means entirely ruled out. In a process of international expansion, it remains inevitable that some of the expanding countries should develop an adverse balance of payments; when this happens, a policy of low-interest rates makes it more difficult than it would otherwise be to raise funds from the rest of the world to fill the gap. A point must therefore be reached (fundamentally similar to the critical point *B* on our latest diagrams) when steps have to be taken to restore equilibrium in the balance of payments. Even though a rise in the internal rate of interest is ruled out, these steps must (from the standpoint of the rest of the world) be of a contractionary character. By devaluating its currency, or imposing import restrictions, the deficit country may succeed in exempting itself from the contraction; but even that is not certain. For either of these actions is equivalent to a reduction in the spendable income of the deficit country, measured in terms of goods available on the world market. It must therefore have a contractionary effect on the outside world; and this contraction may, on occasion, react back on the exports of the country which took the original steps to restore equilibrium in its balance of payments.

The dangers of monetary deflation are no doubt considerably less under the mixed system than they are under the international gold standard; but they do not by any means entirely disappear.

It would take us too far afield to explore this matter farther. I shall even leave unexamined the doubts, which this balance-of-payments application will probably have raised in the mind of the reader, whether the narrowly monetary explanation of the inelasticity of the *L*-curve (attributing it, at bottom, to a limitation on the supply of some sort of monetary reserves), gets to the root of the matter even in the case of the international gold standard. I have some doubts on this question myself. But it would not be profitable to examine that matter more closely without paying attention to the relation between the monetary cobweb and the 'real' cycle induced by the accelerator. To the consideration of the mutual influences of these two cycle-making factors we must now turn.

2. In our statement of the monetary theory, we have assumed

that the *SI*-curve remains unchanged in position during the course of the cycle; it is, of course, this assumption which is inconsistent with what we learned in the earlier chapters of this book, and which has to be abandoned if the two approaches are to be brought together. If the acceleration principle and the monetary factor are both at work, we shall have to think of the *SI*-curve as being subject to systematic shifts, these movements having themselves a cyclical character. This is how the problem will look approached from the standpoint of the monetary theory; but it is, in fact, more interesting to look at it the other way round, approaching it from the accelerator side.

Let us begin from a position (supposing that it could be attained) in which both the real system and the monetary system are in equilibrium. The economy is advancing, in real terms, along the equilibrium line (supposed, for the present, to represent a *steady* progress) and in doing so it imposes, as yet, no strain upon the monetary system. Such a state of affairs could exist, consistently with the monetary theory, in a situation of ample money supply and low interest rates (in which case the expansion might continue for some time without getting into monetary difficulties, even if the money supply was constant) or in a situation of more restricted money supply and higher rates of interest. But in this latter case the expansion would soon be checked by monetary scarcity, and the real equilibrium accordingly broken, if the situation were not saved (as it might be saved) by a steadily increasing supply of money, or by such a process of development in monetary institutions, involving the creation of money substitutes, as caused the *L*-curve to have a steady tendency to shift to the right as time went on. Any of these conditions would make it possible for full equilibrium on both sides to persist in a state of steady progress; but they would not guarantee that it did persist, for they would not remove the underlying instability of the *real* equilibrium.

Let us then suppose, as we have supposed when considering similar problems before, that some chance disturbance causes an upward displacement from the equilibrium path. In view of the lags in the monetary reaction, we shall not expect to find that the consequential upward movement will at once be checked by monetary scarcity; in the opening steps, at least, of the ensuing expansion, the monetary system is likely to be quite passive, and the expansion will proceed just as we found it to do when we were elaborating the *real* theory—before we paid any attention to monetary reactions at all. Now, with the monetary system remaining passive, the expansion will come to an end in one or other of two ways[1]—either it must die away through weakness of the accelerator, or it must be killed by hitting the real ceiling. When we allow for the monetary reaction, we have to add a third possible way—that the monetary system may find itself over-extended, so that it breaks the boom by monetary contraction, with the object of restoring monetary equilibrium. We already know, from the monetary theory, that such action is unlikely to restore monetary equilibrium, but will tend to overshoot the mark, setting up a monetary cobweb. It now appears, when we consider both sets of forces, that there is not only this danger, of the rate of interest being raised above the equilibrium rate, so that the monetary forces compel contraction; there is the certainty that the stop to expansion will put the accelerator into reverse, causing expansion to be turned into contraction on that side too.

Now although it is possible that a boom may be broken in this way, it seems to me to be distinctly more natural that the immediate cause of the downturn should be real than that it should be monetary. For the actual process of real expansion is very favourable to the expansion of credit. Profits are good, and risks appear to be low; even though there is some strain on the ultimate money supply, the opportunities for the development of money substitutes are vast, and the strain is therefore not very likely to be effective so long as the boom continues. It is not very easy to see why a monetary reaction should suddenly appear out of the blue at the top of the boom. It may do so, for special reasons; but they would have to be special reasons.[2] It

---

[1] Presumably it might also be brought to an end by purely exogenous influences—but that may be left out of account.

[2] A case in which we might expect to find such special reasons is in the crisis at the end of a war, or post-war, inflation. During the war it may have been impossible for the monetary system to take any effective action to check the boom; but when the war is over, the situation changes, and a sharp change in policy may occur. There is thus an exogenous cause for a monetary reaction. For my own part, I find it hard to believe that this did not happen in 1920, so that the 1920 crisis may be one of our exceptional cases. But the

is much more understandable that the boom should continue
until the real causes bring it to an end.

3. But even when the cause of the downturn is real, not
monetary, the monetary factor loses little of its importance; for
the monetary cobweb still operates, and can still have a formidable effect upon the course of the ensuing slump. For even if the
downturn has not been caused by the monetary reaction, the
two will still be closely associated; if the downturn did not have
a monetary cause, it will still have a monetary effect. Thus the
subsequent course of events is not so very different in the two
cases. The distinction between the causes of the downturn does
not develop into a distinction between different sorts of slumps,
real slumps, and monetary slumps working quite differently; all
slumps are both real and monetary. Once the downturn has
occurred, the same real factors, and the same monetary factors,
will be at work in the slump.

One of the weaknesses of the monetary theory, when it is
considered in isolation (as we considered it in the last chapter)
is that it provides no adequate reason why a sharp monetary
reaction should occur at a particular stage in the process of
expansion. We can see, from that theory, that an over-expanded
monetary system will be unstable; but no reason is provided why
the instability should be 'touched off' at some particular point. As
soon as we combine the monetary theory with the real theory, this
difficulty disappears. In the downturn of the real cycle we have
a most effective agent for the detonation of the monetary mine.

For consider what must happen if the boom has proceeded
without effective monetary check until the real downturn is
reached. Output then begins to fall, and effective demand to
fall; sales become difficult and fixed costs oppressive; the rate
of bankruptcy rises; all these things are inevitable even in the
absence of monetary strain, but they breed conditions in which
there is bound to be a sharp rise in liquidity preference. This
rise in liquidity preference is itself the monetary reaction, or
what, in common speech, is called the crisis.

contrary interpretation can be defended; Professor Pigou's *British Economic
History 1918–1925* maintains that the 1920 downturn was almost wholly
due to real causes.

Thus even a real downturn is almost certain to be accompanied by monetary crisis; and the monetary deflation is an additional contractionary force, of which pure accelerator theory has taken no account, and which must tend to aggravate the depression. We have already seen[1] that this monetary effect has to be called in to explain the rapidity of the downswing, which would normally take as long as the upswing if nothing but the accelerator mechanism were at work; but the damage done by monetary deflation may not be confined to this speeding-up. Credit stringency may do more than cut off the induced investment, which would in any case have fallen off after a time by the operation of the accelerator mechanism; there is no reason why its effects should not be felt even upon that part of investment which accelerator theory regards as autonomous. In so far as autonomous investment is financed by long loans, it has, indeed, some protection against the deflation; doubtless this does mean that autonomous investment is likely to be somewhat less affected by credit stringency than induced investment tends to be. But some effect on autonomous investment is to be expected. This effect does more than speed up the downswing; it causes activity to fall, at the bottom of the depression, to a lower point than it would otherwise have reached. It is therefore peculiarly dangerous.

What this means, considered from the point of view of accelerator theory, is that the monetary crisis is liable to cause a dip in the lower equilibrium line[2]—a dip which may be quite deep, and which may be rather prolonged. How prolonged it is depends partly on the length of the crisis itself, on the length of time for which dear money, or restricted credit,[3] has to be maintained; partly on the length of time for which the lagged effects of the crisis persist. For not even 'autonomous' investment will recover at the moment the deflationary pressure is removed; the familiar time-shape,[4] which we have found to be charac-

[1] See above, p. 117, a passage in which we began to step outside the pure accelerator theory.

[2] Cf. Fig. 13 (p. 121 above).

[3] The two things are not necessarily the same. Thus in Britain in 1932 credit remained very tight, in any sense which is economically relevant, for many months after the fall in quoted interest rates (both short and long) had begun.

[4] See above, Fig. 5, p. 41.

teristic of investment in general, is relevant here as elsewhere.
The lags may possibly be shorter when it is a question of
restarting old projects than they are when it is a question of beginning new ones; but even a restarted project will not rise
to its maximum employment of resources the moment that
financial obstacles to going ahead are removed. All such things
have to be allowed for; but the main factor governing the size
of the dip in the autonomous investment curve (and the consequential deepening of the depression) must surely be the
violence of the crisis, or monetary reaction, itself. And that
depends, in its turn, mainly on the extent of the previously
existing monetary disequilibrium.

4. The whole of the monetary complication does, indeed, go
back to this previous disequilibrium; its seriousness mainly
depends upon the degree to which the monetary and financial
systems, at the moment the storm breaks, are over-extended.
But for the full appreciation of this essential matter, it is necessary to distinguish between different kinds of over-extended-
ness, corresponding to the different layers of the monetary
pyramid. It is almost inevitable that at the top of the boom,
trade credits (as distinguished from banking credit) will be over-
extended; but the collapse of trade credit need do no more than
limited harm, if the reserves of more widely acceptable money,
in the hands of the banking system, or creatable by the banking
system, are unimpaired. If the whole expansion has been
moderate, reserves will be available at many levels which can
be thrown into the fray; the restriction of credit need not then
be lasting, or go deep. But the vital thing is that the base of the
monetary pyramid should be secure. So long as the banking
system itself is sound, or the central part of it is sound (for we
are talking, it will be remembered, in world terms) it will be
possible for the banks, and especially for the stronger Central
Banks, to do much to mitigate the crisis. The classical remedy
of Thornton and Bagehot—active lending by the central bank,
so as to replace unsound credit by sounder credit—comes into
its own. But the deeper the disequilibrium extends, the harder
it becomes to apply the classical prescription. Even if it is
applied, it may have to be reversed, so that a further monetary

crisis supervenes at a stage when depression is already well advanced. These are the real horrors. Really catastrophic depression is most unlikely to occur as a result of the simple operation of the real accelerator mechanism; it is likely to occur when there is profound monetary instability—when the rot in the monetary system goes very deep.[1]

5. So far we have considered the monetary system in its role as destabilizer—a part which it has, in practice, too often played. Economists have, however, often dreamed of an ideal monetary system, of one which should not merely avoid the grosser errors of illiquidity, but should play an active part in maintaining the balance of the economy against the disturbances induced by real fluctuations. We have seen enough to be able to tell that such monetary control cannot be at all an easy matter. It is, however, interesting to ask what it could achieve, if it were carried out with the greatest imaginable wisdom and patience and restraint.

[1] My interpretation of the Great Depression of the twentieth century (that of 1930–4) is therefore, in broad terms, the following. I do not see that there is any adequate reason to suppose that the *real* boom of 1927–9 was at all an exceptional boom; if the accelerator mechanism, and nothing else, had been at work, it should not have been followed by an exceptional slump. But the slump impinged upon a monetary situation which was quite exceptionally unstable. The main cause of this instability was not the purely superficial speculative over-expansion which had occurred in New York in 1928–9; its roots went much farther back. The monetary system of the world had never adjusted itself at all fully to the change in the level of money incomes which took place during and after the war of 1914–18; it was trying to manage with a gold supply, which was in terms of wage-units extremely inadequate. Difficulties in the post-war adjustment of exchange rates (combined with the vast changes which the war had produced in the creditor-debtor position of important countries) had caused the consequential weakness to be particularly concentrated in certain places; particular central banks, as for instance the Bank of England and the Reichsbank, were therefore particularly incapable of performing their usual function as 'lenders of last resort'. The weakness of the Bank of England, in view of the extent of the sterling exchange standard, was especially damaging. Even in the early phases of the depression (in 1930 and early 1931) this monetary weakness was no doubt an aggravating factor; but the full dimensions of the catastrophe were only revealed when a deep monetary crisis developed, not in its 'proper' place, shortly after the downturn, but in full depression, in the summer of 1931. The real cycle was then at a point which should have been its bottom; but the new monetary disaster caused it to plunge to yet lower depths. From these depths, in view of the lagged effects of so vast a crisis, recovery was inevitably slow and difficult.

What we must do, in order to explore this problem, is to go back to our equilibrium economy, the economy which was in monetary equilibrium, and which was advancing, in real terms, along its equilibrium line. Once again we must suppose the equilibrium to be disturbed by an expansion in activity. But now, instead of allowing the expansion in activity to proceed unchecked, we have to suppose that the monetary system reacts after no more than a very moderate lag. The boom will then have developed only a short way before the rate of interest rises; and the rise in the rate of interest must be expected to damp down the accelerator. This first rise in the rate of interest may not break the boom, but will certainly weaken it; and if the boom is not broken, there will (under the same assumptions) be further applications of the same treatment, and these must inevitably break the boom before it has gone very far. But though this means that the boom will be broken before its due time, the ensuing slump (for there will be a slump) will be very moderate. For, on the one hand, the monetary disequilibrium is small, and the monetary complications in the slump will therefore be minimized; and, on the other hand, the damping down of the boom has a directly favourable effect in the same direction. For if the boom is made less violent, it follows from the accelerator theory that the slump will probably be less violent and will certainly be less prolonged.

As against these favourable effects on the course of the slump, it may perhaps be argued that the maintenance of relatively high interest rates during the boom will have an unfavourable effect. We have granted that the effects of these high interest rates may be lagged, and may therefore persist into the slump. But in the present case it is quite possible that this difficulty may not be serious. For if the boom has been checked in the way described, the rate of interest should never have risen to any great height; a moderate rise, applied in time, should have been sufficient.[1] The adverse effects in the slump should therefore be quite inconsiderable.

It does, therefore, appear that we do here have a policy which can in principle act as an efficient stabilizer. The stabilization might not be complete; booms and slumps might still be dis-

[1] See above, p. 149.

tinguishable. But the booms would be quiet affairs, and the slumps would be far short of being major disasters.

It must, however, be noticed, when assessing the results of such a policy as this, that it can only claim to stabilize the economy on (or in the neighbourhood of) the equilibrium line; and in consequence it only achieves a true stability, if the path pursued by the equilibrium position is one of steady progress. If the equilibrium line is itself subject to fluctuation, the economy, though it is in a technical sense stabilized, will not be stabilized in the more natural sense of the term. Now we have seen that fluctuations in autonomous investment will induce fluctuations in the equilibrium line—a bulge in one is reflected in a bulge in the other. Must we say that monetary management can do nothing to remove these 'autonomous' fluctuations?

Theoretically, I think, even this problem is not quite hopeless. For variations in the rate of interest should be able to do something to damp down the bulges and dips of autonomous investment; and, so long as the monetary management does not involve serious departures from the L-curve, such variations in interest rates are not ruled out. In this respect, indeed, there is some positive advantage in having an inelastic monetary system. For the purpose of controlling induced investment, it is not necessary that the monetary system should be particularly inelastic; the important thing there is not that the rate of interest should move much, but that it should move promptly. The prompter the movement is, the smaller (in that case) it will have to be. But when we turn to fluctuations in autonomous investment, promptness is not enough; a large movement in the rate of interest may then be necessary if the fluctuation is to be smoothed out, even if the movement takes place at the best possible moment.

It is theoretically possible, if monetary institutions are such that the L-curve is decidedly inelastic, and if adjustments are prompt, so that no serious departure from the L-curve takes place, that income and output may be stabilized, even in the face of large autonomous fluctuations, but at the expense of large fluctuations in the interest rate. But it is hardly more than a theoretical possibility. For some of the effects of the varying interest rates will be lagged, so that the assessment of the correct moment to make the changes must be extraordinarily difficult. And since (as we have seen) it is almost inevitable that any monetary system will behave elastically at low rates of interest, any serious dip in the autonomous investment line must fail to be controllable in this way. It is still likely (as the whole of our argument tends to show) that fluctuations will be worse if the monetary system remains passive than they will be if it makes some (not too ill-timed) movement in the right direction; but if autonomous investment is seriously unsteady, the most that can be hoped from interest-rate policy does not go very far.

6. These are no doubt, in substance, some of the reasons which have caused so much economic opinion to swing violently against interest-rate policy, and to place its hopes for stability at full employment in the direct control of investment, combined with fiscal controls over consumption. Many of the problems which are raised by that alternative are political, or administrative, or international, and as such fall outside the scope of this book. There are, however, two points in which the present analysis has a direct bearing on these problems; it will not be inappropriate if I add some remarks on them by way of conclusion.

In the first place it has to be emphasized that the characteristic time-shape of investment, on which so much of our work has been based, holds for all investment, whether it has been induced by previous changes in output, or is a consequence of trend rates of growth, or is deliberately contrived as a matter of policy. It is therefore much easier to devise measures which will cause a hump or bulge in autonomous investment, than it is to stabilize it on a steady course. This is a simple point, but easily overlooked. If the technique developed in this book does something to cause it to be allowed for more automatically in economic discussion, one of my objects in writing will have been achieved.

The second point which I want to make only arises when one has appreciated this first difficulty. It is tempting to say, once one has grasped the difficulty of keeping autonomous investment steady, that perhaps steadiness will not matter if the general level of autonomous investment can be kept sufficiently high. For output cannot rise above the full employment ceiling; and we have granted that it may remain for considerable periods on, or nearly on, the ceiling, without inflation (the Keynesian bogy) necessarily getting out of hand. Thus if autonomous investment can be so stimulated as to prevent the equilibrium line from ever falling much below the ceiling, it would not seem to matter very much if it rises above the ceiling from time to time. As long as the equilibrium line remains above the ceiling, there is no danger of a downturn; from the cyclical point of view this is therefore an excellent position. But it is not an excellent position in all respects. Even if it does not explode into inflation, it has its own dangers, of which we ought to be well aware.

It is of the essence of this 'over-employment' situation that at least one of the constituents of output must be less than what people desire to make it to be in the ruling conditions. One or other of them must be less than its equilibrium amount. Now it is impossible that autonomous investment should be less than its equilibrium amount, for it is what is responsible for the equilibrium level; that alternative is self-contradictory. It is possible that consumption may be kept down by fiscal controls; but experience does not suggest that these are so very effective; certainly it is not easy to make them effective enough to fill the whole 'gap', if it is a large one. There is, therefore, a strong presumption that a considerable part of the necessary adjustment will fall on induced investment. We have, I think, to expect that that is what will happen.

Induced investment has so often appeared in this book as the villain of the piece (which is what it is, from the cyclical point of view) that we may easily be tempted to forget its very important positive function. It would, of course, be absurd to claim that induced investment, as a whole, has greater economic significance than autonomous investment; there will be some investment of great economic importance in both categories. Investment needed to take advantage of new inventions will reckon, for the most part, as autonomous investment; and there can be no question that such investment is very important indeed. But the mere property of being closely tied to the movement of current output (which is the distinguishing mark of induced investment) means that induced investment is generally likely to be the more urgent; it is, as a general rule, more necessary for induced investment to be carried through at its own time, than for autonomous investment to be carried through at its own time, if the efficiency of production is to be maintained. There are, no doubt, cases in which, by the exercise of foresight, investment which would naturally have been of the induced type, and which would have come at a cyclically inconvenient moment, can be transferred to a time at which it is more convenient; by this means induced investment is, in effect, converted into autonomous investment, and into autonomous investment of a stabilizing sort. Obviously such transference as this is extremely advantageous. But the existence of such opportunities does not remove the general presumption that induced investment will tend to be disorganized if autonomous investment is boosted too greatly; and that the effects on efficiency of such disorganization will be very deleterious.

If the only alternative before us was between a continuance of the trade cycle, as experienced since 1914 (a trade cycle, that is, which has had its real oscillations enormously magnified by monetary instability); and a 'Full Employment Economy', always verging on over-employment, with violent balance of payments crises, and shortages due to productive inefficiency; we should, I think, be obliged to admit that the second was the lesser evil. But if a third alternative were offered: of monetary reform to re-establish monetary security, combined with a moderate use of public investment and fiscal controls, designed to quieten, but hardly to eliminate, the real cycle—should we still make the same choice? It seems to me, at least, so far as I can see at present, that it is this third alternative alone which holds out Hope.

MATHEMATICAL APPENDIX

1. IN the text of this book I have usually been able to avoid the direct use of mathematical methods; it will, however, have been obvious to the reader that a good deal of mathematics has been going on behind the scenes. In this Appendix the implied mathematical work is formally set out. Much of the argument (though not, I think, by any means all) will be familiar to mathematical economists; but even for them a more systematic statement than seems elsewhere to be available may be found convenient. I have, however, endeavoured to keep in mind the needs of another class, the growing body of economists who, without being mathematicians, have learned to think mathematically, and can appreciate a mathematical argument if reasonable care is taken to keep it within their reach. I have therefore taken some trouble to find ways of avoiding the use of the advanced methods which a professional mathematician would probably employ in dealing with some of these problems. For the purpose in hand, the nutcracker seems to be sufficient; economy and clarity alike must advise its use, even though the steam-hammer is available.

2. The verbal discussion in the text has proceeded in terms of 'period analysis'—with time divided into discontinuous periods—and the mathematical theory which follows will do the same. From the mathematical point of view, this is not quite necessary; some of the mathematical models on which I have drawn (including those of Frisch and Kalecki) work in terms of continuous time, and therefore use differential equations, instead of the difference equations which I have to use. To a mathematician this looks a more natural proceeding; I have two objections against it. In the first place, I want to maintain a close relation between the argument in this Appendix and that in the text; in the text I used period analysis, and that is a good reason for using period analysis here too. The other reason is more fundamental. It is actually only the simpler sorts of lags which it is convenient to study by means of differential equations; some of the problems I want to study would not reduce to differential equations at all, if time were treated as continuous. They would reduce to *Integral Equations*; though I suppose that a professional mathematician would be able to make something of them in this guise, to do so would be quite beyond my own competence. In any case, I suspect that the easiest way of dealing with these integral equations would be to treat them as limiting cases of difference equations; and so we should come back to the sort of method I propose to adopt. I can therefore adopt that method with a clear conscience.

3. A much more serious limitation on the theory which follows is that all the basic relations (such as the consumption function and the accelerator) are assumed to be linear. I am very conscious that this is an over-simplification; but I would plead some things in extenuation of it. First of all, it is possible to see from our diagrams that many important propositions are not dependent on the linearity assumption—in simple cases where the diagrammatic method is sufficient; this independence does not need to be verified here. Secondly, it may be questioned whether we derive any advantage from extensions into non-linearity, when we come to the more complex cases, with which this Appendix is mainly concerned. The dependence (for instance) of current consumption on past income is a thing which is sufficiently indisputable for the fact of such dependence to have to be taken into account; and the fact of the dependence is registered by the linear form. But the exact nature of the dependence (such as would be indicated by terms of higher order) is not a thing about which we can generally hope to know anything appreciable, or to which we can attach much importance. There may be some special cases where this is not true; but I think that these cases can usually be covered in more convenient ways than by assuming non-linearity. The limitation imposed by my linearity assumption may therefore be not so bad as it looks.

Appendix to Chapter II

4. We may begin by setting out the familiar theory of the Kahn multiplier in difference equation form. This will tell us nothing new, but it will give us a basis from which to generalize. As in Keynes, Y is income, C is consumption, and I investment. Suffixes denote the periods to which the magnitudes refer.

The consumption function is $C = cY + K$, where c and K are constants, of which c (the marginal propensity to consume) is less than 1. With a consumption lag of one period, this will be written

$$C_n = cY_{n-1} + K.$$

Current income equals current consumption plus current investment:

$$Y_n = C_n + I_n.$$

In the static case, where current investment is a given constant, we may suppress the last suffix, and write $I_n = I$.

We now have the materials from which to deduce the basic equation of the system, which is

$$Y_n = cY_{n-1} + K + I. \tag{4.1}$$

We shall solve this equation in the standard manner, in order to serve as a model for what follows.

We first notice that there is an equilibrium level of income, at which income could remain constant from period to period; this is determined by putting $Y_n = Y_{n-1} = Y$. (4.1) then gives

$$Y = cY + K + I \tag{4.2}$$

whence $Y = (K+I)/(1-c)$, the equation from which Keynes's 'static' multiplier properties are derived. Here, however, we must subtract (4.2) from (4.1), which gives

$$Y_n - Y = c(Y_{n-1} - Y) \tag{4.3}$$

a difference equation which may be repeated for any value of n. Thus

$$Y_n - Y = c(Y_{n-1} - Y) = c^2(Y_{n-2} - Y) = \dots = c^n(Y_0 - Y).$$

Thus if we start from a given initial level of income (Y_0), Y_n is determined

$$Y_n = Y + c^n(Y_0 - Y). \tag{4.4}$$

We see from this *solution* that if income starts at the equilibrium Y (if $Y_0 = Y$), it will remain at that equilibrium level indefinitely. If, however, it does not start from equilibrium, it will get nearer and nearer to it as time goes on, provided that $c < 1$. The condition $c < 1$ is the condition for the *stability* of the equilibrium (in the 'dynamic' sense which concerns us here). If c were > 1, the equilibrium would be unstable, with actual income tending to move farther and farther away from its equilibrium position as time went on.[1] But in the Kahn theory we assume that $c < 1$, so that the equilibrium is stable.

5. Before going farther, we should notice that it is directly apparent from the original difference equation (4.1) that *one* initial position has to be known in order to determine the path. For if Y_0 is given, it is possible to determine Y_1 directly from the original difference equation; having done that, Y_2 can be determined in the same way, and so on. But this process of repeated substitution, though it suffices to determine the path, will usually fail to show us

[1] In the unstable case, the equilibrium position is negative (I being positive). But this only means that there is an indefinite *expansion* whatever the initial level of income.

the full characteristics of the path. For that purpose an explicit solution, such as (4.4), is generally necessary.

In the more complex cases to which we now turn, more than one initial position will generally be needed to determine the path. But it is important to notice that the number of such positions which are needed can always be determined from direct inspection of the original difference equation. This number expresses the *order* of the equation. Thus the Kahn equation is of the *first order*.

6. Retaining, for the present, the *static* assumption of a constant level of investment, let us next proceed to ask what happens when the time-reference of the consumption function becomes more complex. Instead of assuming a uniform lag of one period, let us now assume that consumption depends in part on the income of the preceding period, in part on the income of the period before that, in part on the income of the period before that, and so on for p past periods. The consumption relation then becomes

$$C_n = c_1 Y_{n-1} + c_2 Y_{n-2} + ... + c_p Y_{n-p} + K$$

which will still reduce to the form $C = cY + K$, where

$$c = c_1 + c_2 + ... + c_p,$$

in equilibrium. All the c_r's $(r = 1, 2,..., p)$ are positive, and we continue to assume that c (in the sense of $\sum c_r$) is < 1.

Using as before $Y_n = C_n + I$, we get our basic difference equation

$$Y_n = c_1 Y_{n-1} + c_2 Y_{n-2} + ... + c_p Y_{n-p} + K + I. \tag{6.1}$$

Equating the Y's as before, we get for the equilibrium solution

$$Y = c_1 Y + c_2 Y + ... + c_p Y + K + I \tag{6.2}$$

whence we derive the same equilibrium value as before, namely, $(K+I)/(1-c)$. The properties of the equilibrium are, of course, unaffected by the change in the lag-pattern.

We next subtract (6.2) from (6.1). If we write y for the deviation from the equilibrium position, so that $y_n = Y_n - Y$, we get

$$y_n = c_1 y_{n-1} + c_2 y_{n-2} + ... + c_p y_{n-p} \tag{6.3}$$

(the constant terms cancelling out). This is the basic difference equation of the multiplier theory.

Equation (6.3) is much harder to solve than (4.3) and we shall for the present make no attempt to solve it in the regulation manner. Instead, we shall establish its general properties in the following way.

7. We are now dealing with a difference equation of the pth order; each y depends upon the p y's immediately preceding it. Thus in order to determine the whole sequence, we need p initial values; call them $y_1, y_2, y_3, ..., y_p$. If all these initial y's were positive, it would follow at once from (6.3) that all subsequent y's would be positive; if all the initial y's were negative, all the subsequent y's would be negative. Let us, however, make a more general assumption, and allow that the initial y's may have various signs. We denote by $|y_n|$ the absolute value of y_n (regarded as positive whatever the sign of y_n). Then it follows from (6.3) that

$$|y_{p+1}| < \text{ or } = c_1|y_p| + c_2|y_{p-1}| + ... + c_p|y_1|. \qquad (7.1)$$

For these two expressions will be equal if all the y's on the right have the same sign; $|y_{p+1}|$ is then equal to the *sum* of all these (necessarily positive) terms. If any of the y's on the right are negative, $|y_{p+1}|$ is equal to the *difference* between the sums of two groups of the terms on the right of (7.1), and the difference between two positive quantities is necessarily less than their sum.

Further, if $|y_m|$ is the largest of $|y_1|, |y_2|, |y_3|, ..., |y_p|$, it will follow that $|y_{p+1}| < (c_1 + c_2 + c_3 + ... + c_p)|y_m|$, except in the case when all the initial y's are equal. Thus we may quite safely write

$$|y_{p+1}| \leqslant c|y_m|.$$

Passing on to $|y_{p+2}|$, we find that we cannot safely say any more about it. Although it must have a similar relation with the largest of its p predecessors $|y_2|, |y_3|, ..., |y_{p+1}|$, it remains perfectly possible that $|y_m|$ is included among these p predecessors. All we can safely conclude is the same limitation $|y_{p+2}| \leqslant c|y_m|$.

And so on, in complete strictness, until we have been through the whole sequence of p values, from $|y_{p+1}|$ to $|y_{2p}|$. But when we come to $|y_{2p+1}|$, there is a change. The p values of $|y_n|$ which immediately precede $|y_{2p+1}|$ have all been shown to be less or equal to $c|y_m|$. We can therefore, using the same principle as before, state with confidence that

$$|y_{2p+1}| \leqslant c^2|y_m|$$

with the same inequality holding throughout the third group of p values.

The same process may be repeated as often as we choose. Consequently, so long as $c < 1$, the deviation from the equilibrium income ($|y_n|$) can always be made as small as we please by taking n large enough. That is to say, the system must always converge to equilibrium.

With almost any actual figures that one might choose, the convergence is likely to be much more rapid than it appears to be from following these inequalities. But the inequalities are *necessary*; they give us a firm assurance that there will be a convergence to equilibrium under the stated conditions.

This rigorous proof from first principles will be of much use to us as we go on, not only in the multiplier theory.[1]

Appendix to Chapter III

8. The next thing which we have to do is to drop the assumption that investment is constant. Our fundamental difference equation can then be written

$$Y_n - (c_1 Y_{n-1} + c_2 Y_{n-2} + \ldots + c_p Y_{n-p}) = I_n, \qquad (8.1)$$

where I_n now varies from period to period according to some given law.[2]

Instead of working out the problem for each of the many special cases which here present themselves for consideration, we will look for a more general principle of solution. Such a principle can be found in the following way.

Each of the various laws which is likely to interest us in a dynamic theory of investment will itself usually be such that it will satisfy a difference equation of the form

$$I_n + \lambda_1 I_{n-1} + \lambda_2 I_{n-2} + \ldots + \lambda_m I_{n-m} = 0$$

in which the coefficients are constant. And the simplest such equation which will be satisfied will usually be very simple indeed.

Consider the following examples:

1. The arithmetical series. $I_n = A + nh$ (A and h being constants). Here we have $I_{n+1} - I_n = h$; and $I_{n+2} - 2I_{n+1} + I_n = 0$. (Repeated differencing of this sort will annihilate any polynomial in n.)

2. The geometrical series. $I_n = Ak^n$ (A and k being constants). Here we have $I_{n+1} - kI_n = 0$; which is in the requisite form without more ado.

---

[1] There is a generalization of the above argument which will be of some use to us at a later stage in our inquiry. Even if the c_r's are not all known to be positive, but some c_r's are negative, it still follows that

$$|y_n| \leqslant |c_1||y_{n-1}| + |c_2||y_{n-2}| + \ldots + |c_p||y_{n-p}|.$$

Consequently, by an exact reduplication of the above argument, the system can still be relied upon to converge to equilibrium, so long as

$$|c_1| + |c_2| + |c_3| + \ldots + |c_p| < 1.$$

It will, of course, be noticed that this sum of absolute values is necessarily greater than the algebraic sum of the c's, so that the restriction imposed by this condition is drastic. It does not follow that if the sum of absolute values is > 1, the sequence will necessarily diverge from equilibrium.

[2] I suppress the constant K, which can be taken to be absorbed into I_n, and will always be annihilated by a first differencing.

3. The sine series. $I_n = A \sin(nh+k)$; with A, h, and k constants. This is the simplest case of a regularly fluctuating series. Here we have $I_{n+2}-2I_{n+1}\cos h+I_n = 0$.

From some combination of such cases nearly any law, in which we are likely to be interested, can be built up.

9. Now suppose that we have found our difference equation for I. It will be sufficient to indicate how we use it if we suppose it to be of the second order, say

$$I_n+\lambda_1 I_{n-1}+\lambda_2 I_{n-2} = 0. \tag{9.1}$$

Substitute from (8.1) in this, and simplify by writing

$$Y_r+\lambda_1 Y_{r-1}+\lambda_2 Y_{r-2} = X_r.$$

We then get

$$X_n-(c_1 X_{n-1}+c_2 X_{n-2}+...+c_p X_{n-p}) = I_n+\lambda_1 I_{n-1}+\lambda_2 I_{n-2} = 0.$$

Consequently

$$X_n = c_1 X_{n-1}+c_2 X_{n-2}+...+c_p X_{n-p}, \tag{9.2}$$

which is precisely the same *homogeneous* equation as we have studied before under the form (6.3).

We already know that (with $c < 1$) the solution of this equation must converge; that is to say, that when n is large enough, X_n must be approximately zero. In view of the definition of X_n, this implies that when n is large enough, Y_n will tend to equality with some solution of the equation

$$Y_n+\lambda_1 Y_{n-1}+\lambda_2 Y_{n-2} = 0. \tag{9.3}$$

It is this solution which indicates the *moving equilibrium* of the system.

10. In order to find this solution, we do not need to solve the equation (9.3) *ab initio*. For we already know one solution of this equation. It is a particular solution, not a general solution; but from it the general solution can at once be deduced.

We have seen that a difference equation of the pth order requires p initial positions to determine the path; this means that the *general* solution (which is to be valid for *any* initial positions) must contain p arbitrary constants, whose values can subsequently be specified from a knowledge of the initial positions. Now if reference is made to the examples listed above, it will be seen that in the formation of a difference equation of the first order, one constant is eliminated; in the formation of a difference equation of the second order, two constants; and so on. *Consequently the original formula for I_n does* *give us the general solution of* (9.3); *but the constants which were eliminated in forming* (9.1) *have to be regarded as arbitrary.* Those constants which still appear in (9.1) are not arbitrary; they are 'fixed'. Thus what we have proved is that the moving equilibrium of Y_n will follow a law of the same form as I_n follows, though the 'free' constants will not necessarily be the same—indeed, they cannot possibly be the same.

Since the moving equilibrium path has got to satisfy the original difference equation (8.1), we have now merely to substitute for Y_n in that equation an expression of the same form as that of I_n, but with arbitrary values for the 'free' constants; and then to identify the 'free' constants from the results of the substitution. By this rule the moving equilibrium path can always be identified.

11. The working of this rule may now be illustrated from the examples given above.

1. *The arithmetical series.* $I_n = A + nh$. In this case both A and h are free constants. We therefore put $Y_n = A' + nh'$, and substitute in (8.1). The resulting equation must be true for all values of n. We can therefore equate the coefficients of n, which gives $h' = h/(1-c)$. Geometrically, this means that the moving equilibrium path must be parallel to the S-curve. Equating the remaining terms, we learn that $A'(1-c) = A - h' \sum r c_r$, so that the path is deflected downwards below the S-curve when h is positive, upwards when h is negative.

2. *The geometrical series.* $I_n = Ak^n$. Here A is the only free constant, so we must put $Y_n = A'k^n$. Substituting in (8.1) we learn directly that $A' = A/(1 - \sum c_r k^{-r})$. Thus the rate of growth is the same, and (with $k > 1$) the path is deflected downwards as a result of the lags.

3. *The sine series.* $I_n = A \sin(nh+k)$. Here A and k are the only free constants, so that we put $Y_n = A' \sin(nh+k')$. Substituting in (8.1) we equate the coefficients of $\sin nh$ and $\cos nh$, or (more conveniently) those of $\sin(nh+k')$ and $\cos(nh+k')$. We thus learn that

$$A'(1 - \sum c_r \cos rh) = A \cos(k-k'),$$
$$A' \sum c_r \sin rh = A \sin(k-k').$$

From these equations A' and k' can be determined. It follows that (1) in all normal[1] cases k' is less than k, so that the phases of the

---

[1] The (unimportant) exception to the first rule occurs when the lags are so long as to make $\sum c_r \sin rh$ negative. What this would mean is that consumption mainly depends upon the movement of income so long ago as to go back to the opposite phase of the cycle. It is safe to say that no attention need be paid to this possibility.

These questions can be further explored by the use of the geometrical method described in § 29 below.

income cycle come *later* than those of the investment cycle; (2) A' is *always* less than $A/(1-c)$, so that the amplitude of the cycle is always less than it would be if there were no lags. The lags have a *damping* effect.

General Note on the Solution of Difference Equations

12. The difference equations which arise in the multiplier theory can all be dealt with by special methods, of the kinds we have hitherto adopted; those which arise in connexion with the accelerator are more difficult, and cannot be treated except by some use of the regular mathematical technique. It may be useful if some outline of this technique is given before we go on to the accelerator theory.

A *homogeneous* difference equation with constant coefficients (which is simply a linear relation between the 'outputs' of successive dates, without constant term or other independent function) can always be written

$$X_n - (a_1 X_{n-1} + a_2 X_{n-2} + ... + a_p X_{n-p}) = 0 \qquad (12.1)$$

as in (9.2) above. We now remove all restrictions on the values of the coefficients, which may be positive or negative. The X's also may be positive or negative.

Let us try whether $X_n = u^n$, where u is a constant, can be a solution. Substituting, we see that it will be a solution if

$$f(u) = u^p - (a_1 u^{p-1} + a_2 u^{p-2} + ... + a_p) = 0 \qquad (12.2)$$

for the factor u^{n-p} cancels out, and the equation (12.2) is independent of n. Thus if (12.2) holds, u^n will be a solution for any value of n, as it should be.

Next, it is easy to verify that if u^n is a solution, Au^n will be a solution, for any value of the constant A. Further, if u_1 and u_2 are two solutions of the algebraic equation (12.2), $A_1 u_1^n + A_2 u_2^n$ will be a solution of (12.1).

Now this *auxiliary* equation (12.2), being of the pth degree, has in principle p roots. Thus, pursuing the same line of argument, we see that

$$X_n = A_1 u_1^n + A_2 u_2^n + ... + A_p u_p^n \qquad (12.3)$$

is a solution of (12.1) if $u_1, u_2, ..., u_p$ are the roots of (12.2).

Provided that the roots $u_1, u_2, ..., u_p$ are all *different*, it is easy to show that (12.3) is the general solution of (12.1). For it contains p arbitrary constants, $A_1, A_2, ..., A_p$; and since (12.1) is of the pth order, it requires p initial positions to determine the path. Now with p initial positions given, the p constants in (12.3) can be exactly determined. (12.3) therefore determines a path which satisfies the difference equation, and it also passes through the initial positions. But it is directly evident that there can be only one path which satisfies the equation and also passes through the initial positions. What we have found must therefore be the solution we were seeking.

13. Further discussion of the difference equation (12.1) now proceeds almost entirely in terms of the properties of the ordinary algebraic equation (12.2). An algebraic equation of the pth degree must in principle have p roots; but some of these roots may be equal to one another, and some of the roots may have imaginary parts, so that they are 'complex'. Complex roots always occur in pairs, one of them being of the form $a+ib$, and the other of the form $a-ib$, where $i = \sqrt{(-1)}$. In the present theory it is impossible to avoid discussion of these awkward cases.

Equal roots. If two roots of the auxiliary equation are equal, we only get $p-1$ arbitrary constants from (12.3), and this will usually make it impossible to determine a path which will pass through all the initial positions. An additional term to the series (12.3) has therefore to be found. It is found in the following way.

If u_1 is a repeated root of (12.2) (so that $u_2 = u_1$) it must not only satisfy $f(u) = 0$, but it must also satisfy the equation got by differentiating (12.2) with respect to u, which is $f'(u) = 0$. Now if $f(u_1) = 0$, and also $f'(u_1) = 0$, it can be shown that nu_1^n must be a solution of the difference equation. For if $X_n = nu_1^n$,

$$X_n - (a_1 X_{n-1} + a_2 X_{n-2} + ... + a_p X_{n-p})$$
$$= nu_1^n - (\overline{n-1} a_1 u_1^{n-1} + \overline{n-2} a_2 u_1^{n-2} + ... + \overline{n-p} a_p u_1^{n-p})$$
$$= (n-p)u_1^{n-p} f(u_1) + u_1^{n-p+1} f'(u_1)$$
$$= 0$$

when u_1 is a repeated root.

Arguing as before, we see that the general solution in this case is

$$X_n = (A_1 + A_2 n)u_1^n + A_3 u_3^n + ... + A_p u_p^n.$$

If there are three roots, all of which are equal, a term in $n^2 u_1^n$ must be introduced for the same reason; and so on.

Complex roots. If two roots of the auxiliary equation are complex, the general principle that the solution is of the form (12.3) still holds, but the complex terms require interpretation. Let u_1 and u_2 be the complex roots. Then we have to consider the meaning of

$$A_1 u_1^n + A_2 u_2^n.$$

If A_1 and A_2 were two unequal real numbers, this whole expression would have an imaginary part—and that is impossible, for we know that X_n takes on real values. Thus if A_1 and A_2 are real, they must be equal; in that case the imaginary parts of u_1^n and u_2^n would cancel out. But they will also cancel out if A_1 and A_2 are a *pair* of complex numbers, like the pair of complex roots defined above. These, in fact, are the cases which we have to consider.

Any pair of real numbers a, b, can be written in the form

$$a = \rho \cos \theta, \qquad b = \rho \sin \theta,$$

where ρ is positive. (For ρ is the positive square root of $a^2 + b^2$ and $\tan \theta = b/a$.) We can therefore write

$$u_1 = \rho(\cos \theta + i \sin \theta), \qquad u_2 = \rho(\cos \theta - i \sin \theta),$$

and $\qquad A_1 = k(\cos \epsilon + i \sin \epsilon), \qquad A_2 = k(\cos \epsilon - i \sin \epsilon).$

(This covers the case in which A_1 and A_2 are real and equal, for then we have $\epsilon = 0$.)

We now apply de Moivre's theorem:

$$A_1 u_1^n + A_2 u_2^n = k\rho^n(\cos \overline{n\theta + \epsilon} + i \sin \overline{n\theta + \epsilon}) +$$
$$+ k\rho^n(\cos \overline{n\theta + \epsilon} - i \sin \overline{n\theta + \epsilon})$$
$$= 2k\rho^n \cos(n\theta + \epsilon)$$

which is real. Thus the effect of complex roots is to introduce a trigonometrical term $\cos(n\theta + \epsilon)$, which fluctuates periodically as n increases. The complex roots are thus of particular importance for the study of fluctuations.

Equal and complex roots. Finally, we have to notice that there may be two equal pairs of complex roots. If this happens, there will be a coefficient of the form $k_1 + nk_2$ before the cosine term.

14. The general solutions of difference equations such as (12.1) are most conveniently classified according to the form which they take for large values of n.

1. If all the roots of the auxiliary equation are real and unequal, and all of them lie within the range -1 to $+1$, each of the components of X_n will become smaller and smaller (in absolute magnitude) as n increases; X_n will therefore tend to zero as n becomes large. If there are some roots which are greater than $+1$, these will swamp the smaller roots as n increases, so that X_n will get larger and larger, at least when n becomes large. A negative root, with absolute value greater than 1, will also tend to swamp smaller roots; if the largest root is a root of this type, the sequence will tend to oscillate between large positive and large negative values of X_n in alternate periods.

2. If there are repeated real roots, the same usually holds. For if $u_1 < 1$, nu_1^n tends to zero as n increases.

3. If there are complex roots, we have to compare the moduli (ρ) of the complex roots with the absolute values of the real roots. It will be the root (or roots) with the largest modulus (or absolute value) which will swamp the others. If the largest root, in this sense, is real, the analysis proceeds as before; but if the largest root is complex, the system will tend to settle down into an oscillation. The fluctuations will have a diminishing amplitude if the modulus is less than 1, and will be explosive (their amplitude will increase) if the modulus is greater than 1. It is only in the case where the largest root is complex, and its modulus is equal to 1, that we get a steady cycle.

15. *The multiplier theory treated by the general method.* Partly in order to illustrate these principles, and partly in order to get some results which will be useful later, let us now re-work the multiplier theory (§§ 6–7 above) in terms of this regular technique. The basic difference equation of that theory was

$$y_n - (c_1 y_{n-1} + c_2 y_{n-2} + \dots + c_p y_{n-p}) = 0, \qquad (6.3)$$

in which all c's were positive and $c \ (= \sum c_r) < 1$. This would have an auxiliary equation

$$f(u) = u^p - (c_1 u^{p-1} + c_2 u^{p-2} + \dots + c_p) = 0. \qquad (15.1)$$

If p is at all large, this equation becomes impossible of solution by ordinary methods. We can, however, discover a good deal about the solution in indirect ways.

It is clear, first of all, that the equation must have one real positive root. For $f(u)$ is positive when u is large and positive, and is negative when $u = 0$. The curve $f(u) = 0$ must intersect the u-axis between these values; but it looks at first sight as if it might cut it any *odd* number of times. It is, however, impossible for there to be more than one intersection. The simplest way of showing this is to calculate the expression

$$uf'(u) - pf(u) = c_1 u^{p-1} + 2c_2 u^{p-2} + 3c_3 u^{p-3} + \dots + pc_p,$$

which is necessarily positive if u is positive. Thus if u is positive and $f(u) = 0$, $f'(u)$ must necessarily be positive. Thus at a point where the curve cuts the u-axis, and u is positive, the curve must have a positive slope; and this could not be true at *every* intersection if the number of such intersections was more than one. There is therefore only one real and positive root.

The location of this root can be further narrowed down. For if

$u = 1$, $f(u) = 1-c$, which is positive, so long as $c < 1$. On the other hand, if $u = c$, we get

$$f(c) = c^p - c_1 c^{p-1} - c_2 c^{p-2} - \ldots - c_p$$

$$= (c_1 + c_2 + \ldots + c_p)c^{p-1} - c_1 c^{p-1} - c_2 c^{p-2} - \ldots - c_p$$

$$= c_2(c^{p-1} - c^{p-2}) + c_3(c^{p-1} - c^{p-3}) + \ldots + c_p(c^{p-1} - 1).$$

Now if $c < 1$, each of the terms in this last series is negative, and $f(c)$ is therefore negative. Thus the real positive root must lie between c and 1.

Notice, further, that these conclusions do not depend upon the condition that $c < 1$. If $c > 1$, there can still be only one real and positive root. $f(1)$ will now be negative and $f(c)$ positive, but they are still of different signs, so that there still is a real root between 1 and c. But in this latter case the root is > 1. We can therefore tell at once from the general theory of difference equations that if $c > 1$, the solution must be explosive, since a root of the auxiliary equation which is greater than 1 has been identified.

It is not easy to get farther than this by considering the elementary properties of algebraic equations; but it is interesting to notice that our other method does indirectly tell us something more about the properties of the auxiliary equation, and provides a means of establishing some conclusions which would usually be proved by quite advanced methods. It follows from the already-established properties of the corresponding difference equation that the real root which we have just identified must be itself the largest of all the roots, the one which determines the ultimate course of the process. The argument of § 7 has shown us that when $c < 1$, all the roots must be such that their absolute values (or moduli) are < 1. And we can see, in a similar way, that the largest root must be real and positive. For if the largest root were to be complex or negative, then (for a sufficiently large value of n) y_n would oscillate about its equilibrium value, which is zero. But we know that if we start from *any* set of positive initial y's, all succeeding y's must be positive. Oscillations, which carry y_n on to the negative side of zero, cannot therefore occur, so long as the initial values are positive. But they would certainly have to occur, sooner or later, if the largest root of the auxiliary equation were complex or negative.

The same argument shows that the largest root of (15.1) must be real and positive, so long as the c_r's are all positive, whether $c <$ or > 1. Consequently we have in fact isolated the largest root, even if we have not solved (15.1) explicitly. The largest root is the real root which lies between 1 and c; such a root always exists.

In the special case when $c = 1$, it will follow from the argument that the largest root must be 1 itself. (It will readily be verified that 1 has now become a root of the equation.) The solution of the difference equation (6.3) is therefore

$$A_1(1)^n + A_2 u_2^n + A_3 u_3^n + \ldots + A_p u_p^n,$$

in which all terms, except the first, tend to zero as n becomes large. The process therefore tends to a constant value for y_n, which depends upon the initial positions, and is easily determined from them.

This is the proposition about 'repeated weighted averaging' which we used in Chapter IV (p. 42).

16. *Non-homogeneous equations.* In concluding this general note, something must be said about non-homogeneous equations (which do contain a constant term or independent function). We have already (§§ 8–11) seen how to deal with non-homogeneous equations in the case where the homogeneous part of the equation converges regularly. But the method of finding the moving equilibrium, which was there indicated, did not in fact depend upon the convergence of the equation; all that did depend upon the convergence was the proof that the system, when displaced, would converge to the equilibrium path. It is, therefore, generally possible to *define* the moving equilibrium solution as the result of applying the process of §§ 8–11 to the difference equation in question, whatever that equation may be. We shall then get a path which the system could follow, if it were not displaced from it. But in the general case, it will not necessarily converge to this path, if it is displaced from it. It may converge to it, or it may diverge from it, or it may oscillate about it in various ways.

It will further be noticed that the independent functions, to which the process of §§ 8–11 can be applied, are precisely those which can be solutions of difference equations of our type. We now see what those functions are; evidently they provide quite a wide assortment.

Appendix to Chapter V

17. The induced investment, carried out in period n, is assumed to be linearly dependent upon previous changes in output; thus

$$I_n = v_1(Y_{n-1} - Y_{n-2}) + v_2(Y_{n-2} - Y_{n-3}) + \ldots + v_{p-1}(Y_{n-p+1} - Y_{n-p}).$$

Consumption, as before, depends upon previous incomes

$$C_n = c_1 Y_{n-1} + c_2 Y_{n-2} + \ldots + c_p Y_{n-p} + K.$$

Autonomous investment is A_n. Then $Y_n = C_n + A_n + I_n$, whence

$$Y_n = A_n + \sum_{r=1}^{r-p} c_r Y_{n-r} + \sum_{r=1}^{r-p-1} v_r(Y_{n-r} - Y_{n-r-1}) + K. \quad (17.1)$$

This is the basic equation, on which all our work (throughout Chapters V–IX) is based.

18. We begin by considering the equilibrium path, under special assumptions.

(i) *The Stationary State.* Here $A_n = 0$, and all Y's are equal, so that $I_n = 0$. If K was also zero, the only constant value of Y which would satisfy (17.1) would be $Y = 0$. Thus we can only make sense of the stationary model if $K \neq 0$. In that case, Y (the stationary output) $= K/(1-c)$, as in the Keynesian multiplier theory (§ 4 above).

(ii) *The Regularly Progressive Economy without Autonomous Investment.* Here $A_n = 0$, and it must be assumed that $K = 0$. But

$$Y_n = E(1+g)^n,$$

where E and g are constants. Hence

$$Y_{n-r} - Y_{n-r-1} = E(1+g)^{n-r} - E(1+g)^{n-r-1} = gE(1+g)^{n-r-1}.$$

Substituting in (17.1) we get

$$E(1+g)^n = E \sum c_r(1+g)^{n-r} + gE \sum v_r(1+g)^{n-r-1}. \quad (18.1)$$

This has a solution at $E = 0$; in view of the absence of autonomous investment and of any stationary element in consumption, zero output is a possible equilibrium output. But it also has another solution, which corresponds to that discovered by Harrod. For if we divide through by $E(1+g)^{n-p}$, we get

$$(1+g)^p = \sum c_r(1+g)^{p-r} + g \sum v_r(1+g)^{p-r-1}, \quad (18.2)$$

an equation in g which is independent of n. If this equation has any roots which are real and positive, the system could remain in progressive equilibrium with g equal to any of these roots. There seems to be no reason, in general, why there should only be one possible value of g satisfying the equation.

(iii) *The Regularly Progressive Economy with Autonomous Investment.* Here $A_n \neq 0$, and there is no need to assume that $K = 0$. When (18.1) is modified by the addition of these terms, the whole situation is changed. When we divide through by $E(1+g)^{n-p}$, we get

$$(1+g)^p = \sum c_r(1+g)^{p-r} + g \sum v_r(1+g)^{p-r-1} + \frac{A_n + K}{E(1+g)^{n-p}}. \quad (18.3)$$

This equation is not independent of n unless A_n+K is a multiple of $(1+g)^n$—unless, that is, both autonomous investment and the trend element in consumption (if there is any) have a constant rate of growth. It is only in this case that a progressive equilibrium is possible.

Let us neglect K, and write $A_n = A_0(1+g)^n$. Then the variable term in (18.3) cancels out, and we get an equation to determine E in terms of A_0,

$$(1+g)^p = \sum c_r(1+g)^{p-r} + g \sum v_r(1+g)^{p-r-1} + \frac{A_0}{E}(1+g)^p$$

or
$$E = \frac{A_0}{1 - \sum c_r(1+g)^{-r} - g \sum v_r(1+g)^{-r-1}}. \qquad (18.4)$$

If E was given, g would be determined as from (18.2); but it is much more intelligible to suppose that g is already determined from the *autonomous* rate of growth of A_n; (18.4) then determines the 'level' of output quite unambiguously, without any possibility of multiple equilibria.

The only condition which must be fulfilled in order to make this progressive equilibrium possible is that the denominator of (18.4) must be positive—which means that there must be enough saving to cover both the autonomous investment and the induced investment induced by the steady progress. We shall assume that this condition is fulfilled.

It should be understood that all the cases discussed in this section are special cases of equilibrium, based on the assumption that autonomous investment is either zero, or changing according to some particular steady law. In principle, there is an equilibrium path corresponding to any movement of autonomous investment, a path which can be calculated by an adaptation of the methods of §§ 8–11 above. An illustration of the properties of such a more generalized 'equilibrium' will be given in the final section of this Appendix.

Appendix to Chapter VI

19. We now come to our central problem, which consists in finding the general solution of a difference equation such as (17.1), or, when that is impossible, in seeing what can be discovered about the properties of the solution. The method of solution has been indicated in §§ 12–14; we have now to apply that method to the particular form of equation which interests us.

The moving equilibrium having been discovered, the deviations from that equilibrium are given by a homogeneous difference equation of the form

$$y_n = \sum_1^p c_r y_{n-r} + \sum_1^{p-1} v_r(y_{n-r}-y_{n-r-1}) \qquad (19.1)$$

with an auxiliary equation

$$f(u) = u^p - \sum_1^p c_r u^{p-r} - (u-1) \sum_1^{p-1} v_r u^{p-r-1} = 0. \qquad (19.2)$$

We can best approach the study of this equation by beginning with the simplest case, called in the text the 'elementary' case, in which it is easily soluble.[1]

20. We accordingly begin by assuming that all v_r's are zero excepting v_1, and all c_r's zero excepting c_1, so that $v_1 = v$ and $c_1 = c$. (19.1) is then of the second order, and (19.2) a quadratic. If we write $c = 1-s$ (where s is positive and may be fairly small), the auxiliary quadratic becomes

$$f(u) = u^2 - (1-s+v)u + v = 0, \qquad (20.1)$$

an equation which can be solved by elementary methods without any difficulty.

The condition[2] for the roots of this quadratic to be real are that $(1-s+v)^2 > 4v$; which, since $1-s$ and v are both positive, implies that $1-s+v > 2\sqrt{v}$, whence $(1-\sqrt{v})^2 > s$. This must either mean that $1-\sqrt{v} > \sqrt{s}$, or that $\sqrt{v}-1 > \sqrt{s}$; whence $v < (1-\sqrt{s})^2$ or $> (1+\sqrt{s})^2$. If v lies between these limits, the roots are complex, with a modulus which must equal $\sqrt{v}$.

Thus we have four cases:

   (i) $v < (1-\sqrt{s})^2$.   Real roots.
   (ii) $(1-\sqrt{s})^2 < v < 1$.   Complex roots, with modulus < 1.
   (iii) $1 < v < (1+\sqrt{s})^2$.   Complex roots, with modulus > 1.
   (iv) $v > (1+\sqrt{s})^2$.   Real roots.

Now notice that $f(u)$ is easily calculable for certain values of u.

$$f(1) = s; \qquad f(0) = v; \qquad f(-1) = 2-s+2v.$$

All these values of $f(u)$ are necessarily positive; and so are the values

---

[1] Samuelson, in his *Foundations of Economic Analysis* (pp. 429 ff.) gives a general method for discovering whether the roots of such an equation 'lie within the unit circle', which means that their moduli are less than unity. But it is an exceedingly difficult method, both to understand and to apply. Although I have made some use of his method in checking my results, I shall proceed in a different way, which seems to give a more intelligible picture of the working of the system.

[2] In what follows, all square roots are, of course, *positive* square roots.

of $f(u)$ when u is large and positive, and when u is large and negative. Thus if $f(u)$ has real roots they must both of them lie within one of the ranges $-\infty$ to -1, -1 to 0, 0 to $+1$, $+1$ to $+\infty$. Since the sum of the roots is positive, the negative ranges are ruled out. Now in the first of the above four cases, where $v < (1-\sqrt{s})^2$, it follows that $1-s+v < 2$. Thus the sum of the roots is < 2, and both roots must lie within the range 0 to $+1$. Similarly, in case (iv), both roots must lie within the range $+1$ to $+\infty$.

Case (i) is therefore identified with the case of steady convergence without fluctuation; and case (iv) with that of explosion without fluctuation. Case (ii) is necessarily cyclic, but the cycles are damped. Case (iii) is the case of explosive cycles. The classification of the second-order equation is therefore complete.

21. In the cyclic cases, the solution of the difference equation will be of the form $A\rho^n \cos(n\theta+\epsilon)$, where

$$\rho(\cos\theta+i\sin\theta) \quad \text{and} \quad \rho(\cos\theta-i\sin\theta)$$

are the roots of the auxiliary equation. (See § 13 above.) It is the cosine term which is responsible for the cycle, and this term returns to its original value when $n\theta+\epsilon$ has increased by four right angles—that is to say, after a number of periods approximately equal to $360°/\theta$. Thus the duration of the cycle depends on the angle θ; it is shorter the larger is θ.

Now from the sum and product of the roots, we have

$$2\rho\cos\theta = 1-s+v \quad \text{and} \quad \rho^2 = v.$$

Thus
$$\cos\theta = \frac{1-s+v}{2\sqrt{v}}.$$

The value of θ derived from this expression can conveniently be constructed geometrically. Construct a triangle with sides 1, $\sqrt{v}$, and $\sqrt{s}$; then the angle opposite the side $\sqrt{s}$ will be θ. This construction will be found very convenient for remembering the properties of the solution in the second-order case. For if $\sqrt{v} < 1-\sqrt{s}$, the triangle cannot be constructed, and so there is no cycle. As $\sqrt{v}$ increases beyond this limiting value, the angle increases from zero to a maximum; so that the cycle, which is very long for low values of v, gradually shortens. The point where $v = 1$, which is where the fluctuations begin to be explosive, is that at which the triangle becomes isosceles. But θ reaches its maximum value, so that the cycle is at its shortest, when the triangle is not isosceles but right-angled; this is where $v+s = 1$, so that $v = 1-s$. Thus at $v = 1$, the cycle is already beginning to lengthen again. As v rises above

1, the cycle steadily lengthens until $\sqrt{v}$ reaches $1+\sqrt{s}$, when the angle again vanishes, and the system explodes without a cycle.

The minimum length of the cycle is given by $\sin \theta = \sqrt{s}$. Thus if s is fairly small, θ cannot be very large, and the cycle cannot be shorter than a quite considerable number of periods.

22. As a first step towards the solution of the more general problem, let us notice what would happen, in this second order case, if the marginal propensity to save were zero, so that $s = 0$. The auxiliary quadratic then takes the form

$$f(u) = u^2 - (1+v)u + v = (u-1)(u-v) = 0.$$

The roots are 1 and v; the solution of the second-order difference equation is accordingly $A_1(1)^n + A_2 v^n = A_1 + A_2 v^n$. It is therefore evident that the sequence will converge to A_1 if $v < 1$, and will explode if $v > 1$. The cyclic solutions do not occur; for, with $s = 0$, the three 'points' coincide.

Now let us consider what happens, still under the assumption that $s = 0$, if induced investment is spread out over several periods, though there are no consumption lags. The auxiliary equation (19.2) then becomes

$$f(u) = u^p - u^{p-1} - (u-1) \sum v_r u^{p-r-1}$$
$$= (u-1)(u^{p-1} - \sum v_r u^{p-r-1}) = 0. \qquad (22.1)$$

One root is therefore unity; the others are given by the equation

$$u^{p-1} - v_1 u^{p-2} - v_2 u^{p-3} - \ldots - v_{p-1} = 0, \qquad (22.2)$$

and this is an equation which we have seen before. All the v's must be positive, just as the c's had to be positive in the multiplier theory; the equation (22.2) is therefore formally identical with the equation (15.1), the properties of which were explored in § 15.

What we discovered there was that an equation of the type (22.2) in which all the coefficients are positive, will have one real root between 1 and $\sum v_r$ (which, in accordance with our earlier notation, we may henceforward write simply as v); and that this real root must be the largest root of the equation. Returning, therefore, to (22.1) which has an extra root, equal to unity, we can say that we know something about two of its roots. If $v < 1$, the roots about which we have knowledge (the *major* roots, we will call them) are known to be the *two* largest roots; if $v > 1$, this is not certain, for (22.2) can then possess complex or negative roots with a modulus greater than 1. But in any case the largest root of (22.1) is identified, and the solutions of the corresponding difference equation can therefore be classified.

(i) If $v < 1$, the largest root is unity; y_n must therefore converge to a constant, which depends on the initial values.

(ii) If $v = 1$, two roots are equal to unity, and these are the largest roots. Applying the rule for repeated roots, we see that y_n will converge to the form $A_1 + nA_2$—an arithmetical progression. The process is therefore divergent or explosive.

(iii) If $v > 1$, the largest root is greater than unity, and the process is therefore explosive.

The case in which there is no saving is therefore completely cleared up; convergence depends upon the total investment coefficient (v) being < 1.

23. Let us now, still without allowing any consumption lags (beyond the first period), allow s to be > 0. We may now write the auxiliary equation as

$$(u-1)(u^{p-1}- \sum v_r u^{p-r-1})+su^{p-1} = 0. \qquad (23.1)$$

Let us call this expression $F(u)$, still retaining $f(u)$ for the expression (22.1) without the *saving* term. Thus $F(u) = f(u)+su^{p-1}$. What difference does this extra term make?

It is clear at once that if u is small, this extra term must be very small; so that the value of $F(u)$ for small values of u will differ very little from the value of $f(u)$. It follows, therefore, that the small roots of $F(u) = 0$ (whether real or complex) must be very near to the small roots of $f(u) = 0$. It is the largest roots which are likely to be most affected by the introduction of the *saving* term.

FIG. A

Now we know that if $v < 1$, the two largest roots of $f(u) = 0$ are the *major* roots, the only roots which are real and positive. In the neighbourhood of the major roots, $f(u)$ must take the form shown in the diagram (Fig. A). If $v > 1$, we cannot be sure that the major roots will be the largest pair of roots, but it is still true that in the neighbourhood of the major roots, $f(u)$ will take the form shown. Now when the additional term su^{p-1} is introduced, the curve must be raised (since $s > 0$, and in this region $u > 0$). It must therefore move into something like the dotted position shown. As the curve rises, the two roots draw together, and the larger root is therefore reduced; this must have a damping effect. At a certain stage the roots become equal, and thereafter complex. When the major roots become complex, they of course yield a cyclical solution.

All this, it will be noticed, is exactly what happens in the quadratic case. But in the quadratic case, the larger root goes on being reduced, until the roots become equal; after that the modulus remains constant at $\sqrt{v}$. Does this property hold generally? It soon becomes clear that it does not.

24. Consider, in the first instance, the cubic. Here

$$f(u) = (u-1)(u^2 - v_1 u - v_2)$$

so that it has three real roots, the two major roots and a third (minor) root, which must be negative. As s increases, the major roots are drawn together, in the way that we have seen; but whereas in the quadratic case the product of the major roots remains constant (being equal to v, which is unaffected), in the cubic case it is the product of all three roots which remains constant, so that the product of the major roots will only remain constant if the minor root remains constant, which (in general) it will not do. It is, indeed, evident from geometrical considerations (such as those used in the figure) that $f'(u)$ must be positive at the negative root; su^2 is positive, even when u is negative, so that the curve must be raised, even in the neighbourhood of the negative root, as we pass from $f(u)$ to $F(u)$. The absolute value of the negative root must therefore be raised, and the product of the major roots must be diminished.

The same thing can be proved to be true when we go on to the quartic. Here there are two minor roots, which may be real or complex. It is, however, possible to ascertain, by consideration of the symmetric functions of all the roots, that the minor roots are either real and negative, or complex with a negative real part. Equipped with this knowledge, we can also show that a rise in s will diminish the product of the major roots and increase the product of the minor roots. The principle that saving damps down the major roots holds here also.

I have, however, not been able to show that this principle holds for equations of still higher degree; indeed I suspect that it is not universally true. But enough has been proved to show that it will be a reliable guide in most cases. The quartic case is already sufficiently general to provide us with a rough representation of an investment 'hump'; thus it looks distinctly improbable that there will be any exception to the principle which need trouble us.

25. It is important, on the other hand, to notice just how far it takes us. It has been shown that an increase in the saving coefficient can ordinarily be relied upon to damp down the major roots; but this does not prove that there will be a damping effect on the process as a whole. For though the increase in the saving coefficient tends to damp down the major roots, it tends, at the same time, to expand the minor roots. It is possible that some of these roots, which will have been smaller than the larger of the major roots (and will usually have been smaller than either of them) when $s = 0$, will become larger than the major roots when s increases sufficiently. This is the serious way in which an increase in s may be anti-damping.

In order to see what conditions are necessary for this to happen, let us look again at the cubic case. The negative root will then have to become greater in absolute magnitude than the square root of the product of the major roots (this condition is necessary whether the major roots are real or complex). Since the product of all the roots is $-v_2$, this implies (if $-\alpha$ is the negative root) that $\alpha > \left(\dfrac{v_2}{\alpha}\right)^{\frac{1}{2}}$ or $\alpha > (v_2)^{\frac{1}{3}}$. Now if the equation $F(u) = 0$ has a negative root beyond $-(v_2)^{\frac{1}{3}}$, $F(-v_2^{\frac{1}{3}})$ must be positive. On substituting, we find that this cannot happen unless

$$-(1-s+v_1)(v_2)^{\frac{2}{3}}-v_1+v_2 > 0$$

and this is not possible, for moderately small values of s, unless v_1 is very small, while v_2 must in any case be greater than $(1-s)^{\frac{3}{2}}$, the minimum value of v_2 rising as v_1 increases.

Thus the cubic case, in which the negative root becomes dominant, turns out to be one in which the second partial investment coefficient must be fairly large, while the first must be relatively small, and is likely to be very small indeed. It has been shown in the text that there are general reasons why this kind of thing should happen. It is possible, when the induced investment is concentrated in a late period, for short cycles to be set up, which will be reinforced by an increase in the saving coefficient. In the cubic case, these short cycles are two periods in length; they are thus represented by the dominance of a negative root, which produces a term which changes in sign from period to period.

It is not necessary to do more than verify this result in the quartic case. There are then two possibilities of short cycles, one arising from a concentration of the induced investment on v_2 (which must have broadly the same effect as that found in the cubic case just discussed), and one arising from concentration on v_3. It will be sufficient if we consider this last possibility in its simplest manifestation.

Suppose that v_1 and v_2 are zero, while v_3 is greater than zero. Then $f(u) = (u-1)(u^3-v_3)$. This has major roots at 1 and $(v_3)^{\frac{1}{3}}$; its minor roots are

$$(v_3)^{\frac{1}{3}}\left(\cos\frac{2\pi}{3}\pm i\sin\frac{2\pi}{3}\right),$$

and these minor roots generate a cycle of three periods. If v_3 is not much short of unity (and *a fortiori* if it exceeds unity), the s term will cause the minor roots to become the larger roots, and a cycle of approximately three periods will become dominant.

As explained in the text, I find it hard to believe that these short cycles can have much economic significance. They can only arise as a result of extreme bunching of investment after a lag. It seems much more likely that the cycles with which we are concerned are the relatively long cycles associated with the major roots, than that they are the short cycles associated with the minor roots; it seems safe to conclude that these longer cycles will be damped by a rise in the saving coefficient.

26. Something must now be said, in order to complete the analysis, about lags in consumption. The general auxiliary equation (19.2) can be reduced to a form similar to that which we have been studying if we sum the c's and write

$$c_1+c_2+c_3+\dots+c_p = k_1$$
$$c_2+c_3+\dots+c_p = k_2$$
$$c_{p-1}+c_p = k_{p-1}$$
$$c_p = k_p.$$

(All the k's are < 1, and $k_1 > k_2 > k_3 > \dots > k_p$.) We now have $c_r = k_r - k_{r+1}$, and (19.2) becomes

$$u^p-(k_1-k_2)u^{p-1}-(k_2-k_3)u^{p-2}-\dots-k_p-(u-1)\sum v_r u^{p-r-1}$$
$$= u^p-k_1 u^{p-1}-(u-1)\sum(v_r-k_{r+1})u^{p-r-1} = 0. \quad (26.1)$$

If k_1 is written $(1-s)$ (so that s is the coefficient of *outright* saving) then (26.1) becomes the same as (23.1), except that the investment coefficients (v) are now adjusted for consumption lags, by the subtraction of the k-coefficients.

If the consumption lags are fairly small, so that no adjusted coefficient $(v-k)$ becomes negative, the adjustment makes no difference whatsoever to the preceding analysis. All that happens is that the reduction in the size of the (adjusted) investment coefficients has its regular damping effect. Where we have to look a little farther is where the adjustment goes so far as to make some of the adjusted coefficients negative. It has been an essential assumption of the preceding argument that the v's were positive. How much difference is made if some of them take negative values?

Since the k's are in descending order of magnitude, it is clearly the earliest v's which are in most danger of going negative, at least to a serious extent. Even though some of the later v's may go negative, the absolute magnitude of such late negative terms must be quite small. It is therefore reasonable if we test the importance of negative values by considering the effect on our analysis of a negative value for the first v, namely, v_1.

Consider the cubic case. If v_1 is positive, and $v_1+v_2 < 1$, the preliminary equation $f(u) = (u-1)(u^2-v_1 u-v_2) = 0$ must have a negative root which is smaller than either of the positive roots. If v_1 becomes negative (though v_1+v_2 is still less than 1), the negative root becomes larger than the smaller of the positive roots. But the negative root only becomes larger than the larger of the positive roots if $f(-1)$ is positive, which implies that $1+v_1-v_2$ is negative, so that $v_2 > 1+v_1$. As long as v_1 is positive, this is impossible unless $v_1+v_2 > 1$; but if v_1 is negative, it is possible even though $v_1+v_2 < 1$.

Conceivably, therefore, the negative root can become explosive, even though $s = 0$ and $v_1+v_2 < 1$, when v_1 is negative. And in accordance with the preceding argument, the chances of this happening are greater as s increases.

It thus appears that a negative value of v_1 increases the chance that a minor root, with its short cycle, will become dominant. It seems fairly clear that this result will hold quite generally, and there is, indeed, one fairly simple general proposition (given below) which enables us to generalize it a good deal.[1] But it is the violent change from a negative v in one period to a relatively large positive v in the next period which has this effect—and we have already seen that violent changes of this sort are conducive to the dominance of minor roots. If such violent changes are ruled out, the possibility of small

---

[1] We saw in the note to § 7 above that a system which was generated by the difference equation
$$y_n = \Sigma\, c_r y_{n-r}$$
could be relied upon to converge, even if some of the c's were negative, so long as $\Sigma\, |c_r| < 1$. It follows that all the roots of
$$u^{p-1} - \Sigma\, v_r u^{p-r-1} = 0$$
will lie within the unit circle, even if some of the v's are negative, so long as $\Sigma\, |v_r| < 1$. This condition is therefore sufficient to ensure that unity is the largest of the roots of $f(u) = 0$, even if some of the v's are negative.

This test is evidently consistent with what we have just learned about the cubic case; it is indeed directly suggested by what we have learned about the cubic case by other methods.

negative values for some of the v's (after adjustment for consumption lags) does not much affect the preceding argument. So long as the consumption lags are sufficiently moderate not to disturb the dominance of the major roots, we can rely upon them having a damping effect.

Appendix to Chapter VII

27. Erratic shocks. It will be sufficient, in our discussion of this theory, if we work with the basic difference equation in its 'elementary' form

$$y_n - (1-s+v)y_{n-1} + vy_{n-2} = 0. \qquad (27.1)$$

A single shock (or deviation of autonomous investment from its equilibrium path) of e_1 in period 1 would then give

$$y_n = e_1 \rho^{n-1} \frac{\sin n\theta}{\sin \theta},$$

where ρ and θ are defined as in § 21 above. (For with these values of the constants we have $y_0 = 0$ and $y_1 = e_1$.) A series of shocks, $e_1, e_2, e_3, \ldots$, in successive periods, would give

$$y_n = e_n + e_{n-1}\rho \frac{\sin 2\theta}{\sin \theta} + e_{n-2}\rho^2 \frac{\sin 3\theta}{\sin \theta} + \ldots + e_1 \rho^{n-1} \frac{\sin n\theta}{\sin \theta}, \qquad (27.2)$$

for the effects of successive shocks are additive. (ρ is assumed to be $\leqslant 1$.)

In order to investigate the consequences of the hypothesis that the shocks $e_1, e_2, e_3, \ldots$ are random, we have to calculate the serial correlation coefficient of the y series.[1] This is the correlation coefficient between y_n and y_{n+k}—the same variable lagged for an arbitrary number of periods (k). It is defined as

$$r_k = \lim_{N \to \infty} \frac{\dfrac{1}{N} \sum_1^N y_n y_{n+k}}{\sqrt{\left(\dfrac{1}{N} \sum_1^N y_n^2\right)} \sqrt{\left(\dfrac{1}{N} \sum_1^N y_{n+k}^2\right)}} = \lim_{N \to \infty} \frac{\sum_1^N y_n y_{n+k}}{\sum_1^N y_n^2} \qquad (27.3)$$

for the two standard deviations may be taken to have the same limit.

If the e's are uncorrelated,

$$\lim \frac{1}{N} \sum_1^N e_m e_{m'} = 0$$

[1] Kendall, *Advanced Theory of Statistics*, vol. ii, pp. 402 ff.

when $m \neq m'$, and $\quad \lim \dfrac{1}{N} \sum_{1}^{N} e_m^2 = \sigma^2,$

where σ is the standard deviation of the e's. Thus when multiplying y_n by y_{n+k} in order to form the numerator of (27.3) we can neglect all terms in the product except those in e_m^2. Retaining these terms only, we get

$$y_n y_{n+k} = e_n^2 \rho^k \frac{\sin \overline{k+1}\theta}{\sin \theta} + e_{n-1}^2 \rho^{k+2} \frac{\sin 2\theta \sin \overline{k+2}\theta}{\sin^2\theta} + \dots.$$

Summing,

$$\lim \frac{1}{N} \sum_{1}^{N} y_n y_{n+k} = \frac{\sigma^2 \rho^k}{\sin^2\theta} [\sin \theta \sin \overline{k+1}\theta + \rho^2 \sin 2\theta \sin \overline{k+2}\theta +$$
$$+ \rho^4 \sin 3\theta \sin \overline{k+3}\theta + \dots].$$

Putting $k = 0$, we get at once

$$\lim \frac{1}{N} \sum_{1}^{N} y_n^2 = \frac{\sigma^2}{\sin^2\theta} [\sin^2\theta + \rho^2 \sin^2 2\theta + \rho^4 \sin^2 3\theta + \dots],$$

whence

$$r_k = \rho^k \frac{\sum\limits_{s=1}^{s=\infty} \rho^{2s} \sin s\theta \sin \overline{k+s}\theta}{\sum\limits_{s=1}^{s=\infty} \rho^{2s} \sin^2 s\theta}$$

$$= \rho^k \left[\cos k\theta + \sin k\theta \frac{\sum\limits_{1}^{\infty} \rho^{2s} \sin s\theta \cos s\theta}{\sum\limits_{1}^{\infty} \rho^{2s} \sin^2 s\theta} \right]$$

$$= \rho^k (\cos k\theta + R \sin k\theta), \qquad (27.4)$$

where R is dependent on ρ and θ but is independent of k.

The value of R is not a matter of much importance in the theory; the particular value implied in the above formula is, indeed, due to a special assumption which has been made for convenience in the above calculation, but which is not at all necessary. We have supposed that the frequency of the shocks is exactly one per period; and the length of the period, it will be remembered, is not arbitrary, but is a matter of the particular lags implied in the difference equation (27.1). If the shocks had been more frequent than this, the value of R would have been diminished, ultimately tending to zero as the frequency of the shocks was indefinitely increased. Thus r_k would tend to the value $\rho^k \cos k\theta$.

The trigonometrical term in this expression ensures that the sequence will have a periodic component. If ρ was equal to unity, so that the basic cycle was undamped, r_k would become equal to unity when $k\theta$ was a multiple of 2π, so that there would tend to be a regular cycle with a period $2\pi/\theta$. But when $\rho < 1$, though the correlation will rise to a maximum at something approaching the corresponding period, the correlation (at its maximum) may still be quite low. Suppose, for instance, that $v = 0.75$, $s = 0.10$, to take our familiar figures. Then $\rho = 0.87$, $\theta = 17.7°$, and the first positive value of k for which $\cos k\theta = 1$ is $k = 20.3$. But with these figures $\rho^k = 0.05$, and the correlation between 'corresponding' terms of successive cycles is quite small. It is not zero, so that the periodic component does exist; but the periodic component is so swamped by the random component that it would only become distinguishable after careful investigation.

A correlation coefficient so small as this might not be a matter for despair, if we met it in a practical case; for in such a case all of the variables might well be subject to error, and a mere trace of regularity might be a matter for congratulation. But this is theory, not practice. We have assumed a definite difference equation, not subject to error; and even so we get a small correlation, except in the case when ρ approaches near to unity. The conclusion in the text, that the stochastic theory does no more than slightly widen the special case of the regular fluctuation which would occur if $\rho = 1$, seems amply borne out by this more formal investigation.

Appendix to Chapter IX

28. *A particular case of the general difference equation.* Something can be said about the properties of the particular form of equation which we used on p. 114 in the text. As this form of equation may well prove to be a convenient instrument for further analysis, these results may usefully be set down.

It follows, from what has been said in §§ 22–3 above, that the auxiliary equation of

$$y_n = (1-s)y_{n-1} + (v/r)(y_{n-1} - y_{n-r-1}) \qquad (28.1)$$

which is $\qquad f(u) = u^{r+1} - (1-s+v/r)u^r + v/r = 0 \qquad (28.2)$

will have two major real roots if $s = 0$, and that these roots will draw together, becoming first equal and then complex, as s increases. It is, at first sight, conceivable that a cyclical solution might become dominant through an increase in minor roots; but arithmetical experiment with the sequences generated by this type of difference equation seems to show that the minor roots can be relied upon to remain relatively small. It may therefore be assumed that the significant cyclical solutions are those which arise when the major roots become complex. The values of s for which this will happen can in fact be quite easily determined.

We have only to discover what are the values of s for which two roots of (28.2) become equal. If $f(u) = 0$ has two equal roots, it must have a common root with $f'(u) = 0$. But

$$f'(u) = (r+1)u^r - r(1-s+v/r)u^{r-1}.$$

Thus if $f'(u) = 0$, either $u = 0$ (which cannot satisfy $f(u) = 0$ unless $v = 0$), or

$$u = \frac{r}{r+1}\left(1-s+\frac{v}{r}\right).$$

Substituting this value in $f(u) = 0$, we get

$$\left[\frac{r}{r+1}\left(1-s+\frac{v}{r}\right)\right]^{r+1} = v.$$

Since $s < 1$ and $v > 0$, the only significant part of this condition is

$$\frac{r}{r+1}\left(1-s+\frac{v}{r}\right) = v^{1/(r+1)}$$

so that s_0, the value of s for which the major roots become equal, is defined by

$$s_0 = 1-\left(\frac{r+1}{r}\right)v^{1/(r+1)}+\frac{v}{r}. \qquad (28.3)$$

The major roots are real if $s = 0$, so that the major roots are complex, and the solution cyclical, if $s > s_0$. This condition is obviously consistent with that found in § 20 above for the case where $r = 1$. Since it is the real positive root of v which gives the significant result, the expression on the right of (28.3) can be treated as single-valued.

Differentiating (28.3) with respect to v, we find that

$$\frac{ds_0}{dv} = \frac{1}{r}\left(1-v^{-r/(r+1)}\right)$$

which is zero when $v = 1$, positive when $v > 1$, and negative when $v < 1$. Corresponding to any given value of s, there are therefore *two* critical values of v—the upper and lower points.

It can be shown in a similar way, but with rather more difficulty, that when v is given, s_0 steadily diminishes with an increase in r. The lower and upper points therefore draw apart. Cyclical solutions become more probable; the steadily convergent case, and the steadily explosive case, tend to be crowded out.

The theory of the upper and lower points, for this type of equation, is therefore quite manageable. Unfortunately there is no such simple formula for the middle point; and there is, in general, no simple way of calculating the duration of the cycle. But there is a useful formula for the duration of the cycle *at the middle point*. Although, as we have seen, this is not the minimum duration for a given value of s, it is bound to be near the minimum duration, and can therefore be used as a means of characterizing the behaviour of the system.

At the middle point, $f(u) = 0$ has a solution of the form

$$u = \cos\theta + i\sin\theta.$$

Substituting in (28.2) and equating to zero the real and imaginary parts, we get

$$\cos\overline{r+1}\theta - (1-s+v/r)\cos r\theta + v/r = 0,$$

$$\sin\overline{r+1}\theta - (1-s+v/r)\sin r\theta = 0.$$

If θ was eliminated from these equations, we should get the value of v (in terms of s) at the middle point; but this elimination does not seem to give any manageable result. If v is eliminated, we get the value of θ at the middle point, and $2\pi/\theta$ is the duration of the cycle. Now v is eliminated very easily; we get

$$\sin\overline{r+1}\theta - \sin\theta = (1-s)\sin r\theta$$

or
$$\cos(r+2)\frac{\theta}{2} = (1-s)\cos r\frac{\theta}{2}.$$

From this equation the value of θ, corresponding to any given values of r and s, could easily be evaluated by graphical methods. Since $0 < s < 1$, $(r+2)\frac{1}{2}\theta < \frac{1}{2}\pi$, and the duration of the upswing (π/θ) must always be greater than $r+2$ periods. It can be shown that the duration always increases (θ diminishes) with r; and that for given r, the duration always diminishes as s increases.

29. *Fluctuations in autonomous investment.* It is desirable, for completeness, to show how to determine the equilibrium path, when autonomous investment is not expanding regularly (as we assumed it to do in § 18 above) but has a fluctuating component. We showed in § 11 how to determine the equilibrium path when there is no induced investment, but autonomous investment has a fluctuation in the form of a sine curve. We have now to consider the same problem for the case in which induced investment is present.

It will be convenient to begin by making the elementary assumptions, so that the difference equation is

$$Y_n - (1-s+v)Y_{n-1} + vY_{n-2} = A_n, \qquad (29.1)$$

and $A_n = A\sin(nh+k)$. A and k are free constants, so that we have to determine a solution of (29.1) of the form $A'\sin(nh+k')$.

As in § 11, we equate coefficients of $\sin(nh+c')$ and $\cos(nh+c')$ and get

$$A'[1-(1-s+v)\cos h+v\cos 2h] = A\cos(k-k'),$$

$$A'[(1-s+v)\sin h-v\sin 2h] = A\sin(k-k'). \qquad (29.2)$$

Much the easiest way of handling these equations is by a geometrical device, of rather the same sort as that which we used in § 21.

Let OL (Fig. B) be a line of length unity. Make angle OLM equal to h, and LM equal to $1-s$. Continue LM to N where $MN = v$. Make angle MNP equal to h, and NP equal to v. Then it follows from the first of equations (29.2) that $(A/A')\cos(k-k')$ is the projection of OP on OL; and from the second of these equations that

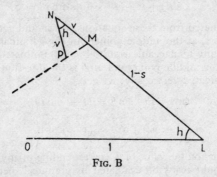

FIG. B

$(A/A')\sin(k-k')$ is the projection of OP on the line through O perpendicular to OL. Thus $A/A' = OP$, and $(k-k')$ equals the angle POL.

We can at once confirm the results we got in § 11. If $v = 0$, P is at M. The phase angle $(k-k')$ is positive, so that the cycle in equilibrium output comes later than the cycle in autonomous investment; while OP must be greater than $OL-OM$ (which is s), so that A' must be less than A/s, which means that the fluctuations in the equilibrium path must be damped.

What happens when $v > 0$? The triangle MNP is isosceles; thus the angle $PMN = 90° - \frac{1}{2}h$, and the direction MP depends only on h. As v increases, P moves downwards along the line MP.

There are evidently two cases, according as MP passes to the right, or to the left, of O. In the first case, the phase angle diminishes as v increases; thus the lag in the equilibrium output continually diminishes, and a sufficiently large v may even cause the equilibrium output curve to turn downwards before the autonomous investment curve does so. (It does not follow, of course, that actual output would turn downwards.) In the second case, the phase angle increases with v; a sufficiently large v may then cause the two curves to have opposite fluctuations, with the peaks of one corresponding to the troughs of the other.

What is the significance of the line between these two cases? If the line MP passed through O, the angle OML would be equal to $90°+\frac{1}{2}h$. It would then follow, from the parts of the triangle OLM, that $\sin \frac{1}{2}h = \frac{1}{2}\sqrt{s}$; so that the duration of the cycle in autonomous investment would be approximately equal to that of the shortest possible induced investment cycle.[1] The second case, in which h is greater than this critical magnitude, may therefore be referred to as that in which the cycle in autonomous investment is shorter than the shortest induced investment cycle. The first case is that in which the autonomous investment cycle has the same duration as some cycle which could be set up (through induced investment) by a single displacement from a stationary or progressive equilibrium, for an appropriate value of v.

In either case, a rise in v begins by reducing OP, and thus has an anti-damping effect. But there will, in each case, be some value of v for which OP will reach a minimum, so that further rises in v will be damping. It is clear, however, that these extreme cases are not important. It will be noticed that in the first case the minimum OP is not reached until after the phase angle has become negative.

The same kind of analysis could in principle be used for other cases than the 'elementary'. Its application to the special case studied in the preceding section is indeed particularly simple. For we need then do no more than set the angle MNP equal to rh, and we can proceed as before. With the increase in the angle MNP, the 'second case' evidently becomes more important; and that is as it should be, for we have seen that the minimum length of the 'induced investment' cycle tends to be increased by lags of this sort in the accelerator.

[1] The minimum length of the induced investment cycle is given by $\sin \theta = \sqrt{s}$ (see § 21 above). The equation $\sin \frac{1}{2}h = \frac{1}{2}\sqrt{s}$ gives very nearly the same value for h as this for θ.

INDEX